The
DILEMMA
of Being
MODERN

ESSAYS ON ART AND LITERATURE

by

J. P. HODIN

THE NOONDAY PRESS

New York

Library of Congress Catalogue Card Number: 59-15130

To Doris and George

Manufactured in the United States of America
by Noble Offset Printers, Inc.

CONTENTS

11030

CONTENTS

LIST OF ILLUSTRATIONS

ACKNOWLEDGMENTS

The essays presented in this volume are a selection from my work in this genre produced during the last fifteen years. They were written mainly in England; only a few, 'The Cultural Psychology of Sigmund Freud', 'Art and Criticism' and 'Edvard Munch, the Forerunner' were written in Sweden. All these essays, with the exception of the second meeting with Marc Chagall and the last part of the study on Bernard Leach, have been published previously in cultural or art reviews in England and abroad. The list of these reviews is given below. I would like to take this opportunity of offering any acknowledgments which may be due to their editors. With a few minor additions these essays are reprinted unchanged. Whatever inaccuracies I have come across in regard to wording or the material used have been corrected. Shortly after the Kafka study was written, I felt that the negative approach to our spiritual difficulties should be balanced by a constructive one. The one-sided knowledge of our failures, it seemed to me, in the end only leads to their acceptance. So the essay on Goethe came about. Although it was not primarily written to celebrate the bicentenary of the German poet's birth, it nevertheless served to fulfil this act of homage.

It would be difficult to-day, fifteen years after the essay on Freud was written, to subscribe to the somewhat narrow pro-scientific view which prevailed at the beginning of this century and with which this essay ends. However, as it represents Freud's own conviction, it may stand in its present form, unchallenged, as a historic document.

In this, my first English book, the expression of my sincere thanks to all those who from the beginning of my residence in this country encouraged me in my work, especially Sir Herbert Read and Sir Kenneth Clark, may find its appropriate place. I am greatly indebted also to Professor Anthony Blunt and Professor Thomas Munroe for their help and appreciation. Of great value to me was the support which the editors of *Horizon*, Mr. Cyril Connolly and Mr. Peter Watson, gave me. Last in this chronological enumeration, the Institute of Contemporary Arts should be mentioned, and thanks expressed, especially to its honorary director, Mr. Roland Penrose, and Mr. E. C. Gregory for all their interest and sympathy.

My thanks are also due to Mr. Frank Budgen, Mrs. Eithne Wilkins, Mrs. C. King and Mrs. Ellen Gillett for their patient co-operation, to Miss I. Schrier for her conscientious proof reading, and to my wife for all her understanding and unceasing aid.

*

Franz Kafka was published in *Horizon*, London, January, 1948, and reprinted in *The Golden Horizon*, London, 1953.

Edvard Munch, the Forerunner, is taken from my book: *Edvard Munch, Der Genius des Nordens*, Neuer Verlag, Stockholm, later *Frankfurter Verlagsanstalt*, Frankfurt, a.M., 1948.

James Ensor was published in *Far and Wide*, London, September, 1948.

Marc Chagall, first part, in *The Month*, London, April, 1950, second part, 1952.

Expressionism: Style and Periodicity. The Psychological Background of Expressionism, in *Horizon*, London, January, 1949.

Edvard Munch in *Art News*, New York, May, 1950.

Oskar Kokoschka in *New Writing and Daylight*, London, The Hogarth Press, 1945.

Ernst Josephson and C. F. Hill in *The Norseman*, London, No. 1, 1949.

A Madonna Motif in the Work of Munch and Dali in *The Art Quarterly*, published by The Detroit Institute of Arts, Summer, 1953.

Henry Moore in *World Review*, London, August, 1949.

Ben Nicholson the Pythagorean in *La Biennale di Venezia*, Venice, No. 19-20, 1954.

Graham Sutherland in *Les Arts Plastiques*, Brussels, No. 6, 1952.

Barbara Hepworth in *Les Arts Plastiques*, Brussels, No. 3, 1950

Bernard Leach in *The Studio*, London, March, 1947.

Recent Trends in Contemporary English Sculpture and their Origins in *Aesthetics*, Bombay, International Number, and in *Sele Arte*, Florence, No. 9, 1953.

Goethe's Succession in *Horizon*, London, April, 1949.

The Cultural Psychology of Sigmund Freud in *Ord och Bild*, Stockholm, No. 11, 1940.

Art and Criticism was published as a booklet in Stockholm, 1943.

Herbert Read's Philosophy of Art in *The Norseman*, London, No. 4, 1951.

André Malraux and Goya in *Art News and Review*, London, No. 26, January, 1952.

Part One

THE VOICE
OF THE PIONEERS

I

FRANZ KAFKA

Reflections on the Problem of Decadence

The true speakers are dead cracked in the valley of hate.

Sydney Keyes: THE MESSAGE

THE generation which made an onslaught upon prejudices of every sort, whether social, political, religious or sexual, was capable of destroying but not of building anew. It was necessarily negative, torn, restless. When Joyce's *Ulysses* appeared, it had on literature an influence comparable to that which the splitting of the atom had on physics. A world collapsed, became rubble. The young generation wandered, astray, among the ruins, filled with the lust for self-destruction. The artist of our time treats his object 'as a surgeon dissects a corpse'.[1] Everything sentimental and trivial was destroyed, but together with it everything that was vital. To-day, surrounded by a culture which in reality is smashed to pieces, and with only the pale remnants of a conception of the world in our hearts, we long for an architecture of the soul. We no longer believe that 'the only true artists are those who wish to become inhuman'. We clearly see that the analytical mind is the antithesis of the creative mind. We long for communion with creation. We do not want to be diverted from it by the modern sorcery of supposedly scientific thinking stamped out by the machine age to a pattern of misunderstood and misdirected psychology.

The revolt of man against the Divine (for one of man's ideas of God had once more begun to totter) is over—for our time. By following in the footsteps of Surrealism we can only arrive at the mad-house. A philosophy revolving about the splitting of the

[1] Apollinaire on Picasso. José Ortega y Gasset spoke of *La Dehumanizacion del arte.*

3

atom is not a programme. Cubism was cold speculation. (Of use as a constructive scaffolding, but insufficient as a content.) To-day we see, too, that Franz Kafka, even though he never believed in a purely rational conception of the material world, yet, because he gave his interpretation of the spiritual forces, the divinely destined aspect of life, to which he as a man of the East owed allegiance, a subjective and pessimistic character, can be of no help to us in our search for harmony and the reshaping of the soul. He belongs to the grave-diggers. The sombre despair, the lack of any hope or comfort, which speaks to us from his work, the fear-complexes and persecution-mania, the monotony of seeing no way out, its morbid, self-annihilatory and decadent quality, prevent many of us from enjoying his extraordinary imagination and stylistic power. To-day, in view of the bewilderment of the times, the thirst for a credo that would unite us all, for an all-embracing, unified picture of life, it cannot be the distinguishing mark of great literature for a writer to project solely and monotonously his personal negative problems into the infinite (an infernal auto-dafé with torture and slow death) and so cause us to despair with him.

How the conception of the decadent has changed in the last decades! For Nietzsche 'decadent' meant critical man, as opposed to creative man, 'Christian' man as opposed to the Greek. We called J. P. Jacobsen, Herman Bang, R. M. Rilke, Hugo von Hofmannsthal, Oscar Wilde, Hermann Hesse, Marcel Proust and the Knut Hamsun of 'The Mysteries' decadent. It was a romantic, melancholy weariness of life, reflected splendour of the Byronic *Weltschmerz*, which Leopardi described as in some sort of the 'noblest feeling of man, which cannot be satisfied by any earthly thing or the whole world of phenomena,' and in which he wished to see the chief sign of the greatness of our nature.

For Søren Kierkegaard the characteristic of the great man lay in distress, torment and paradox. The next stage was to seek the sole sources of the spiritual in disease, in misfortune and in madness. ('The nobler type of people are all mentally ill nowadays. Only the mediocre and the untalented are capable of heartily enjoying life.' Dostoevsky: *A Raw Youth*.) From there it was only a short step to the intensification of the experience of the negative, in which negation became an end in itself and assumed the value of the absolute. Yet here it is that the revolt starts against the

4

essence of life itself. Behind Franz Kafka's metaphysical fear one can feel the revenge of the despairing, the rebellion, driving right into the midst of the Absolute, against the logic of creation, against a performance in which man seems to be nothing but a bad joke on the part of Providence. It is the most consistent bedazzlement, much more subtle than Baudelaire's Satanism or Spengler's pessimism or than Heidegger's 'Angst' or Sartre's *Néant*. How different in character is the polarity in Shakespeare of good and evil forces, or his and Hebbel's concept of the source of the tragic being due to the high level of achievement or quality in any respect—pride, fame, justice, beauty—above average, how unlike the tragic conflict between man and destiny in Greek drama, how great the Promethean idea. The present process is one of self-dissolution, which finds in the unbridgeable dualism of divine and human truth the knife under which man must die 'like a dog'.

One can be just to Kafka only by making a distinction between his world of ideas, which arises out of his depressions, his father-complex, tuberculosis, inability to free himself from a hated milieu, etc., and flourishes on the ground of a religion of despair and negation, and his creative power as an artist. One can reject the one and admire the other, even though we must never forget that creative form is, after all, ultimately something very personal, dependent on its thought-content and thus not transmissible. Kafka's time has yet to come, in an artistic sense, when the problems in his work will no longer burn the living flesh, when one will be able to read him in the way we to-day read the masters of adolescent melancholy, an Amiel, a Gerard de Nerval.

Kafka's artistic merits are fully recognized. He moved from a symbolic way of writing ('An old man, naked, exposed to the chill of this unhappy age, I drive around in an earthly carriage, with unearthly horses.' *A Country Doctor*.) to a surreal realism, of which the characteristic is that the earthly and the supernatural interpenetrate each other and become a unity. It is not a matter of allegories, but of the realism of a man who, with his whole being, feels that there is not only a human standpoint but also a standpoint of 'God', and that man in reality undergoes a 'trial', while he believes that he is simply 'living'. Dante's visions, so far as we are concerned, take place outside the real world. Don

Quixote is an example of the interpenetration of two worlds. But there two 'human' worlds are involved, that of idealism—of a lunatic illusion or of an idea that is no longer historically valid—and that of reality. In Kafka's case it is the interpenetration in reality of a human world and a divine one which is hostile to him. To the question whether there is any hope outside this world, since life in this world seems to be without hope, Kafka answers: 'Plenty of hope—for God—an infinite amount of hope—only it is not for us.' That is the basic note of his whole work. Kafka stands on the shadow side of life. And yet he revered Goethe. In his ardent striving, in the overcoming of difficulties, in creation beyond the limits of his own subjectivity, Goethe found the meaning of human life, he found 'salvation'. In Kafka we meet the image of a doorkeeper who guards the 'doors of the law' and admits nobody. The man who longs for admittance spends his whole life patiently waiting, only in the end to hear the answer to his last, feeble question: 'Nobody else could be admitted here, for this door was meant only for you. And now I go and lock it up.' In Goethe we find a drive towards activity, towards renewal, towards health; there is the urge to unite opposites into a higher unity. In Kafka everything has a negative relation to life, passive and broken. The petitioner is not admitted by the doorkeeper, the surveyor never catches sight of the inhabitants of the 'castle', K. in *The Trial* undergoes trial by ordeal (consciousness of guilt, original sin, court of judgement), he is changed into an insect (*The Metamorphosis*), he humiliates himself into the existence of a mole, suffering agonies of fear and suspense in his burrow under the earth (*The Burrow*). The nightmare sense of inferiority towards a vital and despotic father, who nearly crushes him, the hatred of petit-bourgeois life, of a job that is slowly killing him, his weakness of will, his indecision, show clearly the mistake of calling *The Castle* Kafka's *Faust*. If Dante had emphasized only the negative side of his restless life, he would never have become the author of the *Vita Nuova* and the *Divine Comedy*. Did not Proust wring works of a fragrant beauty and sophistication from his sick-room? The overcoming of human inadequacy, the recognition of a cosmos, of a significant order and harmony which prevails in spite of all suffering, is the mark of great and powerful minds. In Kafka's work everything remains dark as the darkest Middle Ages, the most refined self-torture and self-irony. That is why he can contribute so little towards a return to health in our time.

It will be objected that the value of a work of art does not consist of its moral or 'hygienic' function, that it is the product of a pure process of creation, and so on. This attitude was dominant for a long time and could not fail, *eo ipso*, to lead to nihilism. For art is not only form; form cannot live at the expense of the idea. In the views presented here the moral side of the question, in any case, is not decisive. It is a mere expression of indignation against all that is non-vital, against the deification of the neurotic, the inability to face life, of those who are weakened and worn out by doubts and scepticism and who have been made the fetish of the time. We find that such an attitude cannot be maintained after the Second World War and its horrors which were more ghastly than any Surrealist could imagine. Are we wrong in saying that Kafka himself would not have wished to be canonized by decadent intellectuals, for whom thinking is nothing but an exercise in mental acrobatics?

Kleist, who put an early end to his life by suicide and whom Kafka greatly revered, created in *Michael Kohlhaas* one of the most forceful literary documents of the fight for right and justice, a perfect work of art. Heine drew his 'little songs' from his 'great sufferings'. And Dostoevsky, with whose subtle, depressing psychology Kafka has so much in common, did he not balance a Stawrogin, a Smerdjakov against an Aljoscha, a Dolgoruki? In the work of art the trials of life are melted down into the gold of the ineffable, the imperishable; what triumphs is the mysterious quality of the beauty of life and art, the personal element fades into the background. But with Kafka one feels that the personal element poisons his art. That too is the reason for his destructive urge towards his own work. Therein lies the great ethos of his personality. The message which Kafka, with his great gifts, could have brought to humanity, he never did bring. With all sympathy for his tragic fate, his psychic and physical sufferings, a work which has been written for the purpose of fighting off overpowering complexes, fails to produce the catharsis which is the indubitable sign of every great work of art.

To arrive at a clear judgement of Kafka's work means becoming aware of the greatest deficiency of our epoch. Our time calls for spiritual leadership, not for literature. All humanity's strength, self-confidence and ability to suffer are needed to achieve the Herculean task of lifting life out of chaos into the meaningful. How much love, kindliness and faith, how much trust and wisdom we need for that task! What are we to make of a man whom fear has lowered to the state of animal-existence and who says of himself: 'Inside my hill of earth I can of course dream of everything, even of reconciliation, although I know definitely that all that doesn't exist at all . . . ?

It is better to say with André Gide: '*Tu ne t'étonnes peut-être pas assez de vivre . . .*', Gide whose whole work expounds the view 'that the kingdom of Heaven will not be given to us by grace but will have to be sought and conquered: *le Paradis est toujours à refaire.*'

* * *

We are nihilistic ideas born in God's head.
Franz Kafka

In order to understand the inquisitorial determinism of Kafka's work, one has to take into account the epoch in which it came into existence and the ground on which it grew. Of the epoch it is enough to say it was the pre-war and post-war age. But the ground, Prague, the city where East and West interpenetrate and races mingle, the place where peoples and civilizations have met and influenced each other, centuries of history pervading narrow streets like an intolerable burden, and in the lamplight by night the Latin thoughts of Belezza and Reason fight duels with the sombre world of Russian ideas, where religious feuds cast their bloody shadows, and Slavonic melancholy, Jewish Talmudism, Catholic mysticism, Hussite puritanism, carved their runes in the people's faces—only in Prague could fantasies like Kafka's come into existence. Kafka's flight from his parents' house is at the same time a flight from Prague, flight from the weight of tradition, flight from the multitude of tongues into the unequivocal. An analysis of Kafka's work is not complete unless it takes into account the poetic and tormenting character of Prague.

The Prague painter F. Feigl, now living in England, told me: 'It was in the year 1894. Kafka and I went to school together. It was the Altstädter Deutsche Gymnasium. He was about ten years old, a thin, frail boy with very big, black eyes, a long skull and pointed ears which gave him a degenerate look. The reason why I remember him so clearly is that his mother always came to fetch him after school, which struck us other children as strange.

'Then I lost sight of him for a long time. It was not till 1907 that I heard of him again. In the circle of the group of modern painters known in Prague as "The Eight", Max Brod once said during a discussion: "I can tell you the name of a very great artist—Franz Kafka." He showed us some drawings of his, which evoked the memory of the early Paul Klee or Kubin. They were romantic, expressionistic. Kafka did not develop his gift for drawing any further. Then one day the elocutionist Ludwig Hart told me: "Do you realize that Franz Kafka is the greatest writer of Prague?" At that time Rilke was no longer in Prague and Werfel had settled down in Vienna. Later we struck up a friendship, Kafka and I. Kafka was associated with a group of writers who used to read their work to each other. I remember hearing Kafka there when he read his sketch "The Scuttle-Rider". The background of this story is the shortage of coal after the First World War. A man rides through the air on a coal-scuttle, to the coal-merchant's. It is like things of E. T. A. Hoffmann's, only less mystical. It made the impression of something humorous and grotesque. Kafka read it with a right feeling for the fine points and in a boyish voice. Boyishness—that is the characteristic that clung to him all his life.

'Later in Berlin he once introduced me to his fiancée. He had an "eternal" fiancée and always said he was not worthy of her. Behind things like these there lies hidden a sexual development that is by no means normal. I believe Kafka was afraid of bodily contact. He hated reality. He avenged himself on the causality of the world with a microscopically sharp analytical method. Under the microscope the causality of everyday life becomes a drama. Dimensions lose their sense, because they look quite otherwise under the magnifying-glass than they do to the naked eye. Kafka makes the events of a story into a novel. His sentences have beauty and order, they are built up on a long-term policy. That was necessary, because his thoughts had a complicated causal nexus. It made him creative in his use of language, just as he was in the analysis of the soul. One could call his writing psycho-analytical, and now it is exploited by people who visualize nothing and so reduce it *ad absurdum*. For it depends, after all, on what one finds under the microscope.

'Kafka's life was like one of his novels. This lonely man, who had a longing for the picturesque—I remember him living for some time in one of the little houses in the Alchimistengasse in Prague—had to work in an insurance company, for a small salary, with slow promotion every five years. He had a tyrannical father, who forced him to lead a dull and sober life, and with whom he had nothing in common. When we met—we used to go for long walks together—he was very eager to get to know something about the other arts. Once we tried to analyse the elements of art. That was about five years before his death. We came to the conclusion that the essential of painting was space, of music time, and of writing causality. That corresponds to the basic elements of sensual perception: spatial, temporal and causal. Then I realized for the first time that his way of writing expressed a new causality, a new causal connection. Kafka did not talk of it again.

'Once I had a discussion about him with Max Brod, who was his squire and herald. For me the interesting question was how far one can go in this displacement of causality. Then I classified Kafka as a romantic. Brod protested against that and said it was a limitation. For me it does not imply a judgement of values.

'To simplify into microscopic or over-life-size terms was typically continental and basically "baroque". We use a baroque and almost grotesque scale whenever we think of Prague, that fantastic city. Everything fantastic always had a great appeal for the people of Prague. If someone cannot get any coal, it becomes an experience of far-reaching import. The "ride" is an idea realized in visual terms.

'I believe I understood Kafka, but he was shy of letting anyone really get to know him. If I recall to-day the type to which he belonged, picture how he used to move and what he used to do, I understand him better still. Even at that time I assumed that his way of writing was a self-sufficient relief for him. He needed no one else for confirmation. Marriage with a woman, the relationship of author and public, these are realities. He defended himself against reality, creating for himself a reality of his own, in which he took revenge on the apparent senselessness and injustice of reality by caricaturing it.

'In Berlin, we often spoke of the same questions. At that time he bought a picture of mine, a Prague study. There was a touch of Munch about it, something uncanny. I once found Prague an uncanny experience, when returning from rationalistic Germany. It was characteristic of him to choose precisely this picture. He seemes to have had the typical mixture of hate and love for Prague. He gave the picture to his fiancée.

'Then I suddenly heard that he had died of tuberculosis of the larynx. Fundamentally Kafka remained a boy, to whom it was not granted to grow old. He died in the midst of his youth, while he still faced life with all the curiosity of a child, in spite of the fact that he was over forty.

'Concerning the characteristics of Kafka's work I should like to say that it shows all the signs of a deformed imagination. The deformed comic in a circus, the clown, has a nose that is too long or feet that are too big. All grotesqueness contains the comic element of deformity. Kafka put the negative and tormenting aspect of life into the foreground, all his work is like a nightmare; what is typical of it is this dream-like, nightmarish quality.

'Every artist moves between extremes. Yet every liberty has its limits. Cézanne approaches the banal when he paints apples in monumental fashion. Only art-historians and art-dealers, who make a living by it, see things differently. But artists recognize it as the failings of a genius. Even in Prague I felt the torturing quality of Kafka's art. Still more to-day, when we have to find the decisive ethical standpoint in life. Everything that only underlines egotism, everything merely subjective—the asocial approach gives the impression of genius, but it remains asocial—is of an unhealthy influence. It ran wild in politics, almost like Futurism. The whole era was ripe for such ideas, which brought it to the edge of the abyss in politics and in an evolutionary sense to the atomic bomb and to the triumph of analysis. Analysis is a great poison. It is a rhythm of corrosion, a rhythm of the brain.

'True art is always synthesis. Kafka's mind was basically corrosive and analytic. Why is analysis as an end in itself not a mark of genius? Because it has no real content. It has no real meaning. Analysis pretends to be both content and form. Kafka's object was nothing, it was nothingness; he analysed analysis. It was exactly the same in Cubism and in Surrealism. When they had split up the whole into its elements and finally declared form to

be the meaning, these were only human, egocentric delusions.
But here one can see how movements come into existence. The
Surrealists are imitated, Kafka is imitated, Brueghel's picture
comes into my mind: the blind men, who are guided by a blind
man, all fall into the ditch. The less one can see, the more con-
vulsively one clings to a coat-tail.

'About Kafka I should say that he was honest and did not care
about worldly success. He did not want to be praised, and we do
not want to find fault with him. What I have said was only to
point out his characteristics. The forces of which one gains possession, through analysis, can after all lead to good as well. The
artist, too, must be a "critic". The goal appears to me to be a life
in which pulses the life-blood of an ethical idea. We are still
remote from it.'

*   *   *

Then I beheld all the work of God, that man cannot find out the
work that is done under the sun: because however much a man
labours to seek it out, yet he shall not find it; yea, moreover, though
a wise man think to know it, yet shall he not be able to find it.

ECCLESIASTES

Some deny misery by pointing at the sun; he denies the sun by
pointing at misery.

Franz Kafka

In July 1923 Kafka left Prague. He settled down in Berlin, determined never to return to his parents' house and to devote himself
entirely to writing. It was then that he met the woman with whom
he founded a home for the short time that he still had to live.

I have spent many hours with Mrs. Dora Dymant, talking about
Kafka and those last months of his life. I am indebted to her for
all that she told me so simply, warmly and candidly. Before I
begin to retell it, it must first be said, as she herself emphasized:
'I am not objective, I cannot be. It is more than twenty years
since Kafka went. But after all, one can only measure time by
the importance of one's experiences. Even to-day it is often difficult for me to talk about Kafka. Frequently it is not the facts
which are decisive, it is a mere matter of atmosphere. What I tell
has an inner truth. Subjectivity is part of it.

'I met Kafka for the first time on the Baltic, in the summer of

1923. I was very young then, nineteen, and was working voluntarily in the holiday camp of a Berlin youth hostel, in Müritz, near Stettin. One day on the beach I saw a family playing— parents and two children. I was particularly struck by the man. I could not shake off the impression he made on me. I even followed them into the town, and later met them again. One day it was announced in the hostel that Dr. Franz Kafka was coming to supper. At that time I was in charge of the kitchen. When I looked up from my work—the room had grown dark, someone was standing outside the window—I recognized the man from the beach. Then he came in—I didn't know then that it was Kafka, and the woman with whom he had been on the beach was his sister. He said in a soft voice: "Such tender hands, and such bloody work for them to do!" (Kafka was at that time a vegetarian.) In the evening we were all sitting on benches at long tables; a little boy got up and, as he went away, was so embarrassed that he fell down. Kafka said to him, his eyes shining with admiration: "What a clever way to fall and what a clever way to get up again!" When later I thought of these words again, their central meaning seemed to me to be that everything could be saved—except Kafka. Kafka could not be saved.

'He was tall and slim and dark-skinned and had a loping walk that at first made me believe he must be a half-breed Indian and not a European. He swayed a little, but held himself straight. Only he carried his head tilted a little to one side. That was typical of him. It expressed a relationship-symptom. Kafka had the bearing of the lonely man who is always in relation to something outside himself. It was not exactly a kind of listening; there was also something very affectionate about it. I should like to call it the symptom of a need for relations, which expressed something like this: "I on my own am nothing, I am only something when connected with the outer world."

'Why did Kafka make such a deep impression on me? I came from the East, a dark being full of dreams and premonitions, who might have sprung from a book of Dostoevsky's. I had heard so much of the West—knowledge, clarity, style of living—I came to Germany with a receptive soul, and it gave me much. But over and over again I had the feeling that the people there needed something which I could give them. After the catastrophe of the war everyone expected salvation through the intermediary of the

East. But I had run away from the East, because I believed the light was in the West. Later I became less ambitious in my dreams: Europe was not what I had expected it to be, its people had no rest in their innermost being. They lacked something. In the East one knew what man was; perhaps one could not move so freely in society and could not express oneself so easily, but one did know of the unity of man and creation. When I saw Kafka for the first time, his image corresponded to my idea of man. But even Kafka turned to me attentively, as though expecting something from me.

'The essential characteristics of his face were the very open, sometimes even wide-open eyes, whether he was talking or listening. They were not staring in horror, as it had been said of him; it was rather more an expression of astonishment. His eyes were brown and shy. When he spoke, they lit up; there was humour in them; but it was not so much irony as mischievousness—as if he knew of something that other people didn't know. But he was entirely without solemnity. Generally he had a very lively way of talking, and he liked talking. His conversational style was full of imagery, like his writing. Sometimes one got the impression of a craftsmanlike satisfaction, when he succeeded in expressing well what he wanted to say. His wrists were very slender, and he had long, ethereal fingers, speaking fingers which took on shape while he was telling a story and accompanied what he said much better than the hands did. Later on we very often amused ourselves making shadows on the wall with our hands. He was extremely clever at it. Kafka was always cheerful. He liked to play; he was the born playmate, always ready for some mischief. I don't think that depressions were a dominant characteristic of his, except before he began to write. They did not appear at regular intervals; usually there was a reason for them which could be traced. For instance, when he came back from town. Then he was often more than depressed; it was almost revolt. It was the time of the inflation. Kafka suffered badly under the conditions. He had a rigorous attitude towards himself. Whatever might happen around him, he had no right to shut himself off from it. So the way to town was always a kind of Golgotha for him. He almost broke down physically under it. He could stand in queues for hours, not only with the intention of buying something, but simply from the feeling: blood was flowing, and so his must flow, too. In this way he experienced communion with an un-happy people in an unhappy time. I can see it clearly as the theme of *The Trial*, where he condemns K., because he tried to shape his life differently from a life of crucifixion. But there is no life except in "crucifixion", and nobody is acquitted by the highest court of all. That is my interpretation. "How can it ever become different?" he said to me at that time. There are Helferich, Hil-ferding, Rathenau—but no help (Hilfe), no advice (Rat). He felt as if people did not dare to call things by their right names, as if they were trying to hide all tragedy behind fair words.

'We lived in Steglitz, later in Zehlendorf, first in one room, then in two. The first lodgings we left because of the landlady. Kafka described her in *A Small Woman*: "Only out of disgust, out of a never-ceasing disgust that was her perpetual driving-power, did she occupy herself with me"—that was how he put it.

'Kafka had to write; he had to, it was his life-breath. The days on which he wrote were the rhythm of this breath. If it is said of him that he wrote for a fortnight, that means he wrote for four-teen successive evenings or nights. Kafka used to walk around, heavily and uneasily, before he began to write. Then he spoke little, ate without appetite, took no interest in things, and was very sad. He wanted to be alone. In the beginning I didn't under-stand that; later on I always felt when he was going to begin writing. At other times he showed a great intensity towards even the most ordinary things. But on such days that vanished com-pletely. I can only differentiate between these days, in their various tensions, by comparing them to colours: purple, dark green, or blue days. Later on he liked me to stay in the room while he was writing. Once he started to write after supper. He wrote for a very long time, and I fell asleep on the sofa. When I woke up, the electric light was still on. Kafka was sitting at my side. I looked at him. A palpable change was visible in his face. The traces of the spiritual tension were so obvious that they had changed the face utterly.

'*The Burrow*, one of his last stories, was written in one night. It was in the winter; he began early in the evening and had finished by the morning. Then he worked on it again. He told me about it jokingly and seriously. This story was autobiographical. It must have been the foreboding of the return to his parents' house, the end of freedom, which aroused this panic feeling of fear in him. He pointed out to me that I was the "citadel" in the burrow. He often read to me what he had written. He never analysed, never explained. Sometimes it sounded humorous to me, with a sort of self-mockery.

'Time and again he said: "Well, I wonder if I've escaped the ghosts?" This was the name with which he summarized everything that had tormented him before he came to Berlin. He was as though possessed by this idea; it was a kind of sullen obstinacy. He wanted to burn everything he had written in order to free his soul from these "ghosts". I respected his wish, and when he lay ill, I burnt things of his before his eyes. What he really wanted to write was to come afterwards, only after he had gained his "liberty". Literature for him was something sacred, absolute, incorruptible, something great and pure. The literature of to-day is not what Kafka understood by literature. Kafka felt unsure of most things in life and expressed himself very cautiously. But when it was a matter of literature, he was unapproachable and knew no compromise. There he was concerned with the whole. He not only wanted to penetrate to the bottom of things. He was at the bottom. But where the solution of human confusion was in question, he would not have any half measures. He experienced life as a labyrinth; he could not see the solution. He never got further than despair. For him everything was interwoven with cosmic causality, even the most everyday things. One finds this feeling in the East, too, a longing for the wholeness of life. In the East there are spiritual matters which have to be fulfilled unconditionally, or else one is unable to live. Kafka felt that. The West has forgotten it. And that is why God has abandoned us.

'I have been reproached for having burnt some of what Kafka wrote. I was so young then, and young people live in the present. After all, for him all that had been nothing but self-liberation! At that time he had no more respect, no more love for his father. He had already recognized him: the man who dominated through possessions and "possesses" even his family. Kafka was very bitter about his father, and time and again, with biting humour, he would tell the story of how, when he wanted to present his first book to him, his father only said coldly: "Put it on the table beside my bed."

'In Berlin Kafka believed that he had liberated himself from the tyranny of his past. But the earlier problems were too tightly bound up with his life. As soon as one touched even a single string of it, all the others vibrated, too. His inner life was of unfathomable depth and unbearable. He did not really hate Prague. He spoke of Prague in the way a European speaks of Europe. What tormented Kafka most was the fear of becoming dependent on his parents. This dependence endangered the "burrow". Hence his thriftiness. He wanted to accustom himself to a spartan life. In Berlin he believed for a time in the possibility of saving his life, in a personal solution for the inner and outer confusion. He wanted to feel like an average human being, with only a few wishes and needs. We made so many plans. Once we talked about opening a small restaurant. He was to be the waiter. That meant seeing everything without being seen, being right in the midst of everyday life. Indeed, he did do it, in his own way.

'He attached great importance to being carefully dressed. He would have regarded it as a lack of courtesy to go somewhere without having his tie perfectly knotted. His suits were made by a first-class tailor and he always took a long time about dressing. It was not vanity. He looked into the mirror without complacency, quite critical and judicial. It was done in order not to offend the world.

'He liked to go shopping; he liked simple people. His appearance with the shopping-basket or the milk-can was a familiar sight in our neighbourhood. In the mornings he often went for a walk alone. His day was strictly planned, all with a view to his writing. On his walks he always took a notebook with him, or if he forgot it, he would buy one on the way. He loved Nature, although I never heard him say a word about it.

'Among the things of which he was particularly fond was his pocket-watch. When we got into trouble with our landlady about the electric light—for he often wrote all through the nights—I bought a paraffin lamp. He loved its soft, living light and always wanted to fill it up himself; he would play about with the wick and continually found new virtues in it. He did not take a kindly view of the telephone and was distressed when it rang. I always had to answer it. I think he did not feel quite comfortable about machines and mechanical things. He was very fond of my calendar, which had a proverb for every day. Later we had one each and on special occasions Kafka used to "consult the calendar".

Once, when I was washing grapes—he was fond of eating grapes and pineapples—I broke the glass. Immediately he appeared in the kitchen, holding the calendar in his hand, and said, wide-eyed: "One moment can ruin everything." Then he handed me the page. The truth sounded so trivial. He smiled.

'Although Kafka preferred to remain undisturbed, we often had visitors. I still remember Willi Haas, the editor of *Die Literarische Welt* and Rudolf Kayser of the *Neue Rundschau*. Once Werfel came to read to Kafka from his new book. They were together for a long time. Then I saw Werfel go away, weeping. When I entered the room, Kafka was sitting there completely shattered and he murmured to himself several times: "To think that anything so terrible has to be at all!" He was weeping, too. He had let Werfel go away without having been able to utter a single word about his book. Anyone who put himself into Kafka's hands either had the most encouraging experience or despaired. There was nothing in between. He had the same inexorable severity towards his own work. And although he never really believed that he had achieved what he wanted, I believe he never had the feeling that he was a dilettante.

'Kafka never made other people feel uneasy. He attracted everybody, and whoever came to him did so with a kind of solemnity. They walked as though on tip-toe or on soft carpets.

'We were generally alone, and he often used to read aloud to me from Grimms' and Andersen's fairy-tales or from E. T. A. Hoffmann's *Kater Murr*, or from Hebel's *Schatzkästlein*. There was the story of the miner's sweetheart who accompanied her lover to the pit and never saw him alive again. They brought the bodies out into the daylight, but her lover was not among them. Her life passed away; she grew grey and old. Then one day his body was found in a gallery, quite unharmed, preserved by the gases. She came and embraced her lover; she had waited for him all these years and now it was a wedding and a funeral in one. Kafka liked this story for its wholeness. It was as natural as great things always are. And he loved Kleist. He was capable of reading his *Marquise von O.* to me five or six times in succession. He also used to read to me from Goethe's *Hermann und Dorothea*. He, too, was moved by the love of everyday life that is described there. The chance to live the way he wanted made him enter into a concrete relationship towards home, money and family. In a non-bourgeois sense. I emphasize that because I remember how calmly and objectively Kafka spoke to me about his former fiancée. She was an excellent girl, but utterly bourgeois. Kafka felt that marrying her would mean marrying the whole lie that was Europe. And then there was the fear that he would not find time for writing. On the other hand, his engagement was an attempt to acclimatize himself to middle-class life, and at the same time a sort of curiosity. Really he wanted to know everything and to find out about everything. A haemorrhage, connected with his tuberculosis, cleared away all his doubts.'

In young Dora Dymant Kafka experienced that deep-rooted-ness of the soul of Eastern man. In Western Europe recognition of the tragic situation of the time only rarely goes hand-in-hand with an affirmation of life. Cynicism and pessimism prevail. Martin Buber transmitted to the West the wisdom and cheerful-ness of that East where Dora Dymant grew up, and this gift of hers enchanted him. He even wished to return there with her, in order to enter a community and to live a simple life in it. And that was the question to which he devoted himself in *The Castle*. He would have tried it anywhere, but in the West it was probably no longer possible. The problem of having 'no roots' has much deeper causes in Kafka than his biographer assumes.

Once I directed the conversation towards *The Burrow*, which shows man in his subterranean corridors as a sniffing animal pos-sessed by fear. I pointed to *A Report for an Academy*, in which an ape is forced to become a 'human being'. ('Before that I had so many ways of escape, and now there are none left.') I pointed to the *Investigations of a Dog* and *The Giant Mole*. It is not horror that one experiences in reading them, not the satirical bitterness of Swift, it is not the poetic-moralizing intention one finds in the fables of Æsop or la Fontaine, nor are they socio-political views, as in the *Roman du Renard*, where the author is forced to show humans in animal guise—it is the intention of lowering human existence to the level of creeping things, and it contains disgust. Kafka himself must have felt this disgust.

Dora Dymant said quietly: 'I, too, think *The Metamorphosis* is worse than *The Penal Settlement*.' ('Our verdict does not sound harsh. The commandment which the condemned man broke will be written on his body with the harrow.') All the 'animal' aspect is shown against the background of a universal catastrophe, a cosmic misunderstanding, like the one that stares at us with glassy eyes out of *The Imperial Message*: 'The message has been sent out to you. You are there, and the message is there—only the communications are too complicated. There is no chance that the message will ever reach you.' If we compare that with the loving spirit of Saint Francis, who included even the animals in salvation, the communion of God, creation, and man that lies in Spinoza's 'Deus sive natura', and his gentle 'Amor Dei intellectu', we shall penetrate deeper into Kafka's way of thinking.

Kafka's human tragedy soon reached its end. At Christmas 1923 he caught a chill and was in bed for four weeks with pneumonia. At that time he read a great deal, and he was very busy with the proofs of *The Fasting Man*, which had just come.

Kafka did not recover. He knew how ill he was, and he had long wanted to die. An uncle, who was a doctor, came to take him to Prague. This illness was the last and final 'defeat' for Kafka. What went on in his mind then, Frau Dora Dymant has tried to reconstruct from what Kafka once said to her: 'Tearing himself away from Prague, was, even though very late, the great achievement in life without which one has no right to die. The return to his parents' house was the return to dilettantism in life. That particularly tortured Kafka; one could see it in the mental oppression which conquered him.

'I stayed in Berlin. Kafka did not want me to come to Prague, to the house from which all his disasters had come. A part of his total complex was that he hated his father and felt guilty because of it! I assume that he often murdered him in his dreams. At that time I received daily letters from him. They were taken from me by the Gestapo, together with his diaries, and in spite of all attempts no one has succeeded in finding them again. There were about thirty-five letters. In one of them Kafka mentioned "technical errors" in the way man acts towards himself. He was then preoccupied with the question of Tolstoy's fight for his own liberation and discovered some "technical errors" in that. Another time he told me of a dream he had had. Highwaymen had fetched him from his Berlin lodgings, shut him up in a shed in some backyard and gagged him. "I know that I am lost, because you can't find me." And then he suddenly hears that she is still in sight, he tries to tear himself free, thinks he is already free, and has even succeeded in pushing the gag out of his mouth. She only needed to hear his shout—but at this very moment it is discovered by the highwaymen and they gag him again.

'The uncanny thing about Kafka's mortal illness was its outbreak. I felt that he had brought it about by downright force. It was like a deliverance for him; the decision was taken out of his hands. Kafka positively welcomed the illness, even though in the last moments of his life he once more wished to live.

'He left Prague a sick man, but spiritually in good form. It was in a sanatorium in the Vienna Woods, where his sister had taken him, that I met him again. There for the first time tuberculosis of the larynx was diagnosed. Kafka was no longer permitted to speak, and so he wrote everything down: above all, the devastating effect Prague had had on him. He stayed there for three weeks. When the illness became worse, he was taken to a specialist in a hospital in Vienna. There he lay in a room together with many other gravely ill patients. Somebody died every night. He "told" me about it, pointing once to a bed that was empty. Another time he showed me a patient, a jolly man who walked about a lot, enjoyed eating and had a tube in his throat. He had a moustache and shining eyes. Kafka was very pleased that he had such a good appetite. The next day Kafka pointed at his empty bed. Kafka was not shaken but positively angry, as if he could not grasp that the man who had been so gay had had to die. I shall never forget his malicious, ironical smile.

'From the hospital Kafka was removed to a sanatorium in Klosterneuburg-Kierling, near Vienna. There he lived in a wonderful sunny room with a balcony. I stayed there with him, and later his friend Dr. Klopstock came. Kafka wrote some letters from this sanatorium: to his parents, to his brother and sister, and to Max Brod. The latter came to visit him, after he had given a reading in Vienna, in order not to let Kafka notice in what danger he knew him to be. When he was in the sanatorium, Kafka did no writing, except for the "Conversations" which must be in Dr. Klopstock's possession. He was correcting proofs the evening before he died. At four o'clock in the morning I called Dr. Klopstock, because Kafka had difficulty in breathing. Dr. Klopstock immediately recognized the crisis and wakened the doctor, who put ice-bags on his throat.

About noon the next day, Kafka died. It was the third of June, 1924.

'Years later I often read Kafka's books, always with the memory of how he read aloud from them himself. Then I felt that the German language was a hindrance to me. German is too modern a language, too much of the present day. Kafka's whole world longs for an older language. It was an ancient consciousness in him, ancient things and ancient fear. His brain knew finer nuances than the modern brain is capable of grasping. He is as little the expression of an age as the expression of the fate of a race. Nor is it everyday life that his realism represents: it is an absolute, compressed logic, in which one can live for short moments only.'

With these words Mrs. Dora Dymant closed her story. From the mantelpiece over the open fireplace, in a grey London house, Kafka's eyes looked searchingly into the darkening room out of the last photograph that he had had taken in Berlin, for his passport. They were the eyes of a man who saw the world as split by incurable schizophrenia, the opposing interests of God and man—reflecting in this way his own schizoid mentality. His negative *Weltanschauung* fed on an affirmation of life that could not be fulfilled; his personal dualism drove him into the blind alley of the despairing dualistic theology of this present time. The future belongs to a life-affirming monism, in whose rays man and creation will be reunited and an all-embracing ethos of reverence for life will ripen, like a sweet fruit out of the smoking blood of the generations.

2

EDVARD MUNCH

The Forerunner

IN 1937 a large exhibition of Munch's work was held at the
Academy of Arts in Stockholm. It was an exhibition that pur-
posed to give a comprehensive view of the master's life work—
an impossible undertaking. A year later I went to pay him a visit.
When I arrived in Oslo I wrote a letter to Munch, who was at that
time living on his property at Skøyen, not far from the Norwegian
capital, and waited impatiently for his reply. This was to be my
first meeting with a great artist, and moreover with the very
master whose pictures had made such an unforgettable impression
on my youthful memory. I was given to understand, however,
that for months Munch had refused to see anybody at all, so that
my hope of meeting him was small. Besides, I had little money
and could not afford to wait long. But within three days the post
brought me an answer written in a fine trembling hand with big
spaces between the lines. Munch wrote: 'I telephoned you but you
were not at home. I must speak to you first on the 'phone. Please
let me know when I can reach you.' When I heard his voice on the
'phone it sounded like a broken instrument. Slowly, and at times
with a stammer, Munch begged me to ring again. Yesterday, he
said, a young painter, a political refugee from Germany, had come
to him for help. After agreeing not to come without a preliminary 'phone call the young man had appeared quite unexpectedly again. This had unsettled Munch. I promised to ring
again and waited another three days. Then he told me to come.

As I entered the front-yard a ferocious looking dog hurled itself
barking against the high wire-netting that separated Munch's
property from that of his neighbour. This startled me out of my
train of thought. Another dog of a friendlier disposition looked

at me from his kennel. I went hesitatingly up to the gate. There seemed to be nobody at home. I did not want to ring the door bell, for I thought they must have heard the neighbour's dog. So I walked slowly along the crunchy gravel path leading towards the garden on the left, when suddenly at a side door opening from a glass veranda several steps up I espied the tall figure of Munch, leaning on a stick. He had just come out into the open air, quite silently. His white head was raised skywards like the head of a blind man. I stood stock still for a while staring at him, and to this day I can give no clear account of all that went through my head. But of one thing I have a vivid recollection, and that is that I regretted having come. Nevertheless, how thankful I have been since then for this my first and only meeting with Munch, for a year later, just as I was about to visit the master with the manuscript of a book, I was thwarted by the unexpected occupation of Norway by the Nazis. Munch died before the end of the war, the victim of a severe attack of bronchitis brought on by having to spend several hours in an ice-cold cellar whilst all the windows in Skoyen rattled to the blast of a heavy bombardment of Oslo.

1938. The creator of the Frieze of Life was almost blind. He had completely lost the sight of one eye a year before through the bursting of a blood vessel that flooded the eyeball, and now the other was threatened in the same way, as a result of one of the severe illnesses which had so often endangered his life. The seventy-five-year-old artist had for months been confined to his sick bed, unable to lift a finger to give the much desired finishing touches to the vast edifice of his life's work.

Munch supported himself on the edge of the table with trembling hand.

'I am rather better now,' he said in a hoarse voice. 'In the last few days the blood clot has dispersed. Before that I saw everything as through a lattice. Now I see clearly again. I can see nothing out of the right eye which has completely gone, and with the left eye I can see only a circular shape of space.' Bent over the table, he tapped his eye with his forefinger. 'I started work again yesterday with charcoal on a white canvas. I can see that quite well. Now I shall paint only large canvases, big compositions, wall decorations. That's better for my eye.' After a pause: 'It's no trifle, this danger of going blind. And then there's the pressure on the brain. I have to be careful—mustn't get excited. It all comes of overwork.'

Munch sat down in an easy-chair near the heavy table on which various objects lay strewn about. He spoke quietly, with long pauses, occasionally repeating a few words, as though short of breath—the aftermath of a heavy pressure on the chest. His thin face was clothed with the beauty that belongs to old age. His eyes were a mat grey-blue. The marks of resignation lay upon his tightly closed lips. His ears were big and shapely. Over his reddish brow fell strands of white hair, fine as silk.

We sat in the room which served as Munch's only living quarters. He slept there on a simple white-painted bedstead which was covered with a gaily coloured bedspread. Nearby stood a large wireless, and under the bed a long row of shoes. The table at which we sat had its narrow side turned towards a window through which we could look over one part of the garden, while a second window gave a view of another part of the garden. It was as if we were sitting on a terrace saturated with light. The branches of the trees came up close to the window panes.

'How do things look in the world out there? Such a lot of conflicting rumours come through. Everything seems to be strained to bursting point. War, they say! What do people want? That leads nowhere.'

He looked thoughtfully out into the green, warm light playing round his strong sensitive profile. His face was thin and transparent. His powerful hands rested heavily on the light homespun of his suit.

Munch stood up and again leaned on the table with a trembling hand. On the left middle finger he wore a silver ring of unusual size set with a green stone. This ring, which was made of two circles of different widths, served to cover a deformity, a thickening of the upper finger joint.

He then went slowly towards a tall carved cupboard standing between the two windows, its wide open doors revealing a litter of books, magazines, and all sorts of notebooks, together with cigarette cartons, cigars and a bottle of wine. He took short dragging steps, the soles of his goloshes, which were covered with splashes of colour, shuffling along the floor. It was saddening to

see that Munch was old. I had always imagined him in the full
tide of his strength. Perhaps the weakness due to his illness and
the shadow of danger hovering over him made it especially
touching. But his manner was still youthful, as was also his gaze
which lit up with good-natured irony when a question that
interested him came up for discussion. He never seemed old when
he spoke.

Near the wireless stood a tall canvas primed with the charcoal
outlines of a male figure on it; his painting, *The Negro Wrestler*,
leaned against the door. This picture is in a scheme of warm
brown, blue and violet with a drawing of two wrestlers forming a
vermilion accent in the background. It is a work that symbolizes
the elemental force of a primitive being.

Munch brought back a bottle of port and cigarettes.

Everything around him seemed to be unimportant. He was
wearing a faded blue shirt held together at the neck by a narrow
crumpled cravat. It looked as if it had been knotted hundreds
of times. . . .

We came to speak of the painter Hettner who was a professor
at the Art Academy in Dresden. At one time Hettner, who was
very attached to Munch, belonged to Munch's circle of friends in
Paris. He had many stories to tell of those days. One that he told
with particular relish concerned the portrait of Strindberg that
Munch had been commissioned to paint by a publisher at a time
when the two men were estranged. Strindberg came into the
studio, took his seat and without saying a word drew a revolver
and laid it beside him. Munch also was silent. He started to draw
—took a new piece of paper, and then another. The leaden
minutes ticked slowly away, Munch went on quietly with his
drawing. When the sitting was finished Strindberg put his
weapon in his pocket and left the studio in silence, just as he had
come, without bestowing a single glance upon the drawing.

I asked Munch about the autobiographical work which I knew
he was writing. He answered: 'I have put it aside. It's nothing
but chaos.'

When I was in Oslo I talked, amongst others, with the painter
P. about those pictures of Munch he was said to have painted
under the influence of Strindberg.

'Strindbergian ideas!' said P., and shook his head. Those pictures were the outcome of a painful personal experience. While

26

he was living in Åsgårdstrand (it was in his second great creative period) Munch fell in love with the daughter of a wholesale wine merchant in Oslo. She was rich and beautiful. On account of his Bohemian way of life in Christiania, Munch did not enjoy the best of reputations among the good bourgeois. The lady wanted to bind him to her side, but he feared his work might suffer and left her. Then one stormy night a ship came sailing from Larkollen to Åsgårdstrand with friends of Munch on board, among them the well-known art critic S. Bödtger. They had come to fetch Munch. The lady was at death's door, they said, and wanted to speak to him for the last time. Munch followed them. The lady, wrapped in a shroud, lay on a bier flanked by two lighted candles. As Munch came towards her she rose up and said, 'I knew that you would come.' Munch was shocked by this trick. He turned to leave her again, but she took a revolver, pointed it at her breast and threatened to shoot herself. To quieten her Munch laid his hand on the muzzle of the gun. It went off and wounded his middle finger which has been crippled ever since. After this experience a change came over Munch's attitude towards women. The pictures *Stormy Night* and *Madonna* were painted at this time. The latter of these two bears the features of the lady of this strange story.

Munch wanted to look at some art periodicals I had brought with me, but his reading glasses were not at hand. I went with him into an adjoining room to help him look for them. This room was very typical of the Norwegian master. All sorts of things lay around in utter confusion, but actually, there was system in this seeming disorder. Things were left lying where he wanted them, not where somebody would put them in the course of clearing up. At this moment, however, his eyes were troubling him. We looked on the piano. His fingers glided over countless piled-up gramophone records, tubes of colour, brushes, boxes and tools. A layer of fine dust covered everything. 'You know,' he said, and went over to an open cupboard—all the cupboards, by the way, stood open and were full of books, bottles, pencils and glasses. A piece of paper with something written on it in big letters was made fast to the inside of the door. A similar paper hung also on the opposite side. 'You know, the housekeeper is forbidden to come into this room. The whole house is closed to her. She may do her cleaning only in the room with the bed in it.' We couldn't find the missing spectacles. I caught sight of several pictures—one of two figures under an apple tree, red apples among bright green foliage, a picture sumptuous and rich like an old brocade. A portrait of a woman in springlike colours, painted with a light touch. At last Munch found his thick reading glasses and began to study the illustrations.

'There's a lot of Cubism in this. Cubism hasn't caught on here. Storstein is perhaps the only one. And this: this goes back to Delacroix. Yes. Movement . . .' He soon had enough of looking through the illustrations. 'My eyes are tired. Do you know, it took me three days to read your letter.'

He came back again to the question of Cubism. It was nothing but a set of rules, he said, and laid particular stress on the word 'rules'. Relating everything to cubes, cylinders, cones: hadn't the ancients already thought of it? However, as a reaction against the Jugendstil it had served a useful purpose.

He broke into laughter several times, and always it was a different laugh. On one occasion he spoke of S.'s collection of pictures. He wanted to go and see them, but it was never possible to get in touch with S. This puzzled Munch.

'I have rung him up a lot of times. A rich man like that hides himself in his house like a rabbit in its burrow; no sooner does he come in at one hole than he slips out at another. How can he work? How can he carry on his business if he can never be got hold of? You know, with one stroke S. got very rich. One day, all of a sudden: it was in Amsterdam. Then he started buying pictures, lots of pictures. I can imagine that there's always a queue of painters in front of his house, down the steps and out into the street. Very natural. That's what happens to rich people who buy pictures.' He laughed.

And he laughed again, but there was quite a new tone in his laugh, when I told him that I had just seen his painting in the workers' canteen of the Freia factory. That painting meant a lot to him. It marked, too, a serious break in the continuity of his work. Since painting it he had received no important commission, although he worked at mural decoration and monumental painting had been his chief interest in his later years. I sensed what it meant for him to be without a commission while the others were all busy embellishing new public buildings.

'Youth must be served, that goes without saying. There are

many talented people among them. But they all paint *al fresco*; for years they have talked of nothing but fresco. Books have been written about it. Why? Fresco is an antiquated method, and an unsatisfactory one at that. Often it looks grey; the colour doesn't come into its own. Oil colour has more power and brilliance, so why go back to a method that is outdated?'

'Have you ever painted *al fresco*?'

'No, never—as yet. But I think I could. It is like water-colour, no different. It has a certain charm and something mystical about it, like a dry-point. Everything can turn out differently from what the painter imagined. The result is often a surprise.' He thought for a moment. 'If I painted fresco I should be trying something quite new . . .'

That was Munch, ever ready to accept a challenge; battling against the sickness of his body, caring for his tired eyes with impatient devotion, while all the time his eager spirit was intent on the pursuit of new ideas: a condottiere of art, a Renaissance character. At a time when most men's energies were absorbed in the task of solving problems arising out of the conflicting social and mechanical forces of our day, Munch, a creator in the realm of fantasy, laboured at his task of giving depth to the human aspect of life. He ruled in a world that for us, his contemporaries, is perhaps a lost world, but which he has preserved and renewed for coming generations. Munch dedicated his genius to the inner life of man. His mind never left out of sight our connection with the universe. He unsealed that spring within us without whose virtue life is but empty striving, haste and self-deception. He led us into the realm of dreams, of contemplation and reflection. He saw us in other relationships than those in which we are placed by our mere outward existence, for the life of man was to him a symbol to which he gave back a sense it had lost. Munch saw the artist as a witness to creation. He was admirable in the sincerity and depth of his vision and in the firmness with which he preserved the integrity of his inspiration uncontaminated by the world around him.

A great artist is not the child of his time alone. Munch listened to and obeyed the small but mighty voice of creation rather than the clamorous demands of the day, and this stamps him as one of those geniuses who have taught humanity—and that means our own contemporary humanity—to think, to feel and to judge.

Because he was not the prisoner of his own time he was able to complete a task which was timeless; and in that he was like Rembrandt who stood at his easel and worked while Amsterdam was besieged by enemy soldiers; or like the masters of the Gothic cathedrals who in the tumult of war were shot down from the scaffoldings of their buildings; or, again, like those Persian sculptors who went on chiselling their imperishable reliefs while Alexander the Great marched through their land with fire and sword.

For several decades Munch had not received an official public commission. A Munch Museum was being founded in Oslo, but that was no compensation for the active creative power left without employment.

'I am very lonely here,' said Munch. 'I go on working quietly for myself.'

Yes, Munch and his work were enveloped in silence and loneliness. He put deep and disturbing questions to Nature, and Nature spoke to him with her quiet insistence.

We went into the garden and the change did Munch good. In the room with the black piano he pointed to two pictures standing there. One was *The Modern Faust*: a brightly lit street with groups of people, in the foreground the figure of a man striding forward and by his side the same figure but as a shadow only and without a face.[1] A grotesque face peers out over their shoulders. A Norwegian girl in the middle of the street turns her head and sees only the figure. The meeting with Gretchen. 'Who is Mephistopheles? A second voice within ourselves.' The other picture by the side of it represented the duel scene from *Faust*: a dark and a light figure close together in an attitude of combat. A greenish tone lay over the whole. 'A white night,' said Munch.

The white nights of the North with their deep stillness and mysterious light, the trembling tones of the young vegetation, have to be experienced. Through how many such nights has Munch painted; through how many has he sought for the answer to the riddle of life, alone, seated on a rock on the shore of the fjord!

Munch put on a leather coat and took his stick. I stood aside to make way for him but he said: 'No, you go first. Youth has the right of way.' We came to a stair whose few steps led down to the

[1] The double figure might be explained by the unfinished state of the painting.

garden. The words he had just said pained me. He came down carefully, one step at a time, leaning on his stick. How was this body, perishable in its subjection to the law of generations, related to the spirit that used it, and through it became imperishable, enduring reality? 'The artist,' said André Malraux, 'helps mankind to a consciousness of its inner greatness. Art is not a subjection, it is a conquest. A conquest of feelings and of the means of expressing them. It is a victory over the unconscious—almost always, and over logic—very often.'

Painting was for Munch no mere question of picture construction; rather was it a means of fulfilling his own proper task of human discovery and interpretation. This, too, was the element he looked for in the most recent forms of pictorial art. 'Almost all Cubists have become Surrealists,' he said. 'And did we not make our contribution to Surrealism?' But he broke off as if he had no wish to pursue the subject. 'I can't occupy myself with it. What matters to me is bringing my own work to a conclusion.'

There was only one thing that made Munch forget his bodily condition, and that was art and its problems in general. When the conversation turned to the Exhibition of French Art which brought practically the whole of the Petit Palais of the 1937 Paris World Exhibition to Scandinavia, his face lit up again as Picasso's *Guernica* was mentioned. He stood still and looked at me. His eyes became brighter; his hat was pulled down over his head to his ears. 'There is no frightfulness in that picture: just think how Goya would have painted such a motive? And yet it represents war. It's a good thing that nobody paints bloodthirsty pictures any more. What is really interesting, however, is that this picture is in a scheme of black, grey and white throughout. An excellent idea! Especially after the riot of colour we have seen of late.'

I mentioned that some of the original cartoons for the Guernica picture were in strong colour.

'Look,' said Munch. 'I want to show you something. And if it hadn't been hanging where it is for over six years people might say that I happened on the idea through Picasso.'

We went back into the house and entered a dusty room, the walls of which were covered with small pictures hanging askew. In the middle of the room was a table with all sorts of objects strewn in disorder over it, and under the table—a vacuum cleaner. Munch fetched a big key that resembled an old monastery key, and we crossed the garden which enclosed the house on three sides. The front of the building, which looked more like a simple country house than a villa, faced an empty courtyard shut off from the garden by trelliswork.

The grass grew at least three feet high, and here and there were flowers in thick clusters making colourful patches. A narrow winding garden path led to an open-air studio, to 'my invention' as Munch called it.

'In the part of the country where my family comes from,' he said, 'in a little church there hangs an altar picture some 300 to 400 years old. It is a beautiful piece of work, and it is painted in black, white and grey. You ought to go there: it's a lovely place.'

We came to a brown wooden partition and Munch let us through. A square enclosed room with a narrow strip of roof all around it but open to the sky in the centre. That was his 'invention'. In it he could work in the open air like an Impressionist and devote himself undisturbed and in the deepest concentration on the picture that welled up from within him. He used this 'invention' in summer and winter, and the paintings hung there year in year out, in wind and weather. He could come and look at them in different lights and at different times of the day or year and see them as if they were the work of another. I looked at the big composition that the artist wanted to show me. It was built up of three main groups known from other pictures: his *Workers in Snow*, 1919, his *Navvies*, 1920, his *Snow Shovellers*, 1910-1911. And it was throughout in a scheme of black, grey and white.

Taking another way back, Munch raised his hand at a certain point. 'Look how lovely that is,' he said. It was a group of dark trees, dark green moss and near it a slope sown with pink and red summer phlox. Everything in the garden grew rank and wild. Munch had another open-air studio attached to a new high studio building. Only a few pictures hung there. Again there was a big composition of men at work, and then there was a picture in spray technique, of a Bohemian theme recalling that of *Bohemians*, a youthful work.

We came to speak of van Gogh, 'Ah, he was a really great man. And Gauguin too. One always recognizes him. But isn't he a little bit too general at times?' Munch is said to have developed his style of painting with compact decorative colour masses independently of Gauguin. But so many things leave their traces in a sensitive artist. Certain pictures of Bonnard and Vuillard in which dark figures are placed in brightly lit interiors, may also have meant a great deal to Munch.

We went out into the courtyard, and a young brownish black hunting dog on a chain wagged his tail in greeting. 'One must have a dog in these parts,' said Munch.

I mentioned that in coming to him a similar dog had bestowed on me a friendly greeting when he saw that I waited at the gate.

'They belong together. When one is on watch duty the other runs free.'

Skoyen. Fields between the hills, a peasant behind his horse-drawn plough, on the horizon the serrated line of the forest. And nearby the fjord, as the fjord is ever and always present in Norway.

And loneliness and the timelessness of creation.

Evening came on, the sun set, brooding silence spread over the scene. This was Munch's time of day. Twilight simplifies and deepens; the eye is not caught and held by single details. This was his discovery, his style, his personal message. And at the same time it was the voice of his own generation whose longing forced him to do in art what long ago Plato had demanded: 'not to imitate the outward appearances of things but to depict the deeds of the soul.'

3

JAMES ENSOR

On the Ultimate Questions of Life

NOVEMBER 1949. I was standing in front of number 27, Rue de Flandre, in Ostende, a narrow, three-storeyed house built in the style of Montmartre houses, with its graceful wrought-iron balcony and windows of various shapes. In an empty shop on the ground floor there stood some tall Chinese vases. The house had an aristocratic character. Next to a bronze relief plaque showing the artist at work the following words were chiselled into the stone: LES AMIS DU PEINTRE BARON JAMES ENSOR À L'OCCASION DE SON 75e ANNIVERSAIRE.

I had paused, in those dark post-war days when world politics were being shaped by the rise of the masses, as modern art is shaped by schools, to see one man, one of the last of those artists who were strong enough to stand alone, an independent spirit such as Edvard Munch; to see a man who was the living embodiment of the idea that the personality is creation's highest aim—mass-man only the raw material; to meet a painter who knew how to fight in solitude for an inner world and win the battle. For was it not Ensor who had put into one of his most important pictures the words: FANFARES DOCTRINAIRES TOUJOURS RÉUSSI? Yes, doctrinaire fanfares are always successful. We stand in amazement to-day before the ideological flood which has submerged all human values. Where is there still a human face to be seen? Behind the masks of ideologies and propaganda slogans they are hidden as though in prisons. Ensor has painted these masks on the faces of men. To him at the turn of the century they still seemed to be picturesque and full of individual expression. Humour and the tragic element, delight and despair, were still

34

mingled in them, and death—biological death, not the mass slaughter of our modern analytical civilization—was there too, dignified and top-hatted, and then the Saviour's gentle countenance. It was a carnival of vanities, of short-sightedness, greed and hate, a variegated Ship of Fools, Eulenspiegel's tomfooleries and the wisdom of the men of Gotham, mixed with a dash of bitterness, the kind we have supped our fill of from Goya's *Caprichos*. It was an up-to-date variation of the imaginative world made immortal by the Flemish allegories of Hieronymus Bosch and Pieter Brueghel—not the uniform, soulless mass-face which we encounter everywhere to-day.

When ringing the bell I wondered: Is he still alive? The bell echoed down the long entrance-hall, and I heard dragging footsteps; then the door was opened by a man in a small black cap of the kind that Anatole France used to wear. I learned from Auguste van Yper, who had been Ensor's factotum for more than forty years, that I could see the master only that afternoon, about four o'clock; for he was accustomed to a late lunch. He was well, Auguste told me, but he did not paint now; he had not touched a brush for seven years. The last pictures he had painted were three small panels, no larger than exercise-books. These showed objects from his surroundings, from the first-floor room where he usually sat for the best part of the day—a grandfather clock, statuettes, vases. One of them represented a garden of Eros with small figures on a lawn, a statue, and instead of the sun— a face.

'The devil!' I exclaimed, knowing that the artist's puckish spirit was capable of it, but I could not help thinking too what glorious progress we had made since man had abolished fear and done away with the devil. '*Si vous voulez,*' Auguste said, with a sly smile in his eyes. 'You will see for yourself. And if you have nothing better to do in the meantime, go and visit Antony, Ensor's old friend, in the Rue Euphrosine Beernaert.'

I was grateful to Auguste for his suggestion. From Antony, the photographer, I learned how far I could go with my questions. For after all, I did not want to talk to Ensor about his pictures; they speak for themselves eloquently enough. 'Let there be no bounds to your curiosity,' Antony exclaimed finally. 'You can speak of death, and even about the life beyond. Speak of any-

[1] Ensor, who was born in 1860, died not long after my visit.

35

thing that occurs to you. Ensor is not nervous, even though he stands, as it were, with one foot in the grave.'

Then I looked through the photographs of Ensor's pictures. I saw the masked processions, the *masques scandalisés*, the theatre of life and in it the young artist as melancholy Pierrot, as the pure fool, the innocent sufferer and questioner; or surrounded by demons, pursued by the enigma of life—'*Peste dessous, Peste dessus, Peste partout.*' And I saw, too, humanity 'in need of salvation' like an army of insects, man whose retort to the words of the Sermon on the Mount is a *Mort aux Vaches*. Ensor suddenly struck me as the Molière of painting, a Flemish Rabelais who had sprung from Rembrandt's religious feeling and Rubens' *joie de vivre*. Here were the lyrical pictures of the shells on the seashore. '*La coquille, c'est la fleur de la mer,*' Ensor once said. He preferred them to flowers. Flowers wither and die, but shells were imperishable. And here too was the photograph of the monumental painting of Christ's entry into Brussels, a canvas which hangs in Ensor's studio and which I hoped to be able to see that day. It had been exhibited only three times during his life; first in Brussels in 1929, where some thousand of the master's works were shown;[1] for the second time in Paris, ten years later, and for the third time in the International Summer Exhibition in Ostende, 1949.

When I came in, I saw Ensor sitting near the window, only half turned towards the door. He was wearing a soft black felt hat. His face with its regular features was rosy and his bright forget-me-not-blue eyes were gazing across the room with a kindly expression. Not at me, yet slightly passive, tranquil, waiting. I stated the reason for my visit, raising my voice, for the expression of his face told me that he was hard of hearing. Behind the comfortable armchair stood Auguste with his little black cap and his Mephisto-like gaze. His face beamed with inward certainty, the reflected glory of his master's greatness, a self-confident limitation in contrast to Ensor's understanding gentleness. Ensor pursed his lips before he articulated his words, as though testing them first. We were strangers to each other. I knew that I would have to break the ice of this kindly detachment with my questions, or learn nothing at all in the short time I had at my disposal.

On the walls hung countless small pictures of Ensor's. The

[1] About 350 oil-paintings together with his engravings and drawings: the biggest exhibition of his life, beginning with works from the year 1875.

room was filled with dark furniture; everywhere there was porcelain, big sea-shells and framed photographs. It was like being on a stage, translated into an Ibsen milieu. On the table at Ensor's side stood his three last paintings. Auguste pointed at them emphatically, reminding me of our earlier conversation. On one of the walls hung a portrait in dark tones reminiscent of Courbet, a work of Ensor's early period. On another wall was a larger painting in pastel colours—pink and pale blue—a stage décor for Ensor's ballet-mime *La Gamme d'Amour, Flirt de Marionettes*. In order to start the conversation, I said that I could well understand how difficult it was for the experts to classify his art. It was surreal or super-real because of its subject matter, and that long before the Surrealists, and at the same time it was traditionally felt. It was often symbolic in the conception of its motifs and impressionistic in the handling of the paint. It was expressionistic and fantastic as a spontaneous representation of human emotions.

'*Je laisse les impressions libre,*' Ensor said in a soft melodious voice. The smile on his face was warm and kind. 'I attach no importance to the names of styles, *je n'aime pas les qualificatifs.*'

I mentioned that to me his art was so full of meaning because of the ideas which I could draw from it and how unfortunate I thought the recent development of analytic-constructive painting, which, because of its lack of meaning, has—as André Gide has put it in his essay on Poussin—become the symbol of our time.

'Yes,' Ensor nodded. 'My art tends towards the literary, *est très porté vers la littérature. Mes peintures se promènent à l'autour de la peinture.* But where does generalizing lead us? It is possible to grasp one thing or the other, taking into account the angle from which we see it. *Mais pour faire une règle générale ça devient trop compliqué.*'

I changed the subject. I referred to the restlessness of the time, the disheartenment and nihilism that prevails everywhere, and, I went on, 'there are still people to be found who talk of progress, without recognizing that mechanized civilization has robbed us of our innermost strength and enslaves us more and more.'

'I see no evolution,' Ensor said, pursing his lips. '*Je vois seulement une forte indécision,* nothing but a great uncertainty. *Et des inquiétudes surtout. . . .*'

'Where will it all end?'

He shook his head. 'That probably lies outside our present power of comprehension—*au dessus de la compréhension actuelle.*'

He looked out of the window and I scrutinized him closely. How beautiful old men are, I thought, provided their minds remain alive, while old age exacts its due. I had the burning desire to ask him, just him, about ultimate things and I risked it. 'Do you believe in life after death?'

'No,' he said decidedly. Auguste smiled. '*Je ne crois pas à une autre vie après la mort.*'

'And the meaning of death? Is it enough to regard it as something "natural"?'

'*C'est fort difficile. . . .*'

'But you must have been tormented by the enigma of life and death . . .'

'Certainly. I have searched, *oui, mais pas trouvé.*' He paused. 'Perhaps this is an answer to your question: *Je suis tranquille, je me laisse bercer par les évènements, j'ai confiance dans les forces majeures.*'

'That's resignation,' I exclaimed.

Ensor gave me a lively glance and said: 'You accord the individual too much importance. *L'individu n'a aucune signification spéciale.*'

Auguste had been listening impatiently for a long time, now he burst out with: 'The Master is not a philosopher. After all, he's a painter.'

I would not let myself be put off. A quick answer for Auguste: 'But there is philosophy in his pictures, not only painting!' And so to the next question for Ensor: 'God! How do you conceive of God?'

'*Dieu—c'est une force, c'est quelquechose qui est fort.*' And after a pause: 'God is what we believe in. *Ça change de maître et de maîtresse.* It is a garment in which we clothe our nakedness.' Ensor pointed to a miniature, the figure of a woman. '*Dieu! Pourquoi pas?*'

Auguste threw in categorically: 'The Chinese, think of the Chinese. *C'est évident*, there are very many gods.'

I nodded to him soothingly and said quickly to Ensor, for I felt that I was tiring him: 'But why did you paint Christ on your painting of the entry into Brussels? And why Brussels?'

'I chose Brussels, but it might as well have been another place. And Christ,' Ensor said, drawling . . . Auguste broke in: 'The Master is a bad Catholic but a great revolutionary.'

'You should write a book about it,' I retorted.

'I am waiting until the others have made all the mistakes.'

It was impossible to get the better of this fellow Auguste!

'Christ,' Ensor repeated, '*est une figure très grande. On s'est beaucoup occupé de cette figure-là. Le Christ, c'est une signification obligatoire.*'

After these words Ensor gazed into space for a long time without speaking. He looked at a small picture on the wall, two female figures, one in a red dress, the other in blue. 'At first they were naked,' he said, '*mais elles m'embêtaient, ces femmes nues, elles n'étaient pas belles.*'

I felt I ought to break off our conversation now and asked for permission to see his studio before leaving.

On the next floor Ensor had hung some of his most important paintings. While we—Auguste and I—climbed the narrow stairs, past drawings and engravings, I mused on the life of this man, who for all practical purposes had never left Ostende ('*J'ai saisonné un peu, mais j'ai préféré de habiter ici*') and who had never let his thoughts be disturbed either by wars or by revolutions.

I stood before Christ's Entry into Brussels. A disturbing and at the same time liberating experience! I saw the slogans: VIVE LA SOCIALE, long live humanity, communal life, VIVE JÉSUS ROI DE BRUXELLES! These inscriptions were on red banners carried by fantastic masked figures, and soldiers surrounded the standard bearing the words FANFARES DOCTRINAIRES TOUJOURS RÉUSSI. Death, wearing a top hat, moved about among the masked figures, and our Lord rode in the background on a donkey, almost unnoticed, simple as truth itself, among all the bright, highly-coloured bustle that was on his account. On a stage a curious puppet-play was being performed. Next to this monumental painting hung the 1885 drawing *Jésus Roi des Juifs*, and then the drawings, *Le Christ devant le Peuple* and *Golgathe, Descente du Croix*, experiences reminiscent of Rembrandt. And there, too, was the *Christ Tourmenté par le Peuple*, quite bizarre, like a schizophrenic's painting, an eruption of hot lava from the innermost depths. And the many human heads: perseverations! But here I had not the strength either to condemn humanity or to pity the artist.

There I see him in a portrait from the year 1892 as a young man, kneeling before the Mother of God, praying for her blessing on his work. *La Vierge Consolatrice*. These dunes and windmills he had painted so sensitively as a boy of fifteen, and that *eau forte* of a skeleton rising from its lying position which he had engraved in the prime of life. 'It is a self-portrait—Ensor in the year 1960?' Auguste explained. 'The Master has a sense of the grotesque. Look at this etching, these skeletons p . . . ing at each other. . . . *Les morts qui s'amusent. Peut-être que les morts s'amusent aussi?*'

'Does Ensor play?' I asked, pointing to a harmonium.

'Yes, he likes playing though he never studied it. He does not play from music, only his own improvisations. *Très gai, amusant. . . .*'[1]

I went from picture to picture. Here were the large *La Vive et Rayonnante Entrée à Jerusalem*, the death-bed of his mother and his aunt, the bathing girls with the Mother of God in the sky, the self-portrait (1936) with hat, palette and the grinning mask, all stones combining to make up this rich and curious building of the imagination, in which suffering and darkness were lit up by a liberating self-irony.

We left the studio. I saw Auguste walk down the stairs backwards. It must have been a compulsion-neurosis; perhaps he did not want to turn his back on his master's immortal creations. I felt somewhat uneasy, and still more so when at the same moment I caught sight of an etching on the wall depicting a huge beetle with a human face, a graphic representation which led my thoughts immediately to Franz Kafka's mysterious story of the transformation. It was only when I again entered Ensor's drawing-room that I felt relieved. He was sitting there absorbed in his reading. I glimpsed the title of the book: *Les Ecrits de James Ensor*. He was reading his own writings, as one reads another author's work; he was following with interest the intellectual flashes which he had noted down as a young man.

Downstairs the bell rang insistently. Ensor put the book aside and caught sight of me. But at this moment, with all his Flemish

---

[1] Ensor himself composed the music to his ballet-mime *La Gamme d'Amour*.

joviality and high spirits and smoking a cigar, in came the writer Jean Stevo, who had just published a book about Ensor.

Ensor appeared utterly changed. Suddenly he seemed gay, jocular and youthful. I experienced tangibly the Janus-like quality of his being. When I tried to take leave of him, for I had to catch the train to Brussels, he stamped both feet on the floor like a spoilt boy. And quite unexpectedly he drew the hand which I held out to him to his lips and kissed it. I felt ashamed and could only stammer: 'It is for me to kiss your hand, Master, for I have been moved and enriched.' And I drew to my lips the hand that had created such strangely original things. But I felt as though I were acting in a play together with puppets and masks. Then I left quickly. It was like something in a dream.

Farewell, James Ensor! Earth has become a desert and I have had to travel far in order to speak with a sage who still knows the sweet and bitter secret of Being.

4

MARC CHAGALL

In Search of the Primary Sources of Inspiration

'I was living and working in America at a time when all humanity was involved in a world-wide tragedy. America's hospitality gave me the strength to carry on. And yet my art has remained true to the old ideal.' So Chagall wrote in 1947. Now he has returned to France after seven years' absence. It was Paris that gave him inspiration and the breath of life in the old days; Paris provided the atmosphere in which his art developed and came to full flower. To-day he still believes in France. 'Although the circle of her great masters seems closed, France will produce new wonders in the realm of art. I am sure of that. Nothing can shake my faith in the genius of France.'

Although very lively, Chagall has not become any younger in the interval.[1] He has been shaken not only by the terror of the war, but also by the loss of the one human being, who was a help and inspiration to him from the beginning, his first wife, Bella Chagall, who died of an insidious disease in America.

'I owe everything to her,' he said in a low voice, as though he did not want anyone else to hear what we were talking about; and he gazed long at a photograph showing her in her youth. Now all at once standing quite still, he seemed a legendary figure, as though turned to stone, his face old—a hundred years, two hundred years old. His hands hung down, heavy as lead; his eye was glassy. I have never experienced such a transformation. It lasted only a moment, but he must have travelled far in his thoughts; perhaps he had been listening at the crystal door between this life and the beyond? On the wall hung a version of his famous picture of the pendulum clock with the big bird's wing, giving

[1] In 1949, when this was written, Chagall was in his sixty-second year.

42

one the feeling of the flight of time. It is also a symbol of his own life's journey. To the left and to the right stand the derelict houses of his native town, Witebsk.

Our meeting took place in the Villa l'Auluette in Orgeval, near St. Germain-en-Laye, where Chagall has settled down with his three-year-old son David and the child's young English mother. Ida, his daughter by his first marriage, lives in Paris. Chagall is not likely, however, to stay in Orgeval for any length of time. He longs for the South—Cassis or Vence. He does not feel at peace so near to Paris. 'Wherever I can work,' he says, 'there I feel happy.' His young companion, Virginia, came into his life as Hendrijke Stoffels came into Rembrandt's. I recall that in his book, *My Life*, Chagall wrote: 'Perhaps Rembrandt would have liked me.' She gave him new courage to face life, new joy in his work, and youth renewed. And that explains why, as he said, when we were talking about the nihilism of modern youth: 'I prefer love and optimism to that. *On se trompe tout le temps, la vie est comme ça. Mais je préfère de me tromper avec l'optimisme et avec l'amour.*'

Even before Chagall went to America his art had undergone a fundamental change. This was obvious from the pictures hanging on the walls everywhere in this comfortable house. At first Chagall painted without any teaching at all: a wedding-procession, a funeral, the birth of a child, a beggar, a rabbi, a dream-like fiddler. At that period he was an original primitive *'de la race du Christ,'* as Raïssa Maritain has so beautifully put it. He only had to shut his eyes in order to see. Reality, as he experienced it, was different from the reality that art-galleries had to offer him.

Chagall came closer to me. He is of middle height, supple as a tightrope-walker. He wears a large-checked woollen shirt and a velvet jacket. His face is finely chiselled, his hands are as delicate as a woman's. 'Youth is always in need of orientation. But who gave me orientation?' He smiled. 'There was a picture of Czar Ivan the Terrible, made by Repin. One saw the swollen veins; every little hair, every pore was meticulously painted. The Czar had a tear in his eye. *"Tu ne serais jamais un peintre,"* I said to myself. Purely artistic reasons drove me out of Russia before and after the Revolution. And what was I to find in Paris? When I met Apollinaire, the standard-bearer of Cubism, for the first time, I did not dare to show him my pictures. I understood as little of

French Cubism as of Russian Realism. Personally, I believe that a scientific tendency can never be a fortunate one for art. Impressionism was alien to me too. I grasp everything simply by instinct. Art is for me a condition of the soul. The only master I ever had was my father—not Cézanne, not van Gogh. My father was a simple workman. When I saw his tired hands, or when I saw my mother. . . . And then Surrealism. To me the Surrealists are just the same as the Naturalists. Fundamentally it's all the same thing. All that the Surrealists wanted was to paint a different "pipe", a different "guitar", a different "tree". Automatism never entered into my mind.'

'Why is it that this one figure in your picture stands on its head?' I asked.

'To underline another reality by means of contrast. Art without these psycho-plastic contrasts seems so monotonous. To me it is like a meal without salt or pepper.

'Actually I love all painting, provided that its elements are pure. *J'admets tous.* But abstract art is so intolerant. Everything has to give way, the romantic, the figurative. . . . Even Cubists never went as far as to say: *Seulement nous.* Anyway, abstract painting is not even new, for it is derived from Cubism. Take, for instance, Kandinsky. In the last twenty years he has painted like a cobbler, his work is rigid. Mondrian was more poetical. But I prefer Klee to all of them, a thousand times.'

We left the studio and went down a few steps. Chagall stopped. 'I'll explain to you why the intellectuals never grasp the full meaning of my art. All post-Cubist artists substitute brain-activity for what should be in the heart. Anything constructed can easily be analysed by any brain. When they talk about my work it's always about the poetic element, about the invention in it. But I don't search for the poetic. I have searched for neither poetry nor literature nor for symbols. I only try to be myself. To be honest and simple. Even now I am just like a beginner. When a picture has been sufficiently tortured, when it is sufficiently unhappy, I let it be. Sometimes I work on one subject for several years. It is preferable to work a long time on one subject.'

The dining-room is large and has French windows opening on to a garden terrace. Chagall pointed to one of his early *avant-garde* pictures, *Le Saoul*, 1911. The colour seemed a little cold. A man's

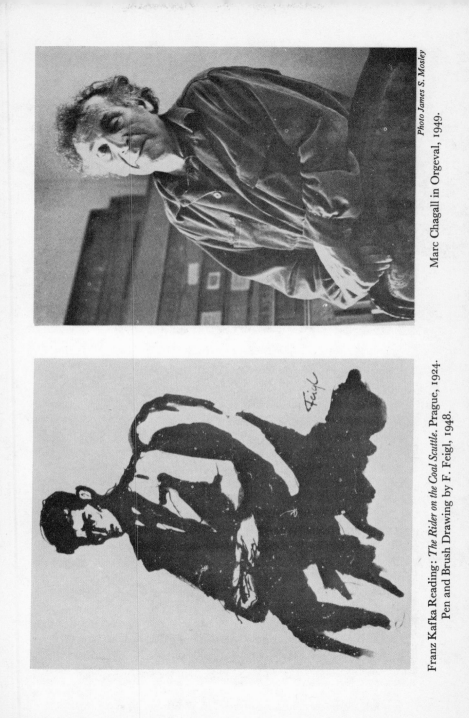

Marc Chagall in Orgeval, 1949.

Franz Kafka Reading: *The Rider on the Coal Scuttle*. Prague, 1924.
Pen and Brush Drawing by F. Feigl, 1948.

James Ensor in His Studio.

Ostend, 1923. In the background the monumental painting: "Christ's Entry into Brussels" (1888).

Edvard Munch, at the age of 75, in his Studio. Skøyen, 1938.

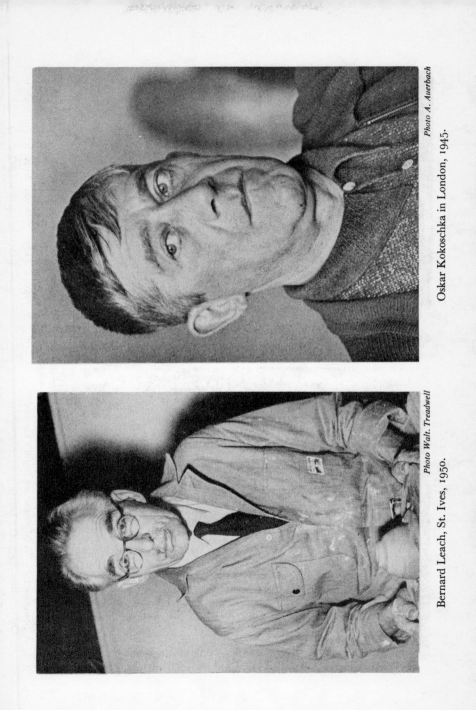

Oskar Kokoschka in London, 1945.

Bernard Leach, St. Ives, 1950.

C. F. Hill: "The Sermon." (Undated) Black crayon. The National Museum, Stockholm, 264/1927.

Ernst Josephson: Portrait of Ludwig Josephson directing Shakespeare's "A Midsummer Night's Dream". Oil painting, 1893. Private collection, Stockholm.

head, separated from the body and flying somewhere in space, must have caused a great sensation before the first world war. Some critics prefer these early pictures to the later ones, where the musical quality of colour is predominant.

'*Des choses folles,*' was all Chagall said. But without this heroic period of his creative life, during which he was formally influenced by Cubism and Fauvism, both of which had to be absorbed by his imagination, he could not have painted the way he paints to-day.

'Avantgardism is necessary. Art must keep on renewing itself. I don't think the present-day generation of artists has less talent than we had. But tell me, how does it come about that art degenerates in quality from decade to decade? Almost all children have genius, if only they have a chance to develop. All this seems to be caused by the restlessness, by the world situation, by politics. It is a sociological problem.'

During lunch Chagall talked about his longing to go back to Russia. 'One ought to travel in foreign countries for a short time and then return home,' he said. 'Van Gogh, Pascin, Modigliani, they all died young. But Munch drew strength from his native soil. Man is like a tree, his roots lie in the earth of his country. Then the branches may spread out over the whole world. Of course, there are trees that hang in mid-air and others that stand in the water. But those that are rooted in solid ground bear the best fruit. Why do I always paint Witebsk? With these pictures I create my own reality for myself, I recreate my home. This flower-piece I painted in 1929, when I was longing for Russia. The flowers I painted at other times were presents. They came to me and I did not want them to wither, so I painted them.'

Here on an easel was Chagall's picture, *The Cock*. It was painted in 1947 in America when he was homesick for France, his second home. It is a picture of a cock holding a palette from which the bride arises like a red flame. It is Chagall's eternal love-song to Bella. In the background, in purple tones, is Witebsk, everlastingly present.

Chagall is the painter of the nostalgic yearning for the first unforgettable impressions that life gives us. These impressions have lingered in his mind as primal images. They are like the letters of an alphabet, like the words from which his language sprang. The candlestick with the burning lights, the moon, the animal playing the violin, Christ, the Wandering Jew, a figure floating in space, the riding girl of the circus-ring. So comes metempsychosis. A fish, a cat, a calf with a human face, a man with an animal's head. For Chagall all life has the same mystic primal source. And so the time element comes in. The clock with the wing, the winged carp, and then the angel falling from on high and the angel that inspires.

Standing before the picture *Resurrection*, which contains some of these primal images, Chagall merely said: 'The resurrection of life, not of dogma, expressed by means of certain colours. There is no rule for the understanding of colour. *Chacun de nous est né avec sa couleur.* One only has to let them come forth, liberate them. *Plus la couleur est riche, plus la vie est tragique.* The truer the colour is, the nearer we are to truth.'

'Perspective? What you see here is not nature. I am not Cézanne, who modulated in order to paint volume. I am concerned with spiritual space. The others *create* objects, the others stand *in front of* nature. I have it inside myself.' And he added: 'Of course, everything contributes to art, even the buzzing of a fly.'

The Naked Cloud. Two reclining lovers, floating like a cloud over a Russian village. Beneath them the moon, above them the animal playing—the animal with the soul—and then the kneeling woman. His delicate hands moved lovingly over another picture, *The Soul of the Town.* He said, '*Il y a une chose d'instantané qui s'épanouisse sur l'éternité, et l'éternité, qui se change dans une minute.*' My gaze followed his hand. It spoke to me of grey tones, of a black in one corner, of the grey blending into purple, and then the red. Colours came alive for me as never before.

'If you knew how many doubts there are within me, you would have doubts of me yourself.' Doubts? I have doubts of those who say that he is only repeating himself. Chagall has just finished work on the illustrations for two of the most beautiful books in world literature, for *Tériade*: *Stories from the Decamerone und La Fontaine's Fables.* And Chagall, who is the first painter since Rembrandt to make us re-experience, in true intensity, the visions of the Old Testament, has some ideas for large religious compositions. Will the old wish-dream of the painter of stage and ballet décors be fulfilled? Will he display, like an old master, his rich imagination on sacred walls?

* *

*

The studio in which Marcel Proust once stayed in Vence and where Paul Valéry tried his luck in painting belongs now to Chagall. It is the smaller of two buildings of the villa Les Collines where he now lives and where he acts as a most attentive host to his friends and admirers. He lets them take part generously in the beauties of his place, the delights of his kitchen and cellar, in the picturesque adventures of his oriental phantasy, his wit, his changing moods, his actor's talent. For Chagall is as much an actor as he is story-teller and a painter. It often seems as if he were watching himself speak, trying to gauge the impression his words make on his audience.

So this is how these gods of the French Art Olympus live! They are few enough to be counted on the fingers of one hand! When I saw this mellow building in the middle of a huge garden, a row of orange trees surrounding the terrace in front of it, the lines of Vasari came into my mind, where he describes Raphael at the height of his glory. 'Raphael's fame and the rewards he received rose more and more so that he was impelled to build a palace to his own memory in the Borgo Nuovo in Rome which Bramante decorated with stucco-work.'

None of his contemporaries has decorated the rooms in Chagall's villa; old and new works by himself are displayed on its walls. And even if in comparison the scale of grandeur seems to turn in favour of Raphael, we must remember the difference between our age and the Renaissance. Raphael remained during his lifetime more or less an Italian master; Chagall is a world master, and the works I saw there in the early spring were exhibited a few weeks later in Paris and the following autumn in New York. Some went to Stockholm, and some to Turin.

We sat under the orange trees overlooking the valley of Vence. Here in the heart of the Mediterranean, the birthplace of our culture, religious and artistic, Chagall felt something new growing in his heart and mind. It is thus that he became a representative, together with Renoir, Bonnard, Matisse, Braque, Picasso, of that drift in art towards the Mediterranean in search of a culture of light and grace. Here everyone smiles at you and artists preach again the gospel of beauty. If I were asked to describe in a few words the characteristics of its atmosphere I would answer: There I met people who were kind and happy. The errant Jew who was haunted by the visions of his native Russian village has taken root in the sweet soil of the Midi. In the midst of mild and fertile nature he is finding his way back to the earth. 'The very earth on which I walk is so luminous,' he said, 'it looks at me tenderly, as if it were calling me. I have wanted to use this earth like the old artisans. . . . It suddenly seems to me that this earth, so radiant, is calling from afar to the deaf earth of the city where I was born—Witebsk. . . . During these threatening times, one is especially eager to attach oneself to this earth, to mingle with it.'

This development started when Chagall left Orgeval six or seven years ago. He turned to me: 'Even then I said to Tériade: "There is something in the air, one is not satisfied. I too am not satisfied. I want to go back to the source. Monet was at the source. Realism, yes, but of what kind? Take a loaf of bread. Would you say it is a primary thing? No. But the grain is primary, the orange, the potato. Monet tastes good. The earth is good. Put an orange beside a painting of Monet—*ça tient*. Put a stone beside a ceramic piece which I have done here in the Midi —*ça tient*. But put a stone beside a ceramic piece of . . ., the stone stays apart because his ceramic is stylization. Monet has not offended the earth. He has not produced decorative things. Do you follow me? This is perhaps a new beginning. Can you realize how they will cry: the traitor Chagall. Why traitor? Because I am faithful to my source?" ' He stopped and slipped, so to speak, out of his skin to have, for an instant, a look at himself.

We went to the studio. I had asked him to show me his recent works. Two large religious paintings stood there, unfinished. The one depicting King David and the other Moses showing the tables of the law to the people. Their strong colour scheme made me think of primitive Italian masters, but in their imagery and delineation they remained typically Chagallesque. ⸳Many well-known French painters have in recent years produced works intended for the decoration of churches: Rouault, Leger, Braque, Bonnard, Bazaine, Manessier, for example. The most famous of all these works is the Chapelle du Rosaire, a few steps from Chagall's house, which was not only decorated but designed and built for the Dominican nuns in Vence by Matisse. The stained-glass windows, the carved door, the altar, the cross on it, the wall decorations, the ceremonial vestments, are all by Matisse. There is even a little museum with working sketches of the master showing the development and the transition from a realistic to an abstract conception of the figural decorations made for the chapel. Apart from his painting and book illustration, Chagall has in recent years also devoted attention to ceramic work, to decorated glass, to sculpture. Small-size sculptures in marble and limestone with typical elements of his compositions, carved directly in the stone in the manner of Romanesque reliefs: Descent from the Cross, Two Nudes with Goat, Lovers. . . .

With a half-ironic and half-communicative smile, so typical of Chagall, he said: 'I have forgotten the history of sculpture, so I had to start in the same way as my little boy would do. I love stone. I love to work with it. It is a primary reality—primary realities are marvellous things. The same is true of clay.'

We looked at his ceramic works, mainly oval or square plates with rounded corners and a few vases decorated with a great variety of motives such as the Circus Clown with Horse, Lovers hidden amongst Flowers, Fish, Sun, and Moon, and other imagery from Chagall's paintings.

'How shape, decoration and glaze are in absolute harmony,' I said to him, 'a perfect unity.' He looked up and used then a word which he uses very often nowadays. 'What you want to say is that it makes an entirely *natural* impression! To do that it has to come from within, it must not be conceived merely decoratively. In . . . ceramics there is *beaucoup d'embrouillage*, much confusion. The source is, in fact, only simulated. The lines, the graphic side are quite favourable. The problem of the source, however, remains. To add this or that colour which then defies the form can never lead to a natural thing. *Il ne faut pas se fâcher.* But . . . gets cross. Goya did not get cross, he was natural. To make ceramics is like baking bread. Colour is not only colour. You see that? The glaze must be true like the human skin. What one feels enters the material. The whole gets enveloped in its own atmosphere and it has to remain ceramic. One simply makes it as one makes love. When looking at the result it is not the motif which interests me.

It is not the primary matter any more, it has become the material of a new reality.'

At the lunch table meat and vegetables are served on ceramic plates. The fine rose, azure and dark blue, the pale yellow, brown-black and olive-green tones mix with the rich colours of the food. Chagall takes up his theme again of 'the chemistry' of Monet. A more theoretical question about his own art he rejects with the words: '*Moi, je ne comprends pas Chagall.*' His disarming, mild voice betrays that he means it as sincerely as when he says: '*Je ne m'occupe pas des choses réelles*' (meaning business; nevertheless he seems to manage quite well); or when, after criticizing the mannerisms of other known contemporary painters, and after having spoken of his own 'stammering' —'painting as a speech is like stammering,' he said—adds: '*Voilà, c'est moi.* I do not say that to please you, or out of false modesty. My eyes are open for the others . . . *Je n'ai jamais fait du mal aux autres.*' —Then again he seems to slip out of his own skin to cast a glance at himself.

When leaving his house I nearly stumbled over an old dog which dragged himself slowly over the path.

'He is blind,' Chagall said, bending his head a little to the one side with a smile of pity and accompanying it with a gesture of his fine hands which expressed—'I need a dog here, this one is blind, but what can I do? I can't possibly have him destroyed!' It is this smile of his which will remain in my memory. For Chagall life is like a big picture book. One does not need to know much. It is sufficient to look at it, with kindness in one's heart, to understand.

Part Two

THE EXPRESSIONISTS

THE EXPRESSIONISTS

Style and Periodicity

The first phase of medieval art has a haunting charm beyond compare: its own intrinsic quality is enhanced by the fact that its message, which stretched beyond art's own self-justification of aesthetic achievement, was the symbolism of things lying behind nature itself. In this symbolic phase, medieval art energized in nature as its medium, but pointed to another world.

A. N. Whitehead

THE newer aesthetics is not exclusively concerned with problems of form, but devotes great attention to the creative processes themselves and the relationship between style and personality. In this one can recognize the influence of modern psychology. For the older generation style was more the expression of a whole cultural epoch's consciousness. The question of style is of the greatest importance in any serious study of art, and aesthetics in Central Europe has been intensely preoccupied with it during the decades before the outbreak of the Second World War. There a comparative science of styles sprang up, and also the beginnings of a morphology of style; the inter-relations between aesthetics and other branches of learning were investigated. All that is more or less absent from England; there has however, been a recrudescence of interest in these matters during the last twenty years in America. A theory of the plastic arts is as necessary as a theory of music. It is impossible to arrive at any really valid results in aesthetic research without agreement as to the use of terms and their exact definition.

In his Principles of Art History, *Kunstgeschichtliche Grundbegriffe* the Swiss art historian H. Wölfflin claims to have discovered two different tendencies in the evolution of European art, corresponding to two different modes of vision and recurring periodically in the course of time. According to Wölfflin these two stylistic tendencies became most clearly manifest in the sixteenth and seventeenth centuries, in the Classic and the Baroque spirit.[1] Wölfflin goes on to point out that the art of the sixteenth century was clear and that of the seventeenth century confused. It is interesting to note that scientists refer to the seventeenth century as the century of genius, in which the names of Francis Bacon, Harvey, Kepler, Galileo, Descartes, Pascal, Huyghens, Boyle, Newton, Locke, Spinoza and Leibniz appeared like stars of the first magnitude in the sky of exact science. Other authorities have postulated a third type of formative will beside the Classic and the Romantic, namely the Primitive, this being regarded not only as an early stage of development in relation to the Classic, but as a mode of expression in its own right. All three styles can appear simultaneously, as it has happened in modern art. Indeed, there is a modern artist who in his work has been inspired by all the wealth of styles from all periods and nations. This global consciousness of styles may lead to a first universal, unified art conception (Malraux), or it may also mean the loss of capacity to create a style in the traditional sense. Style in this sense is bound up with a certain geographical area. (Frobenius' *Kulturkreislehre*, and Spengler.)

When we investigate the elements characterizing the different styles, we can make the following statements about the Classic. The *grouping* in the classic picture is symmetrical and counterbalanced; the *structure* is composite (the individual elements remain distinct, e.g. architecture, landscape, figures); *colour* is based on the contrast of light and shadow; the various components overlap each other to some extent in their *spatial distribution*; *extension* is three-dimensional (geometrical perspective); the *line* tends to be intersected; the *rhythm* is determined by an angular system. As regards *movement*, classic art is static, balanced and harmonious; the *formative will* is constructive, the *state of mind* is a conscious one.

The Romantic style shows asymmetry and torsion (rhythmic sinuosities) in the *grouping*; in *structure* the interpenetration of the various pictorial elements; in *colour* it is opalescent, iridescent; in *spatial distribution* the various components cross each other; *extension* is four-dimensional (three dimensions in space with one psychological or religious dimension extending into the infinite,

[1] In this essay the somewhat wider term 'Romantic' will be substituted for 'Baroque', as being better suited to our purpose.

the eternal); the *line* is violent and varied; the *rhythm* is conditioned by the intersections and interweavings. As regards movement the Romantic style is dynamic, unbalanced, ecstatic, disharmonious; the *formative will* is complex (in our period even destructive; distortions); the artist's *state of mind* is influenced by the subconscious (in our period particularly by negative feelings such as fear and despair). If the seventeenth-century Baroque had faith, the Romantic movement in present-day art is agnostic and solipsistic as a protest against the Zeitgeist itself, and neurotic as well. It is like a cry of despair, a revolt that often oversteps the borderline between the normal and the abnormal.

The Primitive style has symmetry in the *grouping*; the *structure* is simple; the *colour* is even and strong; the *distribution in space* parallel or radiating; the *extension* two-dimensional, the *line* continuous, the *rhythm* established by repetition, symmetry and parallelism. The element of *movement* is supplied by the narrative content. Among primitive people the *formative will* is governed by the magic and the hypnotic; in folk-art and in Neo-Primitivism it is conditioned by a naïve representational decorative and play impulse. (Fr. Lehel.)

This generalizing classification provides us with a measuring rod with which to approach the varied artistic output of the present.

Expressionism has affinities with Romanticism and Primitivism, but none with Classicism. It is hostile to Classicism of any sort. South of the Alps and west of the Rhine, it cannot be found, or only if introduced by foreign artists, such as Chagall and Soutine, who transplanted a Jewish mystical element from Russia to Paris, or van Gogh, who came from Holland. Rouault is the only French exception who may, in a certain sense, be regarded as an Expressionist, although, indeed, his style is characterized by the Primitive formal elements of the archaic Christian art of the catacombs and sarcophagi and Gothic stained-glass windows. In general it may be said that modern Expressionism represents the disintegrating tendency of the tradition-bound formal values of European art, which trace their origin back to Greek culture. This culture spread via Sicily into Italy, from Imperial Rome into its provinces; it was revived in the Renaissance; it later sprang to new life again in France. The feeling of the French for proportion (*la mésure*), repose (*le calme*), *la belle matière* and taste (*le gout*), as the infallible compass for their artistic production, shows them to be the heirs of the Renaissance. It would be wrong to say, as is so often said, that the Classic is the mode of expression proper to the Latin race, since indeed the Greeks were not Latins and the Baroque was of Italian origin. If it is impossible to call the Latin race the sole exponent of the Classic style, then this style must be connected with geographical situation. Perhaps the sun is one of the secrets of the Classic. That is not to claim that the sun is the sole cause of it, but rather that under its kindly rays beauty evolves freely, man finds his way to harmony and to the nobility of balance, that balance which is hardly known North of the Alps, where the lack of sunshine manifests itself in a nostalgic longing, in the Gothic, in Expressionism. While the religion of the North had reorganized itself in rational sectarianism, Italy produced Francis of Assisi, that gentle reviver of the faith, whose love extended beyond human beings to animals, plants, the earth and the wind, and who created the hymn to the sun, *Il Cantico di Frate Sole*:

> Laudato si, mi Signore,
> cum tucte le Tue creature,
> spetialmente messo lo frate sole,
> lo quale jorna et allumini
> noi per loi, et ellu é bellu
> e radiante cum grande splendore:
> de Te, altissimo, porta significatione.

Goethe, perhaps the last European North of the Alps who was classic in his way of feeling, said at the age of eighty, in answer to Eckermann's question whether he felt reverence for Christ: 'I bow before Him as the divine revelation of the highest moral principle. And, indeed, if I am asked whether it is in my nature to revere the sun, I would also say: Certainly! For it, too, is a revelation of the highest, and, indeed, the mightiest one that it is granted to us mortals to perceive. In it I worship the light and creative power of God, by which alone we live and have our being, and all plants and animals with us.' Only in our days does something of the morbid and sceptical spirit of the misty North infiltrate into the South—this time, however, not on the wings of the imagination, but to the brazen rhythm of industrialism. And in industrialism's present anti-cultural stage of development, men waste away from lack of any joy in living, as though touched by the fatal breath of a plague.

The Psychological Background of Expressionism

When we compare the methods of modern science with those of modern art, we are surprised by a peculiar phenomenon. In whatever country a piece of scientific work is carried out, and to whatever nationality the scientist may belong, the methods that he uses are based on internationally recognized and applied principles, and the results bring about changes affecting the whole of mankind. In the plastic arts man's creative urge, the will to expression, has experimented in various directions, and at one and the same time methods of representation have been used that differ from each other in the principles on which they are based. Modern art does not give an unambiguous picture of man's emotional and intellectual life at the present day.

The comparison between science and art would not be justified if a tendency to use the scientific approach in creative art had not become apparent. Cubism was a rational movement. There is rationalism, too, in programmatic Surrealism and in conscious Primitivism. In the first case, it was the shadow of psychoanalysis falling on art; in the second, the shadow of art history. When forms borrowed from Negro sculpture appeared in modern work, it was a rational rather than an irrational process. 'Styles' were rapidly adopted and dropped again just as fast. It was, to vary Picasso's well-known aphorism, more a matter of seeking than of finding.

The uniformity of scientific development all over the world is symptomatic of the fact that science concerns itself only with a part of phenomenal experience, and that, furthermore, only from a particular point of view. The application of scientific methods to other realms of experience necessarily results in an impoverishment of intellectual activity. The analytical spirit and the creative functions of the mind are forces which are diametrically opposed.

When the crisis in modern art is referred to, what is meant is the crisis which occurred in the extreme movements of the Ecole de Paris. It is obvious that the creative energy of Paris is spent. From another point of view there is yet another crisis in art. If we study the art of earlier periods, we are forced to the conclusion that there has been a gradual decay of creative force. In mechanistic civilization the human brain undergoes a profound change. We may go as far as to say that we are witnesses of how the mind is adjusting itself to man's organized and rational world and losing its contact with the primeval forces of creation. This conclusion is not new. Ludwig Klages, in his *Grundlage der Wissenschaft vom Ausdruck* (Rudiments of the Science of Expression), speaks of 'the disturbance in the Soul's power of self-expression' as being due to 'a violation of the instincts by the will'. As the intellect becomes more and more highly organized, so people grow out of the state of instinctive harmony with nature, until, with the appearance of modern civilization, they lose it completely. Evidence of this is seen in children's urge to express themselves; in early childhood they have a capacity for total experience, which later, through the contact with the world of the grown-ups, they lose (Franz Cizek). The formative impulse of the mentally deranged is also part of the same thing, in so far as it is an expression of the creative will's having found new liberty in the disease disorder (Hans Prinzhorn).

When we come to consider the modern schools from the point of view of style, we can say that they fall into two main groups. In one, there is a conscious setting up of formal laws, whose function in our time is 'scientific'. Such are the Impressionists' theory of light and colour, Seurat's Pointillism, the theses of Cubism and Futurism, the geometric imagery of Abstract Art and of architectural Surrealism (de Chirico), Breton's theory of Automatism and, in its over-logical campaign against logic, spatial and physical causality, the Surrealism of Ernst, Tanguy and Dali. The liberation of human imagination from nature, which at first appeared to be a great revolutionary achievement (Ortega y Gasset has hailed it as a triumph, Abbé Bremont has called it the pure act of creation, and André Malraux provided it with a psychological background, when he made the statement, that the origin of a work of art is not to be found in any experience of nature, but in the experience of a picture or a poem), led to a dehumanizing of art. Modern art psychology has defined the problem as being one of abstraction and empathy (*Einfühlung*). Where the creative will produces inorganic, abstract forms, we cannot be dealing with a creative will that arises out of the need to experience by empathy; it is, on the contrary, a need which is directly opposed to empathy, namely a tendency to suppress life. We can go so far as to say that abstraction is nothing less than an escape from life, just as Freud spoke of an escape into neurosis. 'These abstract, logical forms are the highest ones, the only ones in which man can find relief from the overwhelming chaos of the world as he experiences it' (Wilhelm Worringer). 'Abstraction appears as a function which is in opposition to primitive "*participation mystique*".' It is a separation from the object in order to break the attachment to it. Empathy as a principle of artistic creation is based on the magic significance of the subject, which takes possession of the object by a process of mystic identification (Levy-Bruhl). Empathy is the method of Expressionism.

Expressionist and Formalist art in the widest use of these terms are therefore the two currents in which the modern formative will manifests itself. Since art is a language, we may assume that its utterances are those of two human types. Personalities have always been perceived as romantic and classic, or dynamic and static temperaments. Kretschmer (*Körperbau und Charakter*) made other distinctions, Nietzsche spoke of Dionysian and Apollonian, and Jung of introvert and extrovert types. The peculiar fact remains that our modern culture has simultaneously produced two different styles. The art-historian may say that a combination of this kind can arise in an age when one style is being merged into another, as in the time of transition from the Romanesque to the Gothic style or during the early Renaissance (Byzantine style) or the late Renaissance (Baroque). In our time there is no question of a transition period in this sense. Two essentially different styles, different in technique and in tradition, in the artist's approach to his object and his psychological incentives, characterize modern art. Such a phenomenon has hitherto not been known. It is the expression of our rootlessness, when seen from the angle of established values, or maybe of our conquest of noval realms of human experience, when contemplated from the angle of a world-wide culture based on a new science of man. Whether we can speak of a dualism of the expressive and the formal in the art of a period at its height and how far the one lives at the expense of the other in the ascending or descending epochs, according to the formula expressive + formal (element) = maturity in art, is an open question.

Behind Expressionist art stand men who regard it as a sin against the spirit to produce anything by coldly rational means. Van Gogh, Edvard Munch, Oskar Kokoschka have made statements to this effect.

The Expressionist is aware of an archetypal imagery in Jung's sense; that is, he expresses a collective unconscious whose content and functions are of an archaic nature. '*It is not the matter of imitating the archaic*, but of qualities which are in the nature of a relic. All those psychological traits which in essentials correspond to the qualities of the primitive mentality are of such a nature.' The artist's images are archaic when they have unrecognizable mythological parallels. Hence the Expressionist artist is associated with the myth-building force, that truly creative, primordial spiritual force out of which the symbols were created that gave form to men's conception of life and the world.

In Expressionism we are less concerned with a school than with personality. The relationship between personality and style seems obvious, when it is a question of those processes which have their source in the unconscious. The relationship between style and epoch was investigated by the Viennese philosopher Dilthey, the founder of '*Geistesgeschichte*' and explored with great ingenuity by Oswald Spengler and by the Viennese art historian Max Dvorak, who saw the history of art as the history of the human spirit and stated emphatically that the history of art must not remain under the spell of the mechanico-materialistic outlook of natural science.

Expressionism is a style which appears in times of great spiritual tension. The Viennese art historian Alois Riegl showed in the example of the Baroque that one of its characteristics is a profound religious emotion. Michelangelo's *Pietà* in the Palazzo Rondanini, or the *Descent from the Cross* in Florence Cathedral, both belong to this type of expression, as do works of El Greco, of the old Rembrandt, of the late Goya, of Mathias Grünewald, the master of the Isenheim altar in Colmar,[1] or those of the Baroque. It is a sombre, passionate art, the art of van Gogh,

---

[1] It is a significant symptom that Picasso's *Guernica* bears traces of the influences of Mathias Grünewald. In 1936 Christian Zervos redirected French artists' attention to this German Expressionist master, in his book *Le Retable d'Isenheim*. What Zervos admires in Grünewald's work is 'L'exacte conscience de la réalité et du reve'—here meaning the religious idea—'Leur fusion sans que le moindre dualisme puisse s'y observer, l'action prolongé sur la sensibilité, la concentration dans une image de l'emotion spirituelle, etc.'

Lovis Corinth, Edvard Munch, Ernst Josephson, the later Turner, James Ensor, Oskar Kokoschka, the painters of Die Brücke, Rouault, the early Chagall, Jack B. Yeats, Soutine, in which spiritual experience asserts itself against the tyranny of mathematical thought, belief in causality and technical progress, in fact against the mechanization of civilization.

Edvard Munch

The spark from van Gogh's later work, the meditativeness of Symbolism and the liberating fury of the Fauvists brought to maturity in Edvard Munch (1863-1944), the Norwegian painter, this trend of contemporary art which is called modern Expressionism. This great and lonely artist, so completely absorbed in his work, has been appreciated at his real importance only by a handful of initiated people in the West. He has remained practically unknown to the Americans as well as to the English and French up to the middle of this century.

Sheldon Cheney and Herbert Read are among the few critics who recognized Munch at an early date. The latter, realizing that Expressionism stands clearly in isolation and distinct from the Paris school, wrote: 'Munch is an artist whose work is little known in England, but there is no doubt that he has been one of the most important influences of the last fifty years.' He comes to the conclusion that Munch's work 'ought to be sympathetic to our own Northern temperament' because of its 'dramatic values, the emphasis on emotional unity in art, on the element of human feeling'.

Here we are *in medias res* of a problem which can be sketched as follows:—First: that an artist of Munch's standing has not been given an opportunity of making himself heard because of the one-sided orientation of criticism and art dealing. Second: that in the solution of the difficulties into which contemporary art must inevitably be led when rigidly following the abstract and analytical line of development, Munch, probably more than any other modern artist, will be appreciated because of the emphasis in his art on the human idea, the oneness of content and form. To-day we do not fear to specify as the ultimate aim that the human idea shall be the nucleus and final meaning of all plastic art.

The human idea as a central creative element in the work of art loses its importance in the new development since David, Daumier and Delacroix; becomes attenuated in the work of Manet and Monet until, in Post-Impressionism, it finally disappears altogether.

To-day it might be of interest to know why Munch made such a deep impression on art east of the Rhine. We shall find that he not only influenced other painters but that he created what we may call a spiritual climate. No other artist, not even van Gogh, can be compared with him in this respect. Munch is the only artist who can be named, along with Dostoevsky, Nietzsche and Ibsen, as having formed a whole generation's attitude to life.

He started to paint as a Realist with a fine sense of values. Among his earliest works there are landscapes, portraits and scenes of family life. For some time he belonged to the small group of artists who worked under the supervision of Christian Krohg, and fought for the recognition of a Realism with a social tendency. In 1885 Munch spent a few weeks in Paris and was able to return there, thanks to a state grant, in 1889. He stayed in Paris, with the exception of the summers which he spent in Norway and short trips to Italy and Germany, until 1892. Neither the idyllic line of his first Plein-Air pictures, nor the social Realism, nor the French Impressionist manner in which he painted in the years 1890-91 could satisfy him. There was something else he wanted to say, something closely related to the deep and dark experiences of his childhood—the early death of his mother and sister Sophie— and later on a love affair with a macabre background. In being submitted to these personal trials he was being submitted to something more than personal, so that the atmosphere of morbidity, pessimism and melancholy of the *fin-de-siècle* turned him into a representative of his time. The change in Munch's style can easily be studied in two works, depicting the same theme and connected with the death of his sister. The realistic *Spring*, 1889, shows the sick girl sitting beside her mother, looking towards the window through which the sunshine flows into the room. It is the youth of the new year whose cool breath causes the white curtains to swell like a sail of hope and of dreams. In *The Ailing Girl*, on the other hand, painted in six different versions, we notice the concentration on the two figures, the elimination of all realistic details, the emphasis on colour and expressiveness. We read in a diary entry of Munch's from St. Cloud in 1889: 'No more interiors with men reading and women knitting shall be painted. They must be living people who breathe, feel, suffer and love. I will paint a series of such pictures; people shall understand the holy element in them and bare their heads before them, as though they were in church.' It was some of the pictures from this series, called the *Frieze of Life*, which made such a revolutionary impression on Berlin towards the end of the century. Munch worked on the *Frieze* practically throughout his life and thus, understandably, the pictures show a great difference in their stylistic conception. The serial character of Munch's work is very typical of him and reveals the strength of the human idea as a driving force in his creative efforts. Even the nudes, as he has painted them in the beginning of his career and later, tend to develop into a continuous series—*The Life of a Model*.

In Paris Munch was confronted with the newest trends in French art. Impressionism gave him the sensation of light colours, though the first pictures of the *Frieze* are painted in a dark scale—Gauguin and the Synthetists strengthened his feeling for rhythmical composition, for a summarized form, for contours and for strong colour accents. Van Gogh and the Fauves had a very decisive influence on Munch's paintings too. But all these influences have no primary importance; Munch took only what he could use for his own vision. He was too strong a personality and too different from Gauguin or Bonnard or Matisse to be diverted from his imagery.

The *Frieze of Life* depicts the soul of modern man in connection with two main vital powers: love and death, both conceived as destructive forces. To give a few examples: *Ashes*, 1894, evokes the despair and emptiness after fleshly union; *The Dance of Life*, 1900, one of the most moving scenes in the whole Frieze, is a variation of another theme of Munch's, The Three Stages of Woman—the flowerlike nature of girlhood, the seductress and renunciation—which Munch painted later; *The Yellow Boat*, 1891, portrays melancholy, jealousy and loneliness in the foreground figure; *Death in the Sickroom*, 1894-95, is one of the many expressions of Munch's vital dread of the profound unknown; *The Shriek*, 1893, reveals the panic of man facing the mystery of nature.

The impact of such pictures on Munch's generation was tremendous. The Czech painter Emil Filla wrote about that time: 'Munch stood at the beginning of our path: at the very start when we mustered the courage to interpret our own ideas, we had the good fortune to encounter him. For us he became synonymous with our own proper destiny. It was a situation similar to that when Donatello came to Padua and Rembrandt to Amsterdam, when Michelangelo appeared in Florence, or to the influence exercised by Caravaggio in Rome.' This is the evidence of a painter. Let us also hear a critic from those days, F. X. Salda, who wrote in 1905 in Prague of Munch as 'a violator of dreams, a painter in terror-stricken colours ravaged by all the sufferings of life, a man possessed by ashen horror and gloom, a coarse barbarian and skilful decadent in whose work both the old world and the new inferno play their respective parts, in whose pictures objects literally shed the blood of their colours and cry out their sufferings and the mystery of their being; a painter whose colours are no objective manifestation but a lyrical fate.'

Painting East of the Rhine felt the strong impact of Munch's art in Berlin in 1892, in Prague in 1905, in Vienna in 1909 (where Oscar Kokoschka, the greatest living Expressionist, experienced Munch for the first time). It was the ideological force in Munch, his philosophy of life which affected Expressionism most deeply even when formal influences had been drawn from elsewhere. In France, Munch found the inspiration for his future work; in Germany, where he spent most of the years between 1892 and 1908, he developed into the mature master and pioneer. By the beginning of the twentieth century he was recognized in Central Europe, but not yet in his own country. Munch told me himself that he was not generally accepted in Norway until the fiftieth year of his life.

The hectic, restless, melancholy strain in him led to a nervous collapse in 1909. The first half of his life had been under the spell of revolt, decadence and the dark forces in and around us. After his illness Munch returned to Norway, and there painted a great number of landscapes in which he revealed the beauty of his country, such as the extraordinary *Island*, 1901, and *White Night* of the same year. In common with many old masters, Munch was also a portrait painter and very remarkable works from his hand date from as early as 1885, particularly the portrait of Jensen Hjell and that of his sister Inger, of 1892, both showing the conception of the Velasquez-inspired portrait which is so typical of Munch and which he maintained throughout his life: over-life-size and the model generally facing the artist. He was also one of those painters who, at various moments, make self-portraits. In these we can read about him as in the pages of a diary. His first self-portrait is dated 1882, and one of his latest, *Between the Clock and the Bed*, 1940. Everything in this picture is a symbol of death. The clock—the time which passes; the bed, a catafalque, the nude on the wall, a mummy. Here we see him returning to the Symbolism of his former years. Symbolic style is also evident in other self-portraits and in his paintings of the *Bohemian's Wedding and Death*. These later works recall themes from his youth when he was connected with Oslo Bohemian circles. The pictures of *The Modern Faust* allude to the problem of the biological tragedy of the sexes. The dramatic Expressionist style of these paintings stands in contrast to his style after 1909, which followed a more naturalistic and monumental line, as foreshadowed in his triptych, *The Bathing Men*.

The most important works Munch executed after his final return to Norway are the murals of 1909-11 for the Great Hall of Oslo University. They reveal the complete spiritual change in his attitude to life, the harmony he achieved after long years of struggle. Painted in oil on canvas, the outstanding development of modern Scandinavian mural painting started with this work. The main themes are *History*, *The Sun* and *Alma Mater*. Smaller compositions of a more Fauvist character are placed between the main scenes. Munch himself has referred to the association between the *Frieze* and the University decorations. The former, a poem of life, love and death represents the sorrows and joys of man, while the University decorations express the great eternal forces.

Landscapes, portraits and also motifs from the life of workers and peasants complete the activities of Munch's later period. He intended to make a large mural with workers as the main theme, but it was never finished.

Munch's interest in graphic techniques may be seen even in Berlin in the early 'nineties. But it was first in Paris, in 1896-97, that his chief activity was concentrated in that realm of art in which—especially in his woodcuts and coloured lithographs—he achieved such outstanding results. For portraits he preferred the etching or the dry point; for themes taken from his paintings, the lithographic technique. Aquatint also intrigued him, and combinations of the different techniques. Compared with the most important graphic artists of recent times, Toulouse-Lautrec or Daumier, Munch shows himself to be more versatile, and when studying his large graphic production in comparison with Rembrandt, Dürer or Goya we understand that his work is of no less weight.

During the International Congress of Art Critics in 1949 some of the graphic works of Munch were shown in Paris. I discussed the problem of Munch there with leading critics, and perhaps I may be allowed to quote the remarks made by James Johnson Sweeney on this occasion: 'If we consider the Expressionist artists, we see that all of them seem to have developed only one part of their art, which was the emotional. Munch did not. Munch's art with its simplicity, its balance of values, his abstractions, his distortions, has anticipated the twentieth century. But that is not enough. He is stronger than that. Like Gauguin, he turned to life and he found the relationship of the human problem and art again. He never allowed himself to run away with the pictorial conception as the sole embodiment of the emotional in a painting. Munch's art is like a river at a point where it separates into two streams. He is greater than both these streams—on the one hand Fauvism, *Die Brücke*, etc., on the other hand Cubism, Purism, Abstract Art. In his art, the unity of the modern formative elements and the human content are preserved and therein he has outdated his own time.'

If we compare Munch's Expressionist pictures with the early portraits (1907-14) of the Austrian Oskar Kokoschka (b. 1886), we realize how much more disharmonious the world had become for this generation. Kokoschka's Expressionism did not take the form of representing psychological situations, but penetrated far below the surface in an attempt to interpret the psychological states in relation to their mysterious moorings deep in the human psyche. It was the 'inner face' of man that fascinated Kokoschka, and this is what he laid bare with an almost suicidally destructive urge. These early studies in portraiture were painted at the time when Sigmund Freud was announcing the first results of his psycho-analytical research. Kokoschka had to invent new means of expression to enable him to reveal what he saw. In his

early youth he derived considerable inspiration from the art of primitive peoples. Later on, like other artists, he was indebted to the great achievements of French Impressionist and Fauvist art.

Oskar Kokoschka - Revolt

Come hither, Dionysus, to thy holy temple by the sea. Come with the Graces to thy temple, rushing with thy bull's foot.

Greek song from ELIS

The Kunstschau in Vienna in 1908, which was a landmark in the history of Central European modern painting, developed into a scandal. The young Oskar Kokoschka had exhibited in a special room his revolutionary art, which completely upset all contemporary aesthetic ideas. There were four monumental wall paintings (*The Dream-borne—Die Traumgeborenen*) and in a glass show-case his poem, 'The Dreaming Youths'—*Die Träumenden Knaben*', illustrated by himself; flowery poetry in which both East and West had their part and which had a new and challenging effect. Then there were other pictures, and the *Self-portrait* in clay, a head with a gaping mouth, painted in the most vivid colours. The bourgoisie came and were shocked, and there too were the intelligentsia, led by the prophetic Adolf Loos, the first modern architect of Central Europe, who had come from the Czech lands, like many leading cultural personalities of Austria in those days before the First World War; the poets Rainer Maria Rilke and Franz Werfel, the novelists Franz Kafka and Robert Musil, the composer and conductor Gustav Mahler; Karl Kraus the moralist, critic and publisher of the *Fackel*; Sigmund Freud, the art historian Max Dvorak, and Edmund Husserl, on whose phenomenology the philosophy of Heidegger, Jaspers and the French Existentialists is built. Kokoschka, too, is of Czech origin on his father's side; on his mother's he is of Austrian and Celtic descent.

In order to understand how this art exhibition could arouse such excitement among so many people that it came to violence, one must realize that there was perhaps no town in Europe other than Paris which discussed in such a lively manner the questions of the day and of art as the old Vienna. And like Paris, Vienna had produced an individual city culture in which intellect and charm were linked with the courage to experiment with the new. Society there had an almost decadent sensibility which was aware of the deadly danger of the future and despite all its trials in the spiritual field, it felt that it was lost. The peculiar fascination of this Viennese culture was like a rainbow against the dark background of the coming night. It was in this milieu that Hermann Bahr and Peter Altenberg, Hugo von Hofmannsthal, George Trakl and Arthur Schnitzler wrote, that Gustav Klimt and Egon Schiele painted and Sigmund Freud and Alfred Adler explored the realms of psychology. Hardly had the Nestroy-tradition ceased and the tragic voice of Kainz died away from the Viennese Shakespearian stage when already a new theatre had begun to grow up; Reinhardt, Moissi. And the Vienna Opera! And the artists' Cabaret! And the Cafés! The Viennese coffee-house, with its innumerable newspapers and periodicals, was a breeding-ground for new ideas, a cultural centre of the first order. There men of all nations met, and in the melting-pot of cultures and races represented by Vienna, the coffee-house was the Forum in which one passed or failed the crucial test. Kokoschka, too, passed through the 'purgatory' of the Vienna coffee-house and he, the wonder child who came from the suburbs and knew everything, was at that time guided by his Virgil, Adolf Loos. Adolf Loos was among the intellectuals who, on the occasion of the Viennese Kunstschau of 1908, attended the first performance of Kokoschka's play, *Murderer the Hope of Women* (*Mörder Hoffnung der Frauen*) and stood by Kokoschka in the tumult in which the police had to intervene. Already Kokoschka's poster for the performance, which was displayed throughout Vienna, had aroused great excitement. It was a Pièta, the Madonna blood-red, Kokoschka himself as Christ lying in her lap, white as chalk. And then the play itself: an Expressionistic representation of the magic duel between Sun and Moon, the actors and musicians being laymen brought from the coffee-house. The orchestra—cymbals, drums, short and long pipes—shrill, seemingly incoherent and unintelligible, yet conforming to a higher unity. The actors read their parts during the plays from scraps of paper; Kokoschka had written them down at the last moment. 'I didn't write the play,' he said. 'I read it from the faces of those who became the principal actors. I composed everything out of the rhythm of their very breathing.' And the unusual sounds! Improvisations produced as in a trance; not till much later did Hindemith compose music for it.

From that day everyone in Vienna knew who Kokoschka was. He was hated and he was loved, and he himself hated and loved Vienna. But in the foolhardiness of his youthful vigour he bore a deep wound in his breast. He pointed straight to this wound when he painted his generation in his portraits, in which his clear-sighted intuition laid bare, as by X-ray, the true face of modern man, man who was marked with death through technical progress. Kokoschka said, looking back on that time: 'I felt quite intensely and suddenly as if man were stricken with an incurable disease.' To expose this was his duty as an artist. It also set him free. His art was like the cry of a child, who suddenly awakes in a world of grown-ups, whose doings he does not understand and who threaten his life. At that time he lived like a chrysalis, spun round with the mystic forces of which his spiritual life consisted, but he did not see clearly, as to-day, that mankind because it thinks and feels only in ponderable and measurable terms, is not only lost to culture but represents an imminent danger to culture. Yet he lived sunk in a deep dream, and over-sensitive, as if without a skin, almost unconsciously he became at this time the mouthpiece for the anxiety of his generation. In 1945 he wrote in London the fateful words:

Modern portrait painting has become a difficult task—since the artist, who tries to make people see the human being, invisible in present-day man, is apt to make a fool of himself. Since society is at present a mathematical and bureaucratically-conceived mass organization, we cannot hear the last bell toll, although the Apocalyptic Riders already shake heaven and earth. We do not mind the stench of the funeral pyre of our world. Since Humanism is dead, man is soulless, he no longer cares whether he lives or dies. The march of industrial civilization will be marked with utter ruin and destruction, like the path of the hordes which once invaded Europe. There will be no portrait left of modern man because he has lost face and is turning back towards the Jungle.

Every Expressionist is a disappointed idealist. Kokoschka

suffered from the spiritual conflict of his time and was destined to give it form. This stress is apparent in the unrest of his brush-work, as well as in his manner of composition, where everything is in movement and aims at achieving a spiritual relationship.

The Inner Face of Things

A sword cannot sunder it
Nor fire burn it
Nor water quench it
Nor air blast it.
from the BHAGAVAD-GITA

There is something about German Expressionism in the period after the First World War. Expressionism as such is the art of meditative and introvert personalities. It is also a protest against Impressionism and Aestheticism; it restores the relationship between thought and vision and is subjective. The fact that the Latin races stress the importance of form and material means that they incline less to Expressionism than other peoples. Edvard Munch, towards the end of the last century, has set in motion a modern art which has ever since been fighting to preserve the balance between the formal line of the West and the emphasis on the Idea content in painting which was prevalent in the rest of Europe. The so-called 'German Expressionism' stems from Fauvism, from the art of the Primitives, emphasized already by Gauguin, from the Norwegian Munch—though in his generation the young German painters under the leadership of Max Lieber-mann followed French Impressionism—and from Oskar Ko-koschka. With Kokoschka there came from Austria a melancholy Slav element—which saved him from a lapse into the somewhat shapeless art of the members of *Die Brücke*—and a nervousness which one might have called sceptical if it had not displayed a sensitiveness which united in a single awareness the cultural characteristics of different times and peoples. German Expressionism, seen from the standpoint of its foreign influences with the exception of Lovis Corinth and Max Beckmann, is a chaotic movement rather than a true style, which remained amorphous and could not crystallize.

What did Expressionism mean for Kokoschka? Above all, it was a living force, but also a critical attitude. 'The basic feature of our present view of life—so Kokoschka thinks—is Symbolism. One thing represents another; one simplifies, popularizes, generalizes, idealizes but one forgets that that which is thus created is no reality. Slogans are substituted for reality. Two generations ago this was not dangerous, to-day it is fatal. Symbolism needs ideologies and words; culture, however, needs shape and form.[1] Fantasy is creative only when it can produce types and characters like Antaeus, Narcissus, Jacob, Hamlet, Faust, Tartuffe, Don Quixote, Chichikov, Bezuchoff. Or, in painting, imagery such as that of El Greco, Rembrandt, the elder Brueghel, Goya, Hieronymus Bosch. In a world ever more hostile to the spirit, from which no way of escape seemed open— as it still was for Gauguin—there was for Kokoschka only one possibility, namely to cling to the roots which the artist possessed in his own being. These gave nourishment to a world of visions to which Kokoschka trustfully and unreservedly surrendered himself. In 1911 he gave a lecture about the nature of images (*Gesichte*) which is the key to his mystical aesthetics. Here, in a complex Baroque literary style is suggested the significance of images, of visions, which are forms and not abstractions:

The determining feature of life, its essence, is the consciousness of the image. The essence, whether of bodyless or corporeal character. Consciousness is the cause of all things, even of ideas. It is a sea whose horizons are images. Consciousness of images is not a condition in which we recognize or comprehend things, but a state in which consciousness experiences itself.

The perception of images is Kokoschka's creed concerning the creative power of mankind. Philosophically, it corresponds to the idealistic conception of Plato or Berkeley, religiously to that of a Meister Eckhart, a Jakob Böhme, St. John of the Cross. The living source from which the myth-creating, beauty-seeking religious power of the soul pours forth, found in Kokoschka one of its latest prophets. For that reason, too, he is not exclusively concerned with the final result, that a picture should be finished, but with the painting itself, with the creative process. Years can go by during which he may alter a picture in ways not dictated

[1] 1945, in a conversation with the author.

primarily by a formal standpoint but which grows out of the need to approximate more closely to the intensity of his inner vision, painting it, to live it anew.

As long as I can retain an image, I live by it. I know I lack this power more and more as time goes on. That is why I am so ego-centric, because I am compelled to protect myself against a hostile world by withdrawing within myself. There before me is a figure which I have not seen for thirty years. It has the same fascination for me as before, indeed it is more vivid than the present moment. What is this fascination? Behind it there is a hidden force. It is something different from an intellectual process. I can never learn anything. Everything I ever learnt I must forget. Otherwise I should only be copying myself and that would be death. But when this force grips me, all is well. When it leaves me I am empty. That is why I have not had a slow, sure success, but ups and downs, like the ebb and flow of a tide. I could never bring myself to attempt anything deliberately, in cold blood; I should be filled with terror. It is the same as in love. As the image is dependent on me, so am I on it. I have to await the call—and then I must not fail . . .[1]

Out of this primal source grew Kokoschka's work, which is to-day like a mighty tree with broad, strong branches. From the mystic root of his nature, he has found his way to the 'perspective' of the Baroque—in a spacial and above all a spiritual sense, a perspective of infinity, as opposed to the two-dimensional and limited. He abhors the constructivist aspect of modern art and its development into 'schools'. He expressed in drama what could not be conveyed with the brush. (*The Burning Bush*, *Job*, *Orpheus and Eurydice*, *Comenius* or the *Tragedy of Humanism*) and in graphic art what great music called forth in him (Bach: *O Ewigkeit, Du Donnerwort!*)

As he had painted the face of the modern generation, so he painted the face of the earth where Nature and man's work achieve a unity; imperishable paintings of the cities of the world, his *Orbis Pictus*. It is not the object of this essay to deal with the entire work of this artist but with the note which it sounds, the spiritual mood of his artistic metamorphoses which are harmonized by his mode of fantasy; this of itself gives us the sense of unity which has managed to achieve a balance in spite of all the antagonistic, self-conflicting and yet complementary

[1] 1944, in a conversation with the author.

forces in life. It is a microcosm of deed and word. Deep at the foundations of this microcosm slumbers like an enchanted castle, radiant as the Grail, the pure idea of the *unitas catholica*, the union of mankind in the spiritual sense, the unifying certainty, the sure haven from the engulfing storm in which the world is falling to atoms.

The Outward Face of Things

> It is not possible to stem evil but by turning away from evil: for an itch is not cured by scratching, as Plato remarked. Therefore neither are wars put an end to by warfare, quarrels by quarrelling, persecution by persecution, but by reversing all these things.
>
> *J. A. Comenius:* THE ANGEL OF PEACE

The more closely one investigates the life and work of Kokoschka, the more clearly it appears that the subjective world of his art, which is nourished by eternity and the radiant beauty of creation, and the objective world surrounding him—the man-made world of technical, material progress and of spiritual decay—tend to part company, so that even here appears that schizophrenic element of cleavage between the spirit and reality, which is so significant of the experience of the last generations. Yet, just as man does not only do things consciously but also as part of nature and therefore subconsciously, so, too, in Kokoschka the cleavage does not result in an incurable sickness. Like the positive and negative of an electric current, the conflicting visions give life to each other in his fantasy. The product of both these energies, their synthesis, is the series of political pictures of the humanist Kokoschka, which he painted in the years of his English emigration. (1939-53.)

In the first world war, Kokoschka, an officer in the Austrian Army, escaped death by a miracle. A Russian bayonet pierced his breast and grazed the pericardium. He lay bleeding on the battlefield. Visions of intense power and unearthly beauty appeared before the inner eye of the artist. For some years after the war his spiritual equilibrium was upset; he was poised, like Edvard Munch at the time of his great crisis in Copenhagen, on a tightrope between life and death, thought world and reality. Kokoschka found himself again. The colours of his pictures became intense and blooming in the French sense, his mysticism became more imaginative in the mode of Brueghel and Hokusai. He threw himself anew into the great adventure of life and art, he fled from his post as Professor at the Dresden Academy of Art. We find him in Africa, in France, in Italy, in Palestine, in Switzerland, in Turkey, in Holland, in Austria, in Spain. In the years between the two world wars he became more and more conscious of the humanistic mission which he was called upon to fulfil in the midst of universal moral ruin. Following in the footsteps of the Czech philosopher and educator, John Amos Comenius, he took up the thankless task of combating the onslaught of brutal nationalism. When the Viennese wanted to install him as a director of the School of Industrial Art, in which he himself had been a pupil, he made as a condition of his acceptance the reform, in a humanistic sense, of the Austrian public schools. He received no answer. In countless articles, in speeches, in prefaces, he fought during these years for the great ideals of mankind, for the deliverance of man through education. Kokoschka was one of the thirty members of the Prussian Academy of Science and Art. He resigned his membership as a protest against the dismissal of Käthe Kollwitz and Max Liebermann. He left Germany, then Austria. He gave up his Austrian nationality as a protest against the official recognition of the 'Anschluss' in Washington and London. With a Czechoslovak passport he fought as a European for his creed: *Cosmopolitae sumus omnes, ejusdem mundi cives*. In Prague he stood for years by the statesman who was one of the finest men of this last generation, T. G. Masaryk. The picture which he painted of him is dialectic. Masaryk's philosophy, which ethically was built on that of Comenius, is represented there, as he had at one time briefly outlined it to Kokoschka: 'The realization of an international democratic school-front against hate, chauvinism and bloodshed would be the crowning of my ideas.'

What are the basic conceptions of Kokoscha's educational programme? Starting from the assumption that our present crisis, which has seemed incurable ever since the First World War, is due to the misguidance of the masses, he declared at the Pen-Club meeting in Prague in 1936:

The origin of the mental crisis is a disease of the human soul, of man disbelieving in the ethics of his work and incapable of giving, finding, or performing work. This would indicate that the incapability to work must necessarily lead to war, for useful social work needs peace.

For Kokoschka the greatest revolution of mankind against tyranny and barbarism was not the storming of the Bastille, but the recognition, in principle, of the work of John Amos Comenius during the age of enlightenment and its gradual practical application, enforced after 1848 by law—the common, free, and obligatory elementary school.

The elementary school as an image of adult life must convey activity and in accordance with the intention of its inventor must hence be above all a school of work. Since in our time society has lost the creative faculty, since human society has sunk to barbarism, seeing in war the only escape from Chaos, the education of the five senses will bring back to man the natural talent of observation and the faculty of rational utilization of his observations. It will enable him to work with a reasonable conception according to a plan which furthers his own happiness and at the same time that of the greater social unity, humanity. The development of an elementary school for town and country alike which permits of no more double-tongued morality, no *reservatio mentalis*, in which Thou shalt not kill is taught in word and spirit as the first commandment of humanity, and war is condemned as a sin against reason, that will be the best contribution to the creation of a democratic united front against the terror of any group which under this or that pretext of predestination separates itself from the organism of the people to enforce its own morality against all reason.

Sight or Reasoning?

Open your eyes! Behold! These barren mountains have green valleys on their flanks.
Gustave Flaubert: L'ÉDUCATION SENTIMENTALE

The present crisis caused by science is destroying the old culture. 'A world of ideas with a universal aspect is perishing. We are the witnesses of it. These ideas are the opposite of every analytic process.' Kokoschka is a mystic. For him mysticism

75

means a profound sense of the universal, an awareness of totality, and communion with creation. Modern art is for him little more than a formula, a constructive intention. He speaks of the realm of art being invaded by forces that are hostile to life. The Expressionist Kokoschka feels himself aesthetically and spiritually related to the world of the Baroque. The Baroque still had the feeling for the wholeness of life; Baroque man lived at peace with God and creation. For Kokoschka there is no longer any common denominator of a spiritual and human kind, in our time. Only the senses can restore the lost balance. Give man back his innocent sight!

'The eye,' says Kokoschka, 'is like a hand. It grasps some things and ignores others. The eye has its own language. The sense of sight is a deep instinct; it is not merely an optical stimulus. This language of sight is worthy of the same respect as word-language. The eye is not only an instrument. It has an age-long experience. its own philosophy and metaphysics. It is like a brain. Man has developed round it; it has accumulated its own tradition from the time of the cave-dwellings. Man could see before he could speak. Women speak in gestures, they are conservative and retain the best. Everywhere, children, too, speak with their hands. Since the Reformation the link with nature has been undermined, the way to life cut off. The Renaissance had still a means of communication through sight, since then logical intercourse has dominated. Through logic one can prove much, even that green is red. Logic is the oldest conjuror's trick to control the people. Behind logic stands the police.'[1]

Logical thought, modern militarism, technology and material development all form a causal sequence. Where is the way of escape from chaos which man calls progress? Is there an escape from spiritual darkness?

A long period of desert will come, a long period of sterility, after the last outbreak of Satanism. In life there is no progress. But there is a substance of life, a vital power. It appears to me like a great earthworm—behind several parts die off, in front new ones grow. It remains the same organism . . . Because I am a mystic I need no saints. I am against the legends of great men. There are greater times, lesser times. There are artists. I do not understand politicians.

[1] This and the following quotation are taken from an as yet unpublished book on the work and life of Oskar Kokoschka, by the author.

People have wanted to convert me to a belief in progress. I believe in the Goddess, in the return of the Matriarchate. Do you remember in Goethe's *Faust* where Faust turns to the Mothers in his search for the secret of life? The maternal side of life is a reality, not an idea. I believe in this at least as strongly as the Chinese. In the period of spiritual drought which is coming, the essential values will survive in spite of all, and then will come the future. It will follow the same pattern as the myths . . . I am no defeatist, no optimist, no pessimist. That which I know is something which I see, like a stone falling, like stars gleaming. If I think a little further and ask myself: Why then do I commit follies, why do I squander my lifetime painting? Then I can say to you: When I am painting I am in the midst of something living. So true, so concrete can the spirit be. It finds its form in aesthetic realization. In the Upanishads there is a passage which runs: the painted form is a spirit in the hierarchy of the world phenomena: the Maya. It has shape and body and life.

While Kokoschka's imagery is still controlled by the conscious mind, the Swede Ernst Josephson (1851-1906) only achieved his Expressionist mode of representation, and with it his artistic liberation, in a state of uncontrolled vision.

Ernst Josephson and C. F. Hill

A Study in Schizophrenic Art - Its Formative Tendency and Social Background

Ernst Josephson and C. F. Hill stand in the forefront of contemporary Swedish painting. As pioneers they deserve to be known and acknowledged by a wider public. Like Cézanne, van Gogh, Gauguin and Munch, they too belong to the martyrs of modern art. Both these Swedish masters suffered a psychic collapse under the weight of their vocation and the resistance they met with among their contemporaries. They continued their artistic work in the tragic condition of schizophrenia. The countless drawings which they produced during these years give evidence of the fact that the illness, whilst breaking the tyranny of a violent and tortured will, rescued the artists from a tedious reality, and simultaneously freed them from the inhibitions which had hampered their search for form during their period of normality. Their imagination now flourished as lavishly as a tropical garden.

It is to this imagination that we are indebted for works which, if they had come into existence in one of the centres of European art, or had at least become known there, would have made the name of *Ernst Josephson* famous all over the world. In the year 1893, Josephson painted the first purely Expressionistic portrait outside France.[1] It is a picture with an utterly frightening intensity of expression, in its effect stronger than Chagall, and in its conception anticipating the portraits painted fifteen years later by Oskar Kokoschka. Composed in dark colours glowing like blood and jewels, it represents the artist's uncle, the theatrical producer Ludwig Josephson, directing Shakespeare's *A Midsummer Night's Dream*. The small figures sketched into the background of the picture make us think of James Ensor, who, at the same time and quite independently of others, was painting Expressionistic pictures in Ostend, which afterwards influenced Klee. At the same time Edvard Munch had begun to carry out his own Expressionistic programme, as did later the German Lovis Corinth.

Besides a few oil paintings from Josephson's period of insanity —the *Little Goose Girl* with its folk-song-like character, the sombre, poetical *Dream*, *Ecstatic Heads*, the triptych *Zeus*, *Jupiter and Christ*, *The Holy Communion*, *Diana*, *Judgment of Paris* (painted on copper and until lately called *In the Orange Grove*, a picture which shows certain compositional resemblances with Botticelli's *Spring*)—there is a multitude of large water-colours, painted on cardboard (a great master of *belle matière*, Josephson was denied better painting material in hospital) and many hundreds of pen-drawings. The number of the latter is not known exactly, but can be estimated at about 2,000. Amongst these are drawings of astonishing beauty and novelty of manner, which found their way to foreign countries and which influenced one of the epochs of Picasso's many-sided art. This can be seen above all in pure line-drawings like *The Dancers on the Beach*, and in others with voluminous arms and legs like *The Birdcatcher*.

As early as 1918, Gregor Paulsson and Ragnar Hoppe pub-

---

[1]Van Gogh's self-portraits of 1889 and 1890 as well as Dr. Gachet's portrait, 1890, can be considered as earlier examples of this style of portrait painting. But Josephson was quite unaware of them. These painting of van Gogh were unknown at that time.

lished a folio of Josephson's selected drawings in Stockholm. In an introductory essay, Gregor Paulsson pointed out that the best artists of our time are definitely fighting for a freer form of expression.[1] For them, Josephson's drawings are models of supreme value.

In Sweden, Ernst Josephson has always been spoken of with great respect. During the last twenty-five years under the influence of changing taste, this respect has extended also to the works produced during his insanity.

If Josephson is to be accorded the importance of a pioneer of modern Expressionism, this position must be denied to *C. F. Hill*. Shortly before his mental breakdown in 1878, he painted pictures in which the intensity of colour was carried so far that his fellow-painters destroyed them, in the belief that they were saving his reputation as an artist. Some thousands of small pastels and drawings of various sizes date from the time of his illness.[2] What

[1] This publication continues the work of K. Wåhlin, who in 1911 published a Josephson biography. In 1917, in Stockholm, Oskar Kokoschka was shown some of Josephson's drawings. He has stated in a conversation with me what an impression they made on him and that he later showed the folio to everybody likely to be interested, in Germany as well as in Paris. F. Lehel's *Notre Art Dément. Quatre études sur l'art pathologique* contains a Josephson drawing which was put at his disposal by the Swedish painter Isaac Grünewald. The latter also showed the folio to Picasso, in the years 1921-22. Many years later the Dane, Mogens Ellerman, in his essay on *Genius and Madness*, discussed Josephson and Hill. After an exhibition of Josephson's drawings in the Berlin Secession in 1910, German criticism began to reckon with him for the first time. Of the greatest importance was the illustrated essay by Hartlaub in the miscellany on modern art *Genius*, which also drew the attention of the pathologist Hans Prinzhorn to Josephson. Without any doubt Josephson had his influence on German post-war Expressionism. I shall never forget the impression made on me by the first Josephson drawing I saw: it was *The Promenade*. It led me to a closer study of the master's work. In Stockholm, when I had the opportunity of seeing more of Josephson's paintings and drawings, I drew attention to his international importance in an essay in *Konstrevy*, Stockholm, 1940; then again in 1942 in a preface to a Catalogue for a Josephson Exhibition, and in the same year in a booklet published in Stockholm, *Fundamentals of a New Approach Towards the Art, Personality and Insanity of Ernst Josephson.*

[2] Their number has never yet been determined exactly, just as Hill's biography is unfinished, breaking off at the period of insanity. In recent years, in Sweden, collectors have begun to acquire works from this period as well. A final judgement on both artists is difficult, because the preparatory art-historical work, such as the complete *catalogue raisonné* of the works of their insanity and the publication of correspondence has not yet been done. We also lack studies by psychopathologists, psychoanalysts and depth-psychologists *in collaboration* with art historians. A beginning was made in H. Prinzhorn's work, *The Plastic Art of the Insane*. But the study of the art of insane artists, announced in this work, has not been published. Ernst Kris': *Bemerkungen zur Bildnerei der Geisteskranken*, IMAGO, xxii, 1936, No. 3, does not

fascinates one in the Hill drawings more strikingly than in those of Josephson, and which manifests itself on the one hand in the grotesque primitive quality of heavy, earthy shapes (all schizophrenics apparently go back to the form-world of the Neolithic period; see the heaviness of the limbs in Josephson's drawings) and on the other hand in his antique dionysiac raptures, is the soul of those 'who turn, fate-driven, towards the darkness, not towards the ideal of what is generally recognized as the beautiful, but towards the daemonic power of attraction of the ugly, which gushes up, anti-Christian and Lucifer-like, in modern man, creating the sense of a doomed world, and closes in on the bright world of day with the fogs of Hades, infecting it with deadly corrosion, and at last, like a volcanic area, dissolves everything into fragments, broken lines, remnants, rubble, rags and inorganic units.' (C. G. Jung: *Picasso*. In Wirklichkeit der Seele, Zürich, 1932.)

An essential characteristic of Josephson's works up to the outbreak of his mental illness in 1888—van Gogh, too, fell ill in the same year—is his striving to achieve a perfection of form like that of the old masters. Those who had the greatest influence on his development were Rembrandt, the master of Chiaroscuro, Titian, the master of colour, Velasquez, the master of the portrait and of the representation of rich materials, and last but not least Raphael, through the grace of his composition and the musical quality of his line. On his journeys Josephson copied much and searched for his own way in figure-compositions and portraits. The period he lived in was the most unfavourable one possible. After the revolutionary collapse of 1848, reaction made itself felt more and more in *petit-bourgeois* stupidity and complacency, the stuffy atmosphere of the Biedermeier era, for which Heinrich Heine could not find words bitter and scornful enough. The dominating spirit in painting was that of Makart and Kaulbach, of the horse-painter Krüger, the Düsseldorf school with its

tackle the problem from the formative point of view. This study deals also with Josephson and six works of his are reproduced there. (Reprinted in Psychoanalytic Explorations in Art, London, 1953, with reference to the author.) An important contribution to our problem was made by A. J. W. Kaas: *Een Vergelijkend Onderzoek Naar de Beeldende Kunst van Gezonden en Geesteszieken*, Arnhem, 1942. See also: Francis Reitman: *Psychotic Art*, London, 1950, and *Psychopathological Art*. International Congress of Psychiatry, Paris, September, 1950. The most comprehensive work on Josephson was published by Erik Blomberg in 1951. In this work reference is made to more recent psychological research on the subject of Josephson's art and insanity.

romantic pseudo-idealism, the genre-painting, the literary senti-mentality of Böcklin. In Stockholm—at that time a small pro-vincial town, remote from every cultural centre, where intellec-tual impulses found only a belated reflection—at the Academy of Art, drawing was taught from classical plaster-casts. Dark interiors and historical costumes were painted, nature had not yet been discovered. Josephson became the spiritual leader of the opposition to the Academy, organized by the Swedish colony of artists in Paris. Basically a Romantic, in France he was con-fronted with Plein-Air-Realism at a time when Impressionism had already begun to manifest itself, and it shows his tragic uncertainty that, following advice from his artist-friends, one of his romantic works, *The River-Man* (Strömkarlen) into which he put all his artistic longing, was painted in the open from a model, without his being able to grasp the stylistic discrepancy. In order to get an idea of Josephson's quality, one has to look at pictures like *The Merman* (Näcken), the early portrait of *Ketty Rindskopf*, the portrait of *Nennie of Geijerstam*, and, above all, that of *Fru Jeanette Rubenson*. The tragedy of Josephson's fate has to be sought in the obstacles which were put in his way by Biedermeier Sweden: the lack of appreciation of his great ambitions, his failure in the eyes of critics and public, the treachery of his colleagues, who left him when his personality expressed itself too strongly in opposition. In addition there were difficulties of a personal kind, an unhappy love affair, great loneliness and want, because even those who supported him in the beginning denied him their help when he needed it most urgently. (The Art Collector, Fürstenberg.) The full depth of Josephson's despair speaks to us from his letters and poems. When considering his case, we must pay the greatest attention to the demon of his will-power, which once made him exclaim: 'I shall either become the Rembrandt of Sweden or die!' Only where he could dedicate himself lovingly to the motif, as in the portrait of Fru Jeanette Rubenson, where his will grew modest in the face of nature, where he became humble as a monk and subdued himself to the object, did he achieve personal and modern effects, worthy to stand beside the portraits of the sixteenth century.

Born of a wealthy Jewish family, Josephson had to struggle against Jewish conservatism which, though it permitted him to admire Rembrandt's religious realism, yet aroused in him distrust of everything new and also of the titanic-revolutionary element which was his own driving-power. The Jews did not experience the classical age; for religious reasons they took no part in the revival of Greek culture, and besides, there was the commandment against the making of representative images. The earliest Jewish masters of the modern period are Diaz and Israels; after them come Pissarro, Liebermann, Chagall, Soutine, Modigliani. The Jews, late arrivals in the world of painting, suffer from lack of tradition. In comparison with Latin masters they always give the impression of heaviness and gaucheness. A Jewish artist is more likely to approximate the 'style' of Rembrandt than of Raphael. When he attempts to go against this law, as Josephson often did, he is doomed. For a Raphael is a fortunate heir, the fulfiller of an old tradition, and so he is exactly the opposite of a man like Josephson; he has achieved his artistic qualities through generations of healthy intensive cultivation. No individual aspiration can make up for the natural process of intensive cultivation. The same applies to Hill as a representative of the Germanic North and the Germanic artist in general. For the Germanic peoples lack the Latin harmony, the sense of *mésure*. Nobody can begin as a classic. Without the sun, one cannot create an untroubled art. An artist who feels like a peasant (Brueghel) cannot be a Greek. Even Gothic man had to start anew, with the sentimental, and had to return to nature. In addition to that, the Germanic peoples' relations with the South were fatally broken off by the Reformation.

If one tries to tabulate the causes of Josephson's mental disease in the order of their importance, one has above all to consider amongst the external reasons the unfavourable character of the Swedish environment, which he, the battering-ram of modernism in this Northern corner of Europe, had not the power to break through; then the infinitely difficult task which, as a Swedish 'provincial' artist coming to Paris, city of revolutions in art, he had to carry out before he could arrive—if indeed he ever did— at the point at which the Frenchman, the heir of the Renaissance, began to work. The inner cause of his mental disease was, above all, the torturing will to become a great master, and finally personal factors, which would not have had a tragic effect if the artist's constitution had not been worn out by the adverse circumstances of his life.

Hill suffered from a similar atrophy of will-power. One of his letters contains the passage: 'I only want to say that in me Sweden shall have a painter such as it has never seen before.' But even if there was strong moral pressure on Hill from his father's side, yet he did not suffer from want, as Josephson did during those critical months before the outbreak of his insanity, when he had not even the money to buy paints and at the same time was drawing up the most fantastic artistic plans.

Modern psychiatry regards schizophrenia as a disease, the secret roots of which are often nourished by a distorted will-power. It is obvious that a mania for titanic grandeur destroyed both these artists. In order to achieve results in art, it is less important to have great aims in mind, than to make good use of the talent one has been given. Is it not the tragedy of Blake that he had 'the will' to achieve things comparable to those of Shakespeare, Michelangelo and Raphael, and that he tried to achieve them by academic means? When Josephson, before his breakdown on the Ile de Bréhat in Brittany, with an already disrupted nervous system, took part in spiritualist séances and produced drawings which he signed with the signatures of Raphael, Michelangelo or Velasquez, and poems which had been 'dictated' to him by Shakespeare, Milton or Dante, we see how the unfortunate Swede was beginning to identify himself with the greatest spirits of mankind. (Identification with God, Christ or other ideal personages is a usual symptom of schizophrenia.) This fact throws light on the central problem of his disease. His inferiority in the face of the great masters, whom he emulated, finds compensation through the mediumistic consciousness; the anaesthetic of madness permits him to do what in a normal state he would never dare to attempt. The torture of decision concerning his course as an artist is taken from him. Now Josephson, no longer hampered by excessive self-criticism—which had been an obstacle to him when he was sane—found the liberty to create out of his innermost self. By elimination of his judgement he came to a complete self-realization, finding within himself the world which he had not found outside or in others, and gave it shape. It was schizophrenia which made an individual artist of him. Now he was no longer forced to admire either the old masters or Paris. Now his creation not only revealed the instincts which at last had free play, but in his drawings too he showed a real picture of the artistic qualities which he possessed. There his greatest weakness is clearly shown, namely that he could not achieve a direct representation of his visions, i.e., when he drew he was dependent on impressions from nature or from pictures.

It is known that the schizophrenic keeps his chains of association, even if the links with reality are broken off. So motifs from the period of Josephson's insanity point to those of his healthy years (e.g., the Merman motif, which is very familiar to the imaginative world of the North)[1] *et vice versa*; we recognize in works of his sane period elements which are typical of his later one, as in the portrait of Rindskopf, or *The Card-sharper*, in which the dancing movement of the brushwork and the monumentality of conception already express the whole of Josephson's passionate emotion. Such works force us to regard the two periods of his life as a unit.

An important question, already raised by Prinzhorn, is whether Josephson's creative power was heightened by his insanity. Today, when the deformations of Expressionism and Fauvism have become a convention and the programatic dogmatism of the Surrealists fills us with distrust, after the eye has become accustomed to the formal world of a Picasso, the compositions of de Chirico (they have a spiritual affinity with Hill's architectural drawings, which were produced earlier) Miró and Dali, the answer to this question is relatively easy. Many of Josephson's last works show this intensification. We see how in the calligraphy of drawings like *The Birdcatcher*, *The Creation of Adam*, *Ecco Homo*, the drawing signed 'Michelangelo', Josephson found an entirely personal style. These are works where the lines sing like lyric melodies. They anticipate Modigliani's Raphaelism and show the same refinement as drawings of Matisse. They are flashes of imaginative genius, which were denied Josephson in his earlier work. Looking at such works of the years 1888-1906, must one not say what one is inclined to say of Cézanne's *oeuvre*? Had Cézanne died twenty years earlier, he would have been for us just an average painter.

---

[1] Shortly before his illness, Hill also wanted to paint the Merman as an old man, sitting in a river and playing on a golden harp. The Merman in Josephson's work is not only a symbol of Nordic Romantic tradition but also a symbol of nature in general in its contrast to civilization, of the mystery of creation and of man's desire to find unity with it. See also the psycho-analytical explanation in Ingrid Jacobson's *Näckenmotivet hos Ernst Josephson*. Gothenburg, 1946.

Amongst Josephson's drawings are some in which the harmony of the general and specific forms, the harmony of the large and the small forms (details), is destroyed. Here the deformations impress us as insane. We miss the intermediate connections. This applies both to the deformation of shapes and to the incongruity of the style. In drawings like *Self-Portrait—Velasquez*, the monomaniac urge to draw becomes apparent—a monomania which shows itself too in the enormous number of his drawings—just as Klee could find relief for his strained nerves only through his 'scribbling'. There the chain of the 'specific', the details, finds no end. The dots represent longing for a third dimension, but at the same time they break up the two-dimensionality of the flowing rhythmic lines. The difference in the character of lines and dots evokes a feeling of distress. In the drawing *Karin Månsdotter*, for instance, there is a lack of control in the way the pen suddenly jumps from an abstract, large outline, e.g. the neck, to the minutest ornament on the dress. In Josephson's most important drawings, not affected by insanity, we encounter a free, happy and Apollonian mood.

With incredible rapidity, after years of misery at the Academy in Stockholm, *C. F. Hill* found his style in Paris. In the Barbizon school he recognized his own approach, and in Corot his personal master. In the few years which he spent working intensively in France, he often painted two pictures in one day. His art developed not only in an Impressionistic but also in a colouristic sense. Hill was exclusively a landscape painter. His pictures bear witness to his great loneliness. When he fell ill, his art changed fundamentally. In the thirty-three years in which he continued his work, until his death, the human and the animal forms suddenly become the centre of his interest. In the nature-mysticism of his pastels, he expressed the nostalgic side of his Nordic being. Amongst his drawings there are some which are done slavishly from a model (*The Roman Women*). Others, probably also done from models, show creatively transformed shapes of suggestive beauty (*Arabs with Tent*). There are large drawings showing countless figures (urge for repetition, perseveration) amidst a spreading, even rampant architecture. Here the artist gave free rein to his impulses; he built buildings without end as children do, he followed a natural artistic instinct, which has its justification neither in imitating nature nor in solving formalistic problems, but is based on the human urge towards creative occupation for its own sake.

The works which Hill created during his period of insanity are very different from those of Josephson. Even in his insanity, Hill remained much more realistic and dependent on the eye. Josephson is more imaginative, free and uninhibited, his drawing more sensitive, he is more highly-strung, more intellectual and elegant, and has a greater range of versatility. Hill's landscapes are always finished in the formal sense, and in good taste. In his drawings and pastels, in spite of the different motifs, he remains a landscape-painter. In these works we can always distinguish between sky and earth. Hill is heavier, gloomier, more primitive than Josephson, but he is quieter, too, more static. His imagination has not the buoyancy of Josephson. On the other hand, Hill, both in his sane period and after, is not so diffuse as Josephson; as an artist he is more homogeneous, even if less gifted. He held on to the natural element and within it he became expressionistically creative. He did animal-pictures like *The Belling Stag* or the horses in the *Arabs with Tent*, which are an eruption of talent. The stag, for instance, is intensified to the extent of being symbolic. In essence it is a tree, with antlers which branch out like gnarled boughs. Hill paints oaks which grow in their own way, without imitation of nature. There are pines of a luxuriant rhythmical life, drawn without any intellectual check, where the real meaning of twigs and branches has been lost. Now he, who could not master the daemonic principle in nature, is dominated by his own daemon. One can note even in the oil-painting, *Autumn*, these basic elements of his later art. The trees in this picture are like caterpillars. An analogy this to the deer conceived as a tree. The identification of two worlds, the animal and the vegetative principles, is being accomplished. (A Surrealist principle.) This is clearly to be seen also in the picture *The Sermon*,[1] where the clothed figure of the preacher shows no folds but proves itself to be a tree, and in the drawing *Circe*, where the arms turn into branches, or in another drawing, where a figure seems slowly to turn to stone (*Female Figure on a Stone*). The identification of the human and geological element is approached. The gargoyles and the whole scene with the clumsy animals in the prehistoric landscape (*The Sermon*) is of an arche-

---

[1] Hill's and Josephson's drawings were not named till later.

typal character. These are landscapes of the underworld, the realm of the dead. Hill does not always show a liberated and liberating quality like Josephson; his art gives us more of things withering, trees without fruit and leaves, prehistoric animals, desert, the ice-age. This retrogressive development has an uncanny effect on us, which seems to recall the development of mankind and primeval memories of the blood. The schizophrenic artist does not try to transmit emotion. 'Nothing approaches the spectator, everything turns away from him. . . . The grotesque, the incomprehensible is searched for, not for the sake of expression, but in order to be veiled, yet it is a veiling which is not meant for one who searches, but is like a cold mist which descends like a screen on unpopulated moors, purposeless, a mere display.' (Jung, *op. cit.*)

There are drawings of Hill's, such as *The Rape*, where the disharmony between large forms and details is striking. The hands and feet Hill could doubtless actually see on himself, but there is no connection between these strongly accentuated parts and the bodies; there is a leap and no logical link. As there is such a thing as incoherent language, so one can speak here of incoherent drawings, in spite of their apparently coherent appearance on the same sheet of paper. These drawings of Hill's are often of a macabre beauty.

Expressionism was an outcry of creative man in desperation, surrounded by a world which was becoming more and more materialistic and mechanized. Josephson's and Hill's schizophrenia can be regarded as a flight from their age into Expressionism, into the realms of the unconscious, the uninhibited, the Primitive. The schizophrenic is 'under the spell of the secret sense of everything perceptible; he feels himself to be in touch with the fundamental impulses of creation' (Jung, *op. cit.*) The Expressionist, too, in so far as he is genuine, knows of this contact.

Are Goya's *Caprichos* or Hokusai's *Spectres*, or the works of Dali with their paranoiac technique, to be regarded as normal or as abnormal creations of the mind? Where is the border-line between the conscious and the unconscious? Did not Picasso attempt to produce in himself psychic states, which might enable him to penetrate this frontier? 'La différence qui existe entre les peintures de cet homme et celles des autres réside en ce fait que ceux-ci ont aspiré à peindre l'homme comme il est à l'extérieure, lui senta l'audace de le peindre comme il est intérieurement.' That is not a statement about Picasso but the words of a contemporary of El Greco about—Hieronymus Bosch. El Greco, the ecstatic master of Gothic imagination, Mathias Grünewald, the majestic painter of Christ's suffering, Edvard Munch, the nostalgic creator of the *Frieze of Life*—all these by means of mighty fantasies linked the consciousness of reality and of vision, achieving a synthesis of both, a secret, which was revealed to Josephson and Hill only in the condition of schizophrenia.

APPENDIX

A Madonna Motif in the work of Munch and Dali

THE question whether Edvard Munch is to be considered a fore-runner of Surrealism has not been investigated as yet. Munch seems to have thought of himself as such, and in fact he was, as we shall see directly; not only in the wider sense like his contemporaries Lautréamont or Redon, or generations before him, Fuseli and Goya, and after him de Chirico and Chagall, but also in a more specific sense, in having accentuated the power of *libido* as persistently as the psychoanalysts themselves, whose theories are the *motor agens* and the philosophy of Surrealism. It therefore seems to us not a mere chance that in some of Salvador Dali's later works we can trace certain ideas already expressed by Munch. Although deeply rooted in Symbolism, Munch appears in this light, together with the more cynical and deliberate Dali, as the representative of one and the same ideological trend in art which was conditioned by the change of spiritual climate in European culture owing to the impact of scientific thought.[1]

This could be experienced in a recent Dali exhibition[2] in two of his pictures: an oil-painting *Tête Raphaëlèsque Eclatée—A Burst Raphaelesque Head*, and a water-colour of the same motif entitled *Couronnement Céleste—Celestial Coronation*. Munch produced in 1894, more than fifty years before, a painting called *Madonna*. Between 1895 and 1902 he worked on different graphic versions of the same motif, some with and some without a symbolic frame which interprets with the help of physiological pictograms the reasons for the dramatic quality, for the suffering in his subject.[3] These works of both artists seem, as far as concerns their theme and outlook, identical. There is a difference only in the period when

[1] I do not suggest that Dali had necessarily seen Munch's pictures. Sperma, etc., occur also in other works of art in Munch's time.

[2] London, December, 1952.

[3] Already in 1894 in the dry point *Death and the Maiden* there are depicted sperma and the foetus in different stages.

they were created. Munch's work is conceived in the style of the Symbolism of the second half of the nineteenth century, with a dose of pessimism and Baudelairian despair. It is marked by the undulating lines of *Jugend* (*Art Nouveau*) which is used by him as a medium for a strong personal confession and therefore is Expressionist. Dali's picture was painted in the years when the artist, having exalted his art through the use of the paranoiac-critical method, became reconciled to the Catholic Church. (He had previously pronounced madness to be the common base of the human spirit—'madness, visceral cosmos of the subconscious'—aiming at systematizing confusion to help to discredit completely the world of reality.) He then re-interpreted, still with a Surrealist, i.e. Freudian outlook, the old religious images of Christ and the Madonna. Being a Mannerist, which Munch was not, he used for his aims both the formal elements of the High Renaissance, of Dutch Realism and photographic Naturalism.

The outlook which underlies both these paintings was moulded in the workshop of Darwinism, of which Freudianism is only a later derivation applied to the unconscious life of man. (In the same sense Jung's notion of archetypal ideas is only an application of Haeckel's biogenetic law to the life of the soul.) The spiritual tension is expressed in both paintings through the use of the Madonna image.

Why did these artists use this image and what did they aim at expressing through its new interpretation? Let us first examine the Ideal of Mary in the history of the Dogma, and parallel to it contemplate the images through which it is represented throughout the history of art: the Byzantine Madonna; the Sienese Madonna; the Madonna of the Gothic Spirit; the Raphaelesque Madonna; that of the Baroque; they all show an ever-changing image of an ideal of which the main characteristics were her perpetual virginity, her absolute sinlessness, her relation to the Godhead which enables her to intercede on behalf of mankind. The conception of an immaculate eternal womanhood is older than Christianity. (The virginity of Mary was not taught anywhere within the pale of the Catholic Church of the first three centuries, it is of non-Catholic origin.) It is in fact a universal conception which has found in Dante's Beatrice the most poetical expression and in Goethe's Faust its last masterly formulation in Europe. Ibsen's Solveig in *Peer Gynt* is only a pale copy of it.

The title of 'Mother of God' was first applied to Mary by theologians of Alexandria at the close of the third century. Henceforth she was the Holy Virgin and Mother of God. 'Mary was in the Temple of the Lord as a dove that is nurtured and she received food from the hand of an angel.' (*Liber de Infantia Mariae et Christi Salvatoris.*) She was 'the spotless treasure house of virginity; the spiritual paradise of the second Adam; the workshop in which two natures were wedded together . . . the one bride between God and Man.' (First sermon of Proclus, *circa* 430, Constantinople.)

Already in the Magnificat (St. Luke I: 46-55) we can find the nucleus of all her future greatness: 'My soul doth magnify the Lord. . . . For He hath looked upon the low estate of his handmaiden. . . . For behold, from henceforth all generations shall call me Blessed.' And so the Holy Virgin and the Mother of God became the Mediator between God and man. 'Every soul that calls upon Thy name'—Jesus is believed to have said to her (*Transitus Mariae*)—'shall not be ashamed but shall find mercy and support and confidence both in the world that now is and in that which is to come in the presence of My Father in the Heavens.'

Joachim of Floris initiated about the year 1200 a real *Renascita* and *Reformatio* of the Christian belief. He proclaimed that the Christianity of his time was a new, third religion, the religion of the Holy Ghost, going beyond that of the Old and the New Testament. It is the spirit which strengthened the Gothic religiosity and style in art, and brought forth a world of purity and light and ideal beauty. Then also a new image arose of 'Our Blessed Lady' and the 'Ave Maria' came into being at this time. Even about the year 1100 English Dominicans propounded the doctrine of the Immaculate Conception which lifted Mary for ever out of mortal humanity and placed her in the realm of heavenly light. But only in the nineteenth century through the Bull *Ineffabilis Deus* (December 8, 1854), was the Dogma proclaimed by Pope Pius IX that 'the Doctrine which holds that the Blessed Virgin Mary, from the first instant of her conception, was, by a most singular grace and privilege of Almighty God, the Redeemer of the Human race, preserved from all stain of Original Sin, is a doctrine revealed by God, and therefore to be firmly and steadfastly believed by all the faithful.' In 1950 the *Assumptio Mariae* was proclaimed as a Dogma. In Catholic countries one can find that simple people put Mary above Christ because of the suffering she endured for her Son who is accused of not having had a filial respect for her.

It is the *Mater Dolorosa* as she is worshipped in the *Stabat Mater* which has moved the hearts of the people, of the great musicians, and of the great painters.

This ideal of womanhood faded out in the epoch of industrial civilization. It is understandable that modern scientific man does not subscribe to Dogma, but it is deplorable that an archetypal conception should completely disappear. Significantly even hard-boiled dialectic materialists nowadays begin to doubt that it is only economic reasons which transform men into brutes. With the findings of experimental psychology the Christian notion of Original Sin is creeping slowly back into our consciousness, that is, the notion that man is both good and bad and that he is given the free will to decide upon which side he intends to stand. But in the time of Munch's youth the impact of biological science was overwhelming. In 1852 Herbert Spencer had begun to put forward his philosophy of evolution. The year 1859 saw Darwin's *Origin of the Species*. In Germany Haeckel became enthusiastic and with Huxley and Galton pushed the matter further. Instead of an ideal of beauty and grandeur and mildness nineteenth-century man was nourished on a biological notion of natural selection, the survival of the fittest, and so on. Is it not significant that pessimism began to spread? In his famous *Metaphysik der Geschlechtsliebe* (1859) Schopenhauer already illustrates the supremacy of the biological point of view over the idealistic. Man in his love for a woman sees an ideal in her; but in doing so he is deceived as an individual by the sexual urge, the goal of which is to preserve the species. Schopenhauer quotes Plato to support his view: *Voluptas omnium maxime vaniloqua.* Strindberg, Baudelaire, Nietzsche were the protagonists of this disillusionment in literature and philosophy; Felicien Rops, Munch, Redon in painting. This age witnessed also the rise of a conception of womanhood as opposed to that of the Madonna. The rise of the old symbol of Ishtar from the Sumerian-Arcadian culture, the Jewish Lilith, the Babylonian Mylitta in her modern shape as *femme fatale*, a de-romanticized form of *La belle dame sans merci*.

Where an ideal conception ceases to have a place in the human heart the Demons come to dwell in it. This is in accordance with the law of polarity which was not only acknowledged in the myth-creating age of man but is still acknowledged in the scientific age. There is evil and baseness in the human nature; whether it started with Adam or with Satan is unimportant.

Munch's *Madonna* of 1895 is therefore the madonna of the biological age. It is not the image of St. Augustine's Mary who was 'undefiled before God' but it is the image of a woman suffering through conception, a madonna of Eros who suffers as an individual according to Schopenhauer. The sperma, the foetus, state this symbolically, the undulating lines expressionistically. In his work Munch evidently links up with the notion of the *Mater Dolorosa*, not with the mild, smiling Madonna of the Gothic age. It is evident too that Munch from the beginning (and not only after his breakdown in 1909) had a positive attitude to womanhood and that he did not exclusively believe in woman as man's vampire (as did Strindberg) and as he himself might seem to imply in pictures of the same name. In Munch there is evidence of the other side of the problem, also, the age-old conflict between spirit and sex, womanhood and the work of art. This was emphasized by Schopenhauer too.

Let us now turn to Dali. His picture *Tête Raphaëlèsque Eclatée* shows the head of a Madonna with a halo. In the *Couronnement Céleste*, the halo is replaced by a crown of glory in process of melting away. The form is not whole but disintegrated. In contemporary painting it was Picasso who first demonstrated this with his broken forms in the period of analytical cubism. This disintegrated form symbolizes the end of an idealistic notion, that of the Virgin Mary. Moreover the inner volume of the head represents in *Tête Raphaëlèsque Eclatée* a Renaissance cupola. What is here shattered is not only an individual ideal but a whole cultural edifice. Dali, however, does not suffer as Munch did. He is a cold observer of fact.

The Raphaelesque Madonna itself was no longer the Madonna of a profound belief as had been that of the Sienese masters. In the age of Leonardo da Vinci, the other-worldly Christian vision began to crumble under the impact of scientific thought. The constructivist Gabo is conscious of this process when he writes: 'At first sight it seems unlikely that an analogy can be drawn between a scientific work of Copernicus and a picture by Raphael, and yet it is not difficult to discover the tie between them. In fact Copernicus' scientific theory of the world is coincident with Raphael's conception in art. Raphael would never have dared to take the naturalistic image of his famous Florentine pastry-cook as a model for the Holy Mary if he had not belonged to the generation which was already prepared to abandon the geocentrical theory of the Universe.' In the artistic concept of Raphael there is no longer any trace of the religious mysticism of the previous centuries, as there is no longer any trace of this mysticism in Copernicus' book *The Revolution of the Celestial Orbits*. Dali uses a vulgarized, de-idealized Raphaelesque type with pretty features. The beautiful head explodes, as it were, under the bombardment of sperma, which by way of a magnificent trick of the artist are collected inside the head on the stalk of an ear of corn, the symbol of Demeter, of fertility and growth. Both Munch and Dali present a metamorphosis of the archetypal idea of immaculate womanhood in its Gothic and Renaissance form; they illustrate the transformation of a world conception.

I remembered, when standing before Dali's picture, the words which Munch said to me when I visited him in 1938: 'And did we not make our contribution to Surrealism?' I realized only then how true these words were. They were taken up by Edith Hoffmann in an article on Edvard Munch.[1] She said: 'It is amusing to read in Mr. Hodin's book[2] that the old master was conscious of being one of those responsible for the—much later— birth of Surrealism. Surrealism meant after years of aesthetic habit (Impressionist and later Abstract Art), which taught the art public of the West to mistrust subject pictures, the return to subject matter. Munch always made it clear that for him every painting had to have a subject, and the subject had to express an idea. Recently—mainly since the birth of Surrealism— a picture's story has regained importance in France as well as in this country.' When Miss Hoffmann proceeds to say: 'but the ideas expressed are those of a new generation,' then we must join issue with her. We have tried to prove that both Munch and Dali are representatives of an age which replaced a moral, poetic and aesthetic ideal by biological facts. This is true not only as far as motif and symbolism are concerned (only Munch was less destructive than Dali) but also in its psychological consequences. The

[1] *The Burlington Magazine*, December, 1951.
[2] J. P. Hodin, *Edvard Munch, Der Genius des Nordens*, Stockholm, 1948.

writer Przybyszewski said about Munch's pictures, exhibited in Berlin in 1892, that they voiced a revolutionary change of mind. 'The individuality represents that which is eternal in men, and because it is so infinitely older than the modern brain, and because it is so infinitely more receptive than the brain, and its organs of perception are so infinitely more sensitive than those of the brain, it presents the very primal basis of psychic life; it satiates the impressions, imparts life to them, pours into them the powerful blood stream of feelings and passions and thus it represents the power which moves us, the force that convinces, and the source of all warmth, life and pulsation.

'The latest stage of development of art (Przybyszewski meant Academism, Realism, Impressionism) has alienated the psychic and thinking strain in us so much, and so blunted our insight into the profundities, that it is now almost impossible suddenly to begin to transfer one's thoughts to a new art-ideal which does not even employ a realistic technique and which consists solely, as it were, in the psychic and in the most subtle and sensitive spiritual impulses. All those inner reactions which have been portrayed in the pictures of Munch are rooted in almost every differentiated human being. All that is profound and obscure, everything for which the medium of language has as yet devised no system of definition and which is thus inarticulate, all that has manifested itself only as an obscure suspecting compulsion, finds expression in the colours of Munch, and thus enters into our consciousness.

'The old art and the old psychology had been an art and a psychology of the conscious personality, whereas the new art is the art of the individual.'

This was written in 1894. If we replace Przybyszewski's terms 'personality' and 'individuality' by Sigmund Freud's 'Ego' and 'Id' we find ourselves on the threshold of that domain which the psychoanalysts undertook to investigate.

Part Three

THE ENGLISH

I

HENRY MOORE

SINCE the beginning of the war Henry Moore has been established in the small hamlet of Much Hadham in Hertfordshire, not far from London. There, in a seventeenth-century cottage, bearing every mark of intuitively felt proportions and forms, all the works have been brought forth which have made the name of Henry Moore known throughout the whole world as a sculptor who took to himself the fertile seed of the post-cubist impulses in art and brought them to a rich and new development. Not yet has Moore arrived at the zenith of his career and great things are still to be expected from him. Of this we feel assured by the crescendo of his work, the natural rich flow of his ideas and the impression gained by his personality.

He stepped out to meet me from a low whitewashed room whose walls were intersected by black beams. They looked like the bare branches of a tree. Moore is of medium height; his step is elastic, his gestures are controlled, his forehead is well formed. He has an open look and one is inclined to say that the look and the forehead in an interesting way transcend the frame in which the man Moore has been incarnated in this world. His gestures, his friendliness, his quick reactions in thought have a direct and convincing effect. He is straightforward and without pose like a workman. Henry Moore, the son of a workman, has become a workman of art as befits our time; he is far removed from those Bohemians who populated the cafés and novels of the *fin de siècle*. He knows the secret of work, he loves to struggle with stubborn material; he does not fear toil or sweat, there is no studio atmosphere around him, no Sunday mood. With the tenacity of the man who has discovered a vein of gold he clears his path inch by inch. It is strange how the naturalness and ease of this artist from the very first disperse any doubts which may sometimes assail the spectator of works of modern art.

Moore had just been drawing in one of the notebooks which he fills with impressions and formal thoughts. Pastels and pencils were lying on one chair, on another the open sketch book, its pages glistening with the wax with which they had been treated. Moore's drawings are intriguing. His shelter sketches from the beginning of the war are among the most widely-known drawings in England. They are the record of a time which in its horror recalls the darkest days of ancient history. At that time he had volunteered for work in a munitions factory, but many had done so before him and he was never called up. Then Sir Kenneth Clark saw his shelter sketches and through his intercession Moore became a war artist. He showed me one of his wartime sketch books; one day it will be considered a lasting document of our time, as Goya's sketchbooks are of his.

'Come in,' he called, 'I have just done a bit of work. This is the day on which my pupil occupies my studio, so I stay here.' I asked his permission to look through the notebook. There were drawings from life, a sleeping cat, Moore's little daughter in various positions, his wife stretched out on a divan and knitting, and then—in much larger numbers—sketches for compositions of sculptural groups and of single figures seen in Gothic elongation, and again spaces between walls, with figures interspersed, not unlike de Chirico, who paints empty spaces between buildings. I had noticed before that the ideas of contemporary painters, of Picasso, Miró, Ernst, Klee, had had a particular effect on this sculptor. I went on turning the pages. There were new sketches of Moore's by now classical reclining figures, which showed the innumerable possibilities of experiencing one and the same motif in the manner of variations on a musical theme. I realized that this sculptor knows not only the secret of work, he also knows how to be methodical and tenacious. The consequence of his methodical approach may be seen from the fact that Moore always starts from an idea, which may have its origin in Brancusi, Arp, the primitive pre-Columbian sculpture or Masaccio; and there is also much more medieval art in Moore's work than is generally assumed—but this is not important; it is, however, important that he takes it as far as it will go, so that in the end the starting point vanishes and the result bears the imprint of his own intellectual rhythm. One only has to instance the way in which he has developed his recumbent figures until they have culminated in the highly sophisticated creations which, though they originate in a very different cultural climate, remind one, by their finality and suggestiveness, of Tollec-Mayan deities. What the artist in Yucatun projected, a thousand years ago, into symbols of worship, the modern artist searches for in his own psyche. Then with his power of perception and creative metamorphosis he projects it into that mysterious realm of knowledge which has been so aptly named 'Man the Unknown'. (Theism—Existentialism.) That Moore has been able to reach results which are final is due to his tenacity. This tenacity, the directness with which he grasps ideas, added to his intellectual courage and honesty are the true secret of his success. In the case of Moore one might almost speak of an 'exact imagination', which brings this artist nearer to the scientist than to the musician. He enjoys the adventure of his ideas like the physicist who works in atomic research. He has discovered the cavity, the hole, the 'negative fulness' as sculptural opportunity and has adopted it as his special field of investigation in contrast to the concave conception and plasticity which was predominant during the last few centuries. It is space from within which he has started to develop in all its richness. From the cavity Moore has proceeded to the problem of the form within a form, to the tension between concave and convex relations. Besides this there is only one other idea to which he clings as tenaciously as to the concave; it is the idea of the living organism. Moore is as an artist deeply attached to organic life and, but for a few early attempts, his sculptural adventure never led him away from nature towards a merely mechanical or purely formal conception. The idea of organic life is expressed in his sculptures in a higher degree of concentration than even nature itself can give. Each of his works is consequently not only an organic entity but also the result of that inclination of his mind which calls for new ventures. His strongest impulse is the will to express space, not volume, through the human figure. Hence all these elongations and distortions, these hollow forms and excavations, these structural arches in place of limbs. What one might sometimes reproach Moore with in one's mind is that he has no respect for the human figure seen objectively, and one thinks one might explain this by the fact that the artist of the twentieth century has no ideal of beauty to support him as other cultural ages had, whether Renaissance, Gothic or Baroque. But all this appears more comprehensible when one looks at his work from the angle of the intellectual integrity with which he, driven by an irresistible urge, has created them.

I mentioned how unusual it seemed to me that he often gave a narrative content to his drawings which their very colours endow with the quality of paintings rather than the ideas of a sculptor. He retorted: 'It is the general opinion that the drawings of a sculptor should be mere outlines, silhouettes, a recipe for a sculpture, and nothing else. I am concerned with many other things. Here is the space between the walls, it is a sculptural problem for me. The relation between these two figures, the bigger in the foreground and the smaller in the background, is for me not a painter's problem, it is very sculptural and I want to solve it in a sculptural way. The narrative content fades out by itself. It yields to something else, more intense, defying expression, a relation between figures, which increases the feeling of space and fills it with tension. The ancient sculptors knew how to compose single figures and how to bring them into relationship with each other. One can see it on their monuments. I am thinking of something similar. But for me a figure limited by a purpose or only related to a given space or building is not the ideal task of a sculptor. In the same way as I stress the organic idea, I like to see my figures in freedom, in the breadth of a landscape. Then they can breathe; then I can endow them with characteristic forms which together with the landscape melt into a higher entity.'

In the summer of 1948 Moore exhibited three figures in Battersea Park. Their gaze fixed on the horizon, these three female figures, in spite of their relative smallness under a high group of trees, radiated by the very carriage of their bodies an intensity lacking in the other sculptures exhibited there, and transformed the whole surrounding landscape by their power of expression.

'I will make such sculptures,' Henry Moore continued, 'as you can see here in the sketches: a woman sitting on a chair perhaps and another at some distance from her. What takes place here is sculpture in connection with space as I see it.' I looked closely at the pages, and realized how much Moore represents our scientific age, and how subtly his brain works. His sensations are essentially different from the literary and emotional ones of a Rodin. I felt distinctly this palpable drama of space. The traditional style of a group on a vault, a Pietà, seemed to me to be out of date. Rodin had perhaps attempted a space conception similar to that of Moore in the group known as the 'Burghers of Calais'. But Rodin yielded to the old romantic idea while Moore's idea is metaphysical. Moore's work has also little in common with the classical conception of sculpture. Compared with other contemporary sculptors, such as Giacometti, his creativeness is real strength and not merely an outlet for nervous energy. Is it not remarkable that this most productive of modern English artists has grown up in a country which by the iconoclasm of the Puritans was robbed of all sculptural tradition, and where the weakened artistic vitality was almostly completely destroyed by the Industrial Revolution? Later I was more pleased than surprised when we went into the adjoining study, to discover that Moore's pupil was a young foreigner who had come for a time to study under him. Through Moore England has regained the position of an authoritative centre of artistic creation.

Indicative of the improved outlook for contemporary art in England was the strong plea made by the Vicar of St. Matthew's, Northampton, that Moore should adorn his church with a Madonna and Child: and more recently King's College Chapel in Cambridge has asked Moore for a similar work, as has the Barclay School in Stevenage (Family Group), Harlow New Town (Family Group) and the architect of the 'Time and Life' building in London (great reclining figure and a screen of four-figure variations). The first commission, although perhaps a compromise between Moore's individual style of sculpture and a given subject, is nevertheless convincing, even if it is not a genuine piece of 'religious' sculpture. The German Expressionist Ludwig Meidner, a religious man, after studying illustrations of Moore's 'Madonna' declared: 'He shouldn't do it. It is not his world. Don't you see that his hollow figures are idols? They are like Baal in whose hollow belly children were sacrificed by the pagans.'

At the time when I visited Moore some sculptures of his early periods which for many years had been on show in various exhibitions in America and Australia had just been returned to him. Their long absence made them new to him, and he could not avoid recalling how he started and developed his work. In the beginning, even at the art school, his sculptures had some primitive element but they were predominantly massive; they were connected with the structural idea of the Egyptian pyramids and their effect was more architectural than sculptural. 'None of these shapes you see has its own life.' (Mother and Child in Hornton stone, 1925.) 'Years of work were needed to free the forms. In between I made attempts in a more abstract and geometrical sense. Purely abstract thinking is a matter of taste and design, it is not sculpture.' Moore rejects it. 'Did it strike you,' he asked me, 'how lifeless such a sculpture seems in front of architecture? Instead of stressing the contrast, organic forms—architectural forms, these two architectural conceptions kill each other. I dropped all this very quickly.' The egg-shaped bodies as well as the stringed figures were another transitory stage. (Three Piece Carving, 1934; Head and Ball, 1933; Bird Basket, 1939.) 'I would like to say that many of the early works, in particular the abstract experiments, should never have left the studio. But here'—and Moore stepped towards another piece—'you see how I pierced an abstract geo-metrical form because I felt strongly its inadequacy. The hole might be a mouth, and the two points look like the small eyes of a skate; here the will to express the organic is manifest. In a formal sense the two trends are not yet integrated in this work but we approach my final conception of sculpture (Square Form, 1936). The true sculptor is not a modeller. Anybody who models can always produce something round, three-dimensional, without necessarily having a true notion of space. But if one carves or cuts straight into a block the sculptural notion has to be mature, the spatial idea has to be concrete. Not only light and shadow have to be considered; form becomes action, each angle has its fate, each distortion has its reason. One could go on without ending. I stretch and build, and such an arch as formed here by the leg'— Moore stepped to another figure and touched it with his hands— 'has to be as capable of bearing weights as a viaduct. A real sculptor must be a man with the mental equipment of a sculptor.'

As he spoke I was reminded of an essay on Moore's reclining figures, published in The Journal of Aesthetics and Art Criticism by a theorist of the Freudian school. The cliché of the IMAGO writers had been applied throughout; everything was entangled in a web of Freudian terminology. Moore had read it, and only said that he was surprised by what one could see in his sculpture. I felt that the working of his imagination is very different from the implications of this essay; that his fantasy, his intellect—realistic in spite of the logical pursuit of his task—has not much in common with the direct application of the doctrine of Libido. It is distinctly the intellect of a well-balanced man who clearly and vigorously expresses his 'biological formative' will in our technical age.

Again I glanced at the reclining female figure. The breasts stood at an angle to each other, the thighs were stretched, the head was seen as a small mass in relation to the body. No, this was not the presentation of a human being *per se*, but the attempt to express a philosophy of relationships as the only reality, a philosophy of tensions between opposites as against static, isolated, *ergo* non-existent, values. It was not hostile to life, this adventure, as a mere geometrical conception would be. Nevertheless, the organic element in his work does not imply that Moore's mind is not also under the influence of the analytical imperative which is the distinguishing characteristic of our time.

But, I believe, Moore cannot do otherwise. I see him before me, this forceful surgeon of sculpture. He has overcome Constructivism and has achieved his new vision but at the cost of the classic sense of beauty. I know there is no arbitrariness in his work; that he struggles like Jacob with the Angel when he stands in front of an unhewn block of stone; that a reclining female body is all that is given to him to shape the mystery of endless space which lives in his brain, and that he has to create it in a limited volume and through a form as definite as a human body. To this must be added the unyielding character of the material: granite or hardwood. Sometimes he uses also a softer stone or cement, terracotta and then the silent paper, which this skilled artist covers with his hieroglyphics. How, one asks, should one be able to understand all this at the first impact? The man Moore teaches us to respect and to understand it.

The intellectual and emotional development of a contemporary sculptor is that of a complex, not a naïve personality. Most children prefer painting to carving; and as for the layman it is easier for him to enjoy and grasp colour, for colour evokes moods more readily than do forms, and in particular forms in all the complicated transformations in which they are experienced by an artist of the atomic age.

2

BEN NICHOLSON

The Pythagorean

> The kind of painting which I find exciting is
> not necessarily representational or non-
> representational, but it is both musical and
> architectural, where the architectural con-
> struction is used to express the musical rela-
> tionship between form, tone and colour.
>
> *Ben Nicholson*

THE most remarkable tension in the creative faculty of the
people of Great Britain is that which exists between their
rational, practical clarity of conception in all matters per-
taining to life—political, economic, administrative or educational
on the one hand, and their emotional, religious and poetical
urge on the other. This came like a flash to my mind when
I visited the Roman excavations in Bath, that city in Somerset-
shire called by the Romans *Aquae Sulis*, which played the social
rôle of a Versailles in Gainsborough's time. The Roman buildings there originally consisted of a temple and a few houses for
priests, officials and guests, apart from the large baths, which are
still in good condition, with their vaulted *sudatorium* and conduits.
The fragmentary colonnade surrounding this relic, which is
among the most striking of Roman antiquities in Western
Europe, still supports the street and buildings beneath which it
lies, the Roman foundations having been left untouched. The
purposefulness of this establishment conceived in pure geometric
forms [circles, squares, cubes, etc.] is, aesthetically, highly satisfying, leaving one with the impression of primary and at the same
time final values. There is about it a clarity of design and directness of approach, a sense of serenity and measure, of 'noble

simplicity and tranquil greatness,'[1] of virility and strength, typical of that mature spirit, when art and science merge and appear as but two sides of one thing. The Bath ruins are an example of that classic Latin conception which through education and tradition, though not racially, has impressed itself most decisively on the spirit of the English. In the history of English architecture we can follow this line, especially in the enthusiasm with which the civilized taste and the polite learning of the Georgian gentry took up Palladio's style[2] which, although in itself not of purely classic conception, is based—and that is what mainly concerns us here—on those unchanging fundamentals of architectural beauty named by Vitruvius *eurythmia*, which is the value of the repetition of certain elements; *symmetria*, which is the proportion between the various elements and the whole *décor*, which is the perfection of the execution.[3] Most significantly, one can study this line of English development in this same city of Bath, where John Wood in 1728 built Queen Square and designed the Circus, and where his son, the younger John Wood, built the Royal Crescent of 1767-c. 1775, both unthinkable without Palladio. Robert Adam, known as the father of the Classical Revival in Britain,[4] follows in the same line, which explains why places such as Bath are classical in spirit, and why London also, from the main impression made by its outstanding buildings and planning schemes must be called a classical city in comparison with Paris, which is Gothic, or Vienna, which is Baroque.

Leaving the Roman baths I came upon the Abbey Church of St. Peter and St. Paul, which dates from the fifteenth century, and is considered a singularly pure and ornate example of late Perpendicular work. It then struck me as not only the expression of a different spirit—the antique root of our culture on the one hand and the Christian-Barbarian on the other—but also of a mind much more inclined towards a mystical and symbolic conception, having nothing in common with the Euclidian elements of space and definiteness or with Mediterranean clarity, a mind where decoration and volume, having parted company, are often

---

[1] Winckelmann's characteristics of antique art in his History of Ancient Art. *Werke*, 1808-25, Dresden and Leipzig.

[2] Andrea Palladio: *Quattro libri dell'architettura*, Venezia, 1570.

[3] Vitruvius: *De Architectura*. See Jolles: *Vitruvs Aesthetik*, Freiburg im Breisgau, 1906.

[4] Nikolaus Pevsner: *An Outline of European Architecture*, London, 1951.

confusing, overloaded, Northern. It dawned on me then that the classic tradition is the source not only of English philosophy, but also of British statesmanship, parliamentarianism, rhetoric, of the British conception of Empire, of world trade and industrialism, of *civiltá* and humanism, of the rôle that sports play in education and of the balance in the British character, whereas the English form of the Gothic style with its late revival in the eighteenth and nineteenth centuries is a typical expression of the Romantic spirit which has its roots in the septentrional geographic position of the country and also, probably, in the racial composition of the people. [Anglo-Saxon, Norman—which is to some extent Scandinavian—Celtic and others.] These two spiritual forces, the Mediterranean and the Nordic, are not only interwoven but they oppose each other as polarities, creating that cultural entity which we call English. At present we can observe that not only the main trend in poetry and art is in fact romantic, but also that the leading critics are inclined to classify the art style of present-day England as fundamentally romantic. 'If art's vitality,' Herbert Read writes, 'comes from the cross-breeding of styles, its strength comes from stability, from roots that grow deep into a native soil. The typical style of Northern Europe alternates between Abstraction and Expressionism. We may for a time successfully absorb the style of Southern Europe, and we have had idealistic and naturalistic artists of great talent. But our natural talent lies elsewhere—in those styles which spring from introspective and personalistic moods. Such styles are in both the critical and historical sense romantic by nature. The genius of our greatest painters and architects no less than our greatest poets was always romantic. In that sense the general trend of contemporary art may be interpreted as a return to our romantic tradition.'[1] Although the terms used in this paragraph are wide enough to cover all aspects, the Classical, the Romantic and the Modern,[2] I do not think that historically this definition is tenable, although it expresses the view of that group of critics, artists and connoisseurs at the moment most powerful in England. There is no possibility of reducing English art and architecture to one com-

---

[1] *Contemporary British Art*, London, 1951.

[2] A view shared by N. Pevsner who does not see in Adam the direct heir of a classic tradition and who calls the Classical revival 'only a part of a much wider process, the Romantic Movement.'

mon denominator, of covering it with one stylistic definition. Our picture of the polarities is surely nearer the truth, and in the realm of painting Ben Nicholson is the great living example of it. He is the only classic painter of England; indeed, Braque and Morandi are, at the moment, the only names we could couple with his, if we surveyed the whole field of painting in Europe. Ben Nicholson's painting is expressive of those characteristics of the British nation for which it is mainly known amongst other peoples: the clarity and purposefulness of design, the simplicity, and even the modesty [understatements] in the expression of that harmony of emotion and thought which is so typically English, the aestheticism which dominates the taste of England—in spite of the present predominance of a Surrealist biological mentality in the realm of modern art—the feeling for accuracy, characteristic of the scientific and technical spirit of the English as well as of certain of their sports; sailing, for example, with its delicate play of balanced volumes, or golf where the curve of the perfectly formed small white ball cuts through the blue space on the background of the gentle slopes of the English countryside, with the sea somewhere behind, and the exact shapes of the greens, the holes and flags, the tees and clubs. This refined relationship of the small geometric object—the sail or the golf ball—and the wide, coloured planes of landscape and sea, is it not as much an element of Ben Nicholson's art as the basic forms of the Roman baths whose ground plan with its exquisite proportions could be considered as the compositional structure of one of his works from his geometric period? The English might easily recognize their own spirit in Ben Nicholson's work, which is also typical, to some extent, of their puritanic inclinations. They might easily recognize the essence of it with satisfaction, but why is it that they do not? Paradoxically enough, because of their traditionalism which is so deeply rooted in the classic earth. The spirit of the Royal Academy of Arts, an institution still powerful in our days, has, since Reynolds, formed the great English public into an essentially traditionalist people with an anti-modern bias in all questions of art. Being realists in art appreciation, and naturalists in their emotional leanings, the English cannot grasp the break with the visual convention of pictorial art seen in the greater part of Ben Nicholson's work. Although they still cling obstinately to their classical education, they do so in the realm of art more in an academic than in a spiritual sense. In the Autumn of 1953 the Arts Council of Great Britain organized a large exhibition of Roman Portrait Busts. It was at the time one of the most popular exhibitions among the educated classes; and most revealing it was to observe the faces of the gentlemen from the city, the banks and the offices, from the universities and the colonial services, walking pensively through the Arts Council's galleries and resembling the Roman portraits to such a striking degree that one cannot re-member ever having experienced anything like it before. I myself was vastly amused when I recognized in the head of a man from Minturno (1st cent. B.C.) Prof. Anthony Blunt, the director of the Courtauld Institute; in the head of an old man, probably a priest of Isis (1st cent. B.C.) Sir Henry Dale, the biologist and Nobel prize winner; the director of the Fine Arts Section of the Arts Council himself, Philip James, appeared there in the disguise of Julius Caesar (*Castello di Aglie*); the sensitive face of the poet and critic, Herbert Read, was caught in a portrait from Palombara (*Museo delle Terme*), and Lawrence of Arabia's intelligent look, in the head of a man from Caere (*Villa Giulia*) and so on. Nigel Gosling wrote in the *Observer*[1] under the title 'Friends, Romans, Country-men', that the English recognized in these portraits both their power and their effemination. 'First came the virtuous ones—austere, lantern-jawed men, full of "gravitas" and "fortitudo", tramping across Europe or lecturing each other in citizenship; then followed the decadence, with bloated flower-wreathed figures gobbling nightingale pie, drinking, assassinating, and generally letting their private life decline into footnotes. . . . It was much for Roman renown that we are surprised to find they look like the rest of us; surprised and delighted. With a kind of Proustian pleasure we see our contemporaries in these 2000-year-old faces. . . Progressing through the rooms . . . one seems to trace not only individual likenesses but a resemblance between whole centuries. With an agreeable shock we realize that the period which, in physical appearance, is most like our own is the heroic age of the Republic and the early emperors.' This resem-blance to the Romans goes far deeper than the face can reveal. It goes back to the spirit of a basically male society with strong anti-artistic instincts, instead of to the Greeks, a fact which is respon-sible for Ben Nicholson's not being acknowledged to-day as the

[1] Nov. 5, 1953.

English painter who has most decidedly striven for perfection of
form. His art of sophistication can never be popular. But what
sophisticated art is?

*   *   *

Were the English more Greek and less Roman, they would
appreciate the intriguing parallelism of the ideas underlying Ben
Nicholson's geometric work and Plato's aesthetics. Plato wrote
of the pleasures which 'straight lines and circles and the plane
and solid figures give, which are formed out of them, by turning-
lathes and rulers and measures of angles; for these I affirm to be
not only relatively beautiful, like other things, but they are
eternally and absolutely beautiful. . . . And there are colours which
are of the same character and give similar pleasures.'[1]

The English, were they more Greek than Roman, would find in
the recent works of Ben Nicholson an even finer assimilation of
Greek philosophical thought, namely the Pythagorean ideas on
harmony and number. The things of the objective world and their
proportions were to Pythagoras 'analogies or imitations of numbers,' number being for him the essence of the world. The
Pythagorean principles were the straight and the non-straight
[curved] line, the infinite and the finite, which all emerge from one
unity. Pythagoras is said to have discovered a certain relationship
between the length of the vibrating string and the tones in the
octave. He thereupon based his philosophy on proportion [ana-
logia]. Proportion was henceforth declared to be the root of
everything that is most beautiful. The Pythagoreans transferred
the idea of musical harmony to creation itself in which opposites
are united harmoniously. And so Aristotle in his *Metaphysics*[2]
could proclaim that everything is harmony or harmoniously
ordered. What could better define the subtle relationships in the
paintings of Ben Nicholson? It is this harmony of the straight and
the curved lines uniting the different elements of which painting has consisted since its beginning—plane, colour, clair-obscur,
movement and rest, etc.—which is the essence of his artistic
adventure. In its latest phase this adventure bears a certain analogy to musical form, but cannot be defined as expressing music
in painting—a metaphorical way of stating the case which has

[1] Philebus.
[2] I.5.

dominated the writings on art for more than five decades—although the method of composition and the spiritual tendency may obey certain rules similar to those of the composition of a fugue. Out of such rules, out of a formal vocabulary with its grammar and syntax which he has chosen for his purposes, Ben Nicholson has built his world of personal artistic achievement, leaving far behind the primary impulses which he derived, in his early beginnings, from the work of Braque, from Cézanne's austerity and precision—this, however, with an added Fauvist colour accent—from Picasso, Mondrian, and Miró, from Purism [Neo-Plasticism] and primitive Animism.

Let us study further the analogy with the fugue. Rules for the construction of fugue have been prescribed dogmatically by many teachers. Bach, however, the unrivalled exponent of fugue, gives the style a variety and freedom incompatible with the rules of Cherubini and later theorists. Replacing Cherubini with Kandinsky, also a dogmatic, we can speak of Ben Nicholson as the Bach of the fugal composition in so-called abstract painting. The fugue is defined as 'a style rather than a form of composition, in which a melody subject is treated contrapuntally and which exhibits certain clearly recognized features. A fugue is designed for a definite number of voices or parts; its most distinctive and regular feature is the exposition in which each voice enters in turn with the subject. [This time element is replaced in painting by the devices of transparency, super-imposition and multivalence, the equivalent of the space-time continuum in modern physics.] The first voice to enter states the subject in the tonic key; the second enters with the answer, the subject in the dominant key; the voices enter in turn with the subject or answer until all the voices have entered. After the first voice has stated the subject it often continues with a counter-subject, a counterpoint to the subject [or answer]. Sometimes a brief digression called a *codetta* is introduced before the third voice enters; sometimes extra entries—or a complete set of them forming a counter-exposition—occur after the exposition proper. If the subject has any marked statement or implication of tonic and dominant following each other, or a modulation from one to the other, the answer matches tonic with dominant and dominant with tonic—a tonal answer—rather than letting the answer be a straightforward transposition of the subject into the dominant key—a real answer. The exposition is fol-

lowed by a series of modulations in the course of which entries of
the subject may be interspersed with episodes. Generally, the
climax of a fugue is at the end of this middle section, as the return
is made to the tonic key and the final entries of the subject occur.
During the course of the fugue the subject and the counter-subject
may be treated by augmentation, diminution, inversion or other
device. The subject and counter-subject will normally be in
double counterpoint with each other, and their judicious treatment by the less and more erudite contrapuntal devices is one of
the main ways of making the interest grow. *Stretto* and *pedal* are
common features of fugue, usually employed towards or at the
end.'[1]

In Ben Nicholson's work the parallel between the fugue and
his conception is most evident in his still lifes. The *subject* matter
is, from the beginning of his work, a combination of one, two or
several objects (numbers of *voices*). The subject can also be
visualized as the main—central—object of the whole motif of
everyday life, glasses, bottles, jugs, pitchers, goblets, cups, etc.);
from 1921 onwards (*Still Life Villa Capriccio, Castagnola*, 1921-
1922, *Bottle and Goblet*, 1924, *Still Life* (L.L.) 1926, *etc.*) mainly
placed on a table with a 'Cubist' view from the front and from
above. *Variations* of a circular theme, four in one canvas, can be
conceived as modulations of the cold-warm colour scheme or of
the clair-obscur treatment (tonic-dominant key); (*See Painting*,
1923-24).[2] The appearance of linear profiles in 1929-30 (*Prince
and Princess*, 1930 and 1932) or letters and printed words (*Le
Quotidien*, 1934), is comparable to the interposition of episodes
between entries of the subject in a fugue. The development of the
Cubist table still life rendered in a Purist manner (*Still Life*, 1929-
1935) leads to the treatment of subjects (subject and counter-
subject) in a varied way by augmentation (*Still Life*, 1945),
diminution (*Still Life, Mediterranean*, 1933) and inversion. In
Ben Nicholson's flat reliefs the heightening above the main surface corresponds to its inversion, the planes incised lying below
the main surface (*White Relief*, 1934); or the same effect may be
achieved by colour only, e.g., through the use of white and black
as the highest and the deepest layers with primary and tonic

---

[1] *A Dictionary of Music* by R. Illing, London, 1950.
[2] All titles and dates refer to Ben Nicholson: *Paintings, Reliefs, Drawings*, Lund
Humphries and Company Ltd., London, 1948.

colour planes combined (*Two Forms*, 1940-42). Subject and counterpoint to the subject (answer) appear in the treatment of *Project for Two Forms*, 1946-47. *Stretto*, which means narrow in Italian, usually refers to a characteristic device of the fugue in which a second entry of the subject, or its answer, occurs before the first has been completed. *Stretto* in Ben Nicholson's work is a linear device of great sophistication which occurs in several compositions of later date. The *pedal* point is a sustained note round which the harmony and counterpoint continue. The intermediate harmonic clashes resulting from the independent movements of the harmony against the pedal point are one of its most exciting features. This is a device used very often and successfully by Ben Nicholson. It is in *Still Life*, 1929-35, the neutral tone pervading the background, table and some shapes on it, against the 'clashes' of black and Venetian red; or it is the recurring colour scheme, such as the browns and the ochre tones in *Still Life, Winter Landscape*, 1946, against the harmony of the independent white, grey and black tones, whereas the blue accent is analogous to those brief digressions called *codettas*, whose function it is to interrupt the main theme both in colour and in line. In *Painting, Hibiscus*, 1933, and *Coin and Musical Instruments*, 1933, the angular lines in the former, and the undulating lines in the latter, are like voices entering and re-entering against the dominant and tonic keys of the backgrounds. Extra entries—or a complete set of them forming a counter-exposition—are represented in Ben Nicholson's work by the landscapes inserted into a Purist emblematic composition, or the abstract diagrams on the background of landscapes, creating thus a contrast of extraordinary effectiveness and expressiveness of both the visual reality and the ideological pictogram. The title of *Contrapuntal, February 25, 1953*, reveals the factual basis of these analogies drawn up here. Counterpoint means 'the art of combining melodies or, more strictly, adding a second melody to a first. The term counterpoint and its adjective contrapuntal differ in use rather than meaning from polyphony and polyphonic, the former being used for the academic practice of composition embodying the interplay of melodies, and the latter for the compositions displaying this feature as their prime characteristic, in which the interest of the harmony is of markedly subsidiary if not negligible interest.'[1]

[1] R. Illing, *op. cit.*

Beside the musical parallels used here to explain the working method of Ben Nicholson, other comparisons can be introduced to explain *per analogiam* the contemporary spiritual soil out of which his art has grown. The connection with the formal principles of functionalist modern architecture is too obvious to be dwelt upon. Of far greater interest to us here is the fact that those principles have their origins in Japan, which country has developed a high degree of sensitivity where proportion, colour and beauty of material are concerned. Again, whereas the early flat reliefs and similar compositions of Ben Nicholson can be compared with the static principles of Euclidian geometry, which still has a tangible contact with reality, in his later work the whole composition is dissolved into a dynamic rhythm of relationships, no element having an absolute value of its own, but only in its connection with the others. Thus the 'function' of the single elements, as distinct from the single elements themselves, the integral calculus has been adopted in painting as well as in mathematics. Highly abstract conceptions of an almost philosophical purpose, having no relationship to reality, have dominated modern physics since the Quantum theory was developed by Planck and the theory of relativity by Einstein was stated in mathematical language by Minkowski.[1] The dissolution of the materialistic and mechanical world view,[2] the appearance of a highly speculative element in physics—Heisenberg's uncertainty principle, etc. —analytical formulae instead of tactile realities: all this is mirrored in modern art just as it is in modern philosophy. The Neo-Positivists (Petzoldt) accept the relativity principle because they deny an *a priori* principle, and they see in the exclusion of the Euclidian space and the Newtonian time a confirmation of their theories; the Neo-Kantians (Ernst Cassirer) accept it, because the *a priori* principle is for them a condition for all possibility of knowledge although never of absolute knowledge *per se*. Consequently all notions of phenomena conceived in Euclidian and

[1] Albert Einstein: *Über die allgemeine und spezielle Relativitätstheorie*, Braunschweig, 1917. H. T. Pledge: *Science since 1500*.

[2] 'The notion of mass was losing its unique pre-eminence as being the one final permanent quantity. This train of thought leads to the notion of energy being fundamental, thus displacing matter from that position. But energy is merely a name for this quantitative aspect of a structure of happenings; in short, it depends on the notion of the functioning of an organism.' A. N. Whitehead: *Science and the Modern World*, Chapter: The Nineteenth Century, Cambridge, 1945.

Newtonian terms were disclosed as anthropomorphic limitations. The enormous freedom of ideas released in modern physics, mathematics and modern cosmology (Schrödinger, Born; Riemann, Poincaré; Cantor; de Sitter, Milne, Eddington) is basically the same freedom as that at which the modern artist has arrived, and all seems but a new convention of fictitious value in the sense of Hans Vaihinger's *Die Philosophie des Als Ob* (the philosophy of 'As If'). The latest step in this direction was taken by Ludwig Wittgenstein[1] who, proceeding from logic and mathematics as did similarly Spinoza, analyses our possibilities of expressing in language the facts which we can perceive but which we cannot handle directly in speech or in thought except by symbols. Wittgenstein's conception of philosophy as the analysis and criticism of language, as 'the battle against the bewitchment of our intelligence by means of language' is also the conception of Ben Nicholson, who might define his art as the handling of its pure elements without considering any relationship to photographic reality. What metaphysics and philosophy is for Wittgenstein, the narrative, the didactic, the representational for its own sake is for Ben Nicholson: 'the outcome of some insensitivity to the manifold of language.' (Art is a language.)

*　　*　　*

From his early beginnings two main parallel themes appear in the work of Ben Nicholson, the landscape and the still life. The human figure seems never to have interested him to a great extent, although it occurs occasionally as in three drawings of nudes, 1932, and the nude *St. Remy, Provence*, 1933, or, in the shape of faces (*Kate, Paris*, *c.* 1933, *Prince and Princess*, 1930 and 1932, *Auberge de la Sole Dieppoise*, 1932, *Painting*, 1933), and in a primitive rendering of human and animal shapes depicted in *Cumbrian Farm*, *c.* 1929, and others. The theme of the jug and its handle which has become a hallmark, so to speak, of his whole production, goes back to his father, Sir William Nicholson, who not only liked to paint jugs but also collected them. This fact and his fine sense of colour as displayed in some early still lifes (such as *Balearic Islands*, 1925, or *Villa Capriccio*, 1921-22) support the conclusion that Ben Nicholson's work must be considered as a direct continuation of that side of William Nicholson's work where

[1] *Tractatus Logico-Politicus*, London, 1922, *Philosophical Investigations*, London, 1953.

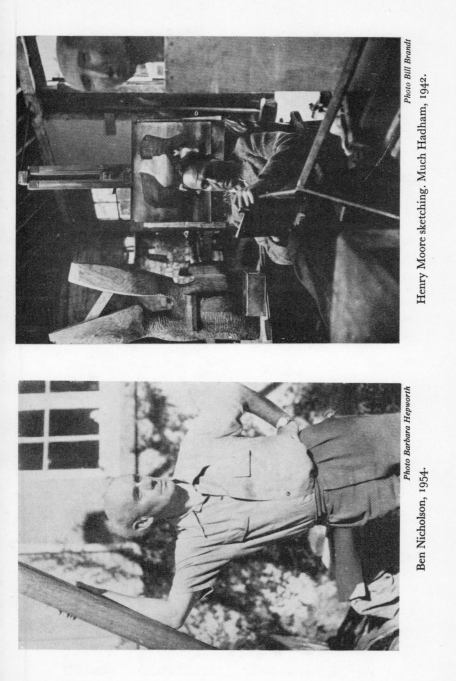

Photo Bill Brandt

Henry Moore sketching. Much Hadham, 1942.

Photo Barbara Hepworth

Ben Nicholson, 1954.

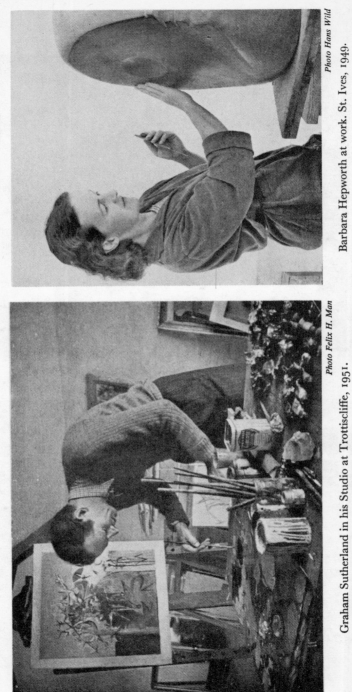

Barbara Hepworth at work. St. Ives, 1949.

Graham Sutherland in his Studio at Trottiscliffe, 1951.

pure forms and near abstractions are dominant. (*Glass, Jug and Fruit,* 1938, *The Lowestoft Bowl,* 1911, *Mushrooms,* 1940, *The Stack, Halls Fields,* 1928, *Plaza de Toros, Malaga,* 1935, etc.)[1]

The stages of Ben Nicholson's still life compositions are: The Impressionist still life, the Cubist still life, the formalized still life (which brings his art near to the lyrical conception of Morandi, without being directly influenced by him) and the Purist still life. About 1932 Ben Nicholson began to change the still life motifs into a completely flat pattern. Playing cards replace jugs, glasses, bottles. Letters are introduced, but more in a decorative, less in a Cubist manner. The decorative element is emphasized from now on; pattern replaces more and more the varied views of still life objects. The year 1933 is a very important one in his development. He experiments in various techniques, as, for example, in combining the techniques of the graphic and pictorial arts, by the insertion of coloured planes into monochrome compositions. In producing interesting textures by means of scratching and scoring the picture surface, he uses the suggestive power of amorphous patches and lines of direction for the release of creative phantasy, a method related to Surrealist Automatism. Stylistically, Ben Nicholson now follows three distinct lines in his work. A Neo-Plastic element makes its appearance in this year, and at about the same time the pure geometric forms, the circle and the square. At first these are not rendered with technical precision. In the years 1937-39, however, they become in general exact in their execution. This is his architectural or geometric period, with flat reliefs in white or grey or, occasionally, with colours inserted. The meaning of these reliefs, apart from their architectural character, is the replacement of the illusion of three-dimensionality, which prevails in traditional painting through perspective, by three-dimensionality itself. With Purism the primary colours begin to dominate. The linear pattern is super-imposed on fine colour values, which increase in number and refinement in his more recent work. Again, in 1933 (*Painting,* 1933, coll. the late Michael Sadler) through the manipulation of twisted lines and different backgrounds, a development is anticipated which only much later (about 1945) began to take shape in the work of Michaux, Wols, Dubuffet and Bryen on the basis of already well-known Surrealist theories. The third line is that of landscape

[1] Robert Nichols: *William Nicholson,* Penguin Modern Painters, London, 1948.

which, from 1939 on, is devoted mainly to Cornwall. About 1945 a higher integration of the linear element takes place, and this leads to the development after 1950. In 1946 the contrapuntal composition of two analogous themes occurs, the one in coloured planes and the other in a linear movement, these, through their juxtaposition, leading to a more intricate form of 'instrumentation'. From 1950 complete mastery is achieved. Spontaneity is combined with definiteness; the composition is enriched with an ever greater number of pictorial elements; the ingenious use of subtle line movements leads to visual sensations reminding one of those of Vivaldi's, Bach's or Mozart's music.

The landscape production shows at first a tendency towards stylization in a Cézannesque or Cubist manner. About 1928 a definitely Naïvist trend develops which bears some relationship to the work of Christopher Wood, and later on also to that of Alfred Wallis. The combination of landscape and abstract elements appears for the first time in 1928 (*Porthmeor Beach, St. Ives*). This line continues in 1942-47, leading to such exquisite compositions as *Trevega*, 1946, or *Mousehole, November 11*, 1947. About 1932 Ben Nicholson aimed at realizing a landscape conception in which the basic elements both of the landscape (tree forms, shapes of hills, paths, etc.) and architecture should be expressed in a kind of shorthand as definite statements reduced to their essential elements. In 1939 landscape drawing forms a considerable part of his production; this was the year when he moved from London to Cornwall, where he has lived ever since. The primitivist trend in his work is now combined with the Cubist sense of form, resulting in great economy in the use of shapes and in an accentuated delineation of those used. From 1945 more Impressionist views appear, linking them with early works. The year 1950 added a series of drawings and engravings of Italian motifs, all of them being bold and characteristically definite statements. An intensified activity in recent years has resulted in the production of works exemplifying all the types of pictorial composition which have engaged his attention over a period of forty years, and in addition he has produced some monumental compositions conceived in a profoundly lyrical vein.

Ben Nicholson is now in full possession of his technical means, of a great refinement of taste and mastery of form. The impressive output of significant works suggests that he is at the beginning of a new fruitful period, for he has arrived at the climax of a development during which he has thoroughly tested all the elements that went into the making of his personal style. In that process he has gone forward step by step, discarding what he could not accept, and these discarded elements express perhaps as well as those that are accepted what he has achieved. His latest work is a mature expression of a personality endowed with a rare gift of sublimating his experiences and with the courage and conviction of a genuine pioneer.

3

GRAHAM SUTHERLAND

The English and the European Aspects of His Art

To enjoy and to understand Graham Sutherland, he should be seen against his English horizon. But to savour him as something typically English is not enough. To accord him his just place in the contemporary flux of artistic ideas he should be regarded and appreciated also as a representative of a wider European conception of art. These two characteristics, the insular and the continental, were strikingly exhibited at the Venice Biennale of 1952 where Sutherland represented British painting.

In an intellectual way the non-British spectator seizes without difficulty the essentially British qualities of Sutherland's work by the contrast with the work of other countries. The Englishman recognizes them more instinctively by the familiar approach, the pantheistic Romanticism, the mystical feeling for nature, the religiousness at once obvious and hidden, all of which form part of the natural English inheritance. To understand Sutherland fully we have to realize that he expresses only one aspect of the English scene. He is a living link with those spiritual values which found their visual expression in the works of Turner, in the English water-colourists, and especially in Samuel Palmer and William Blake. Nordic man is dreamy, nature-bound, hence his lack of attention to architectonic values. What appeals to him is the mysterious, the legendary, the metaphysical, all of which we find gently expressed in Sutherland. Through them he registers a conscious and subconscious protest against that over-rationalization which is the dominant tendency among the Germanic and Anglo-Saxon nations of to-day.

The other trend in English art has roots which do not go so far back in time as to the primitive mind of a pre-civilized epoch, yet nevertheless are planted in a rich cultural soil, that of Roman civilization. The Roman feeling for law, organization and technical efficiency suited the English climate better than did the creative genius of Greece, with its images of archetypal phantasy and its notion of the Classic. We sense this in the work of that other great English painter, Ben Nicholson, a master in his craft, a classical and disciplined mind, who worked his way from the clarity of geometrical design towards a pure poetry and melody, in which, however, the classical mind keeps a firm hold on the reins. His creativity is architectural, governed and shaped, and therefore active in the humanistic, not in the naturalistic sense. Hence also the difference in technique. With Sutherland the line is seismographic, tentative, seeking its way in planes of strong colour, contrasting sometimes with black areas, often undecided in its attempt to translate from naturalistic shapes to artistic forms, whereas Nicholson proceeds with a sensitive but mastered delineation of pure classic intentions. Expressed antithetically the difference gives us Nature-Architecture; Passivity-Activity; religiousness-philosophy; Pantheism-Humanism.

Symbolic of the regeneration of the creative spirit in England (symbolic because every new cultural phase starts with sculpture) yet a third artist must be named: Henry Moore. He is a son of the people, tenacious, direct, free, impulsive, and in no degree corrupted by the aesthetic and academic predilections of the English upper classes who, because they are more interested in sports and hobbies than in art have had in the past, and still have, a disastrous influence on English taste. With a tremendous effort of work and experiment Moore has tried to bridge the gulf which stretches between the past and the present, breaking the continuity of the English tradition.

The line Turner-Palmer-Blake-Sutherland is ideologically unbroken. The Romanticism of the nineteenth century with its tendency to idealize, to flee from the present into the past, from the real into the imaginary, was a protest against the rule of the sceptical, rational mind. The Romanticism of the twentieth century is rather a violent revolt against the domination of the scientific spirit which threatens to overcome and intellectualize the miracle of life, and that revolt takes the form of a quest for the roots of experience, of a search for primitive states of mind and history, for the elemental, the primary in existence. Just because they are romantic movements, however, both display similar characteristics, such as the subordination of form to theme, the readiness to be influenced by imagination and sentiment, the neglect of harmony and balance, the leaning towards the fantastic and extravagant. Hence it is that we find Graham Sutherland coming dangerously near (dangerously near for an Englishman, that is) to a genuine Expressionist like Mathias Grünewald.

In Samuel Palmer's letters he refers to his sketches as 'bits of nature . . . improved by being received into the soul'. He speaks of 'excess' as 'the essential vivifying spirit, vital spark, embalming spice . . . of the finest art'. Compare this with a statement by Sutherland: 'The eye absorbs the extrinsic material. . . . The mind is a reservoir: Memory, the knowledge of previous thoughts and events . . . is fused with the optical impressions of the present. That is the interesting thing. . . . It is necessary to work parallel with nature. . . . The unknown is just as real as the known, and it must be made to look so.' What a step forward from the nineteenth century to the twentieth, above all in the comprehension of the inner processes in man! Did not André Breton in his *Le Surréalism et la Peinture* speak of 'the eye which exists in a wild state . . . It presides over the conventional exchange of signals called for, it appears by the navigation of the spirit.' How important for Sutherland was the Surrealist revolution with its irruption of Freudian psychology into art! And again, Samuel Palmer: 'Though I hope we shall all be severe outlinists, I hope our styles of outline may all be as different as the design of Michael Angelo from his equal Blake, and the outline of Albrecht Dürer from that of Andrea Mantegna. There is no line in nature, though excessive sharpness. The visions of the soul, being perfect, are the only true standards by which nature must be tried. . . . Sometimes landscape is seen as a *vision*, and then seems as fine as art; but this is seldom . . .'

Outlinists! This is as true of Palmer and Blake as it is of Sutherland, although less true of Turner who concentrated on the atmospheric sensation. Sutherland tries to combine both. Sutherland's line is the twentieth century child of its English father, Palmer, and a Latin mother. Compare Palmer's sepia drawing, *Rustic Scene*, 1825, or some sketchbook pages, *A Shepherd and his Flock Under the Moon and Stars, Ancient Trees, Lullingstone Park,*

1828, *The Harvest Moon*, 1830-1 (water-colour) with Sutherland's
Sun Setting Between Hills, 1938, or *Green Landscape*, or *Pembrokeshire
Landscape*, 1944. Before we turn to the maternal Latin side, let us
say a few words here on Blake's mysticism and religiousness, the
other main English characteristic, beside that of nature Romanticism, which has presided over Sutherland's art. I spoke one day
with Sutherland about the religious element in his painting. He
was inclined to dissent from this, at least in the dogmatic sense of
a creed and a moral code, but he could agree in the sense of
religious feeling, of a creative communion with the universe. He
told me that since his childhood his mind had been definitely pantheistic in its disposition, everything in life being holy. The
matter and the individual shapes of the universe were to him both
the expression and the body of the divine essence. This is a notion
admirably set forth in the writings of Anthony Ashley Cooper,
third Earl of Shaftesbury,[1] whose influence on Herder, Goethe
and the German Romantic School, as well as on Diderot, Rousseau and others, was immense. It is here that we have to seek the
religious and philosophic roots in Sutherland's spirit. We catch
the manifestation of that religious mood in his way of seeing in
the humble, the unexpected detail of nature a surprising expression
of life, in his searching for the essence of the vital, universal
energies of Being. Being, Martin Heidegger defines as 'not God,
nor the cause of the world. Being is further away than all reality
and yet nearer to man than any individual piece of reality, whether
it be a rock, an animal, a work of art, a machine, an angel or a
god. Being is the nearest, but the nearest which remains also the
furthest from man. The vital matter is that the truth of Being
shall of itself come into language, find expression in language, and
that thinking shall attain to this language.'[2] It is in a similar sense
of devotion and piety towards life that Sutherland approaches
nature. In this sense he is also representative of that contemporary
spirit in European thought which wages a desperate struggle
against the mechanistic-materialistic conception of life. The
growth of this spirit has been a slow process since its beginnings
in the philosophy of science of the seventeenth century, and
equally long has been the struggle against it. Blake took part in it
on the side of the mystical consciousness. He, too, was undog-

[1] 1671-1713.
[2] *The Meaning of Humanism.*

matic. He brooded over the ideas of the French Revolution, but instead of demanding social upheavals he insisted on a spiritual revolution, on a 'religious vision which was not exactly that of the church'. 'The vision of Christ that thou dost see/Is my vision's greatest enemy . . .' He never ceased from mental fight against the attacks of the rationalists. 'Mock on, mock on, Voltaire, Rousseau./Mock on, mock on: 'tis all in vain!/You throw the sand against the wind/And the wind blows it back again./ —And every sand becomes a gem/Reflected in the beams divine. . . ./Blown back they blind the mocking eye . . . etc./The Atoms of Democritus/And Newton's Particles of light/Are sands upon the Red Sea shore . . . etc./' He hailed imagination: 'The world of imagination is the world of Eternity; it is the divine bosom into which we shall all go after the death of the vegetative body. This world of imagination is infinite and eternal, whereas the world of generation, or vegetation is finite and temporal. There exist in that eternal world the permanent realities of every thing which we see reflected in these eternal forms, in this vegetable glass of nature.' Blake's own imagination saw deep into the mysteries of Nature's workshop. There is a drawing of Blake's depicting Daphne 'root-bound', with her feet rooted in the ground and branches springing from her fingers. Metamorphosis is frequent in Greek mythology, for the Greek mind was swift to perceive and marvellously apt to personify the changing outward face of things, although behind all change and common to all beings, is the one unifying life force. Ta-o, Atman, Bergson's *élan vital*, God. Mythological and philosophical knowledge breeds art forms and expression, gives rise to the symbol and the myth. With Sutherland metamorphosis takes the form of a suggestion of otherness cutting athwart the thing perceived. Thus the root of a tree partakes also of the life of a living undulating animal; a blasted oak is a monster left over from the age of giants; thorns are thorns and also threatening teeth in a cruel mouth, instruments and symbols of martyrdom. When in making a 'close-up' he emphasizes a natural shape, often a very common one; when he enhances tree forms to the dignity of human beings, or debases the human being to the level of lowlier existences, or bestows upon a stone the sensitive contours of living flesh he does but represent the whole with the part or the part with the whole. And with this instinctive interpenetration he expresses a philosophy of life which is older than science, indeed, a philosophy of life to which the empirical science of to-day is turning again for guidance.[1] Sutherland himself once said: 'It is not a question so much of a tree like a figure or a root like a figure—it is a question of bringing out the anonymous personality of these things; at the same time they must bear the mould of their ancestry. There is a duality: they can be themselves and something else at the same time. They are formal metaphors.'[2]

The English brook discharges here into a wide European river, the new metaphysical-mythical art with its symbolic significant imagery, a river full of dangerous depths and whirlpools. And here then we may turn to the Latin ancestry of Sutherland's art. For even if great contributions have been made elsewhere, as by Munch, Kandinsky, Kokoschka, Klee, Ernst, it is the Latin races which, since the decay of Greek culture as an organic whole, have been creative in the primary form-shaping sense of the word. The 'German' Gothic style has produced genuine works of art, but what was new in this style came from France, so that in saying that the North was dominated by the Gothic style we are but saying that it was dominated by French genius. The Roman, the Romanesque, the Renaissance, the Baroque styles were created in Italy. They were eruptions of creativeness out of a race in its maturity, its wealth and power. The French had as yet no great painter who could compare with a Titian or a Tintoretto, no sculptor comparable to Donatello or Michelangelo. Then in the nineteenth century there arose suddenly in Paris an art movement which turned Paris into a new Florence. The art of the other European peoples has been grafted upon the immortal achievements of these Latin countries. In Paris, the Spaniard, Picasso, grew to his superhuman stature, one man representing the soul of a whole people. He unites in his work French *élan* with Spanish *terribilità*. (Goya was, in fact, the first artist who expressed the nightmare quality of our modern times.) Picasso is a volcano of invention, an inexhaustible mine of experiment. He is indefatigable in his search for the face of the new Adam, the man of the new scientific age. One can think of Sutherland as a romantic painter without thinking of his affiliations with Palmer and Blake, but one cannot think of him without taking into account the im-

---

[1] E. A. Burtt: *The Metaphysical Foundations of Modern Physical Science*, London, 1925.

[2] The Listener, London, 19th November 1951.

pact Picasso made upon him. And one is obliged also to recall the influence of de Chirico with his singular feeling for space and metaphor, and that too of the Kandinsky of the early 'Expressionist Abstract' paintings. He is indebted also to Max Ernst's Concretism of the phantastic and to Matisse for intensity of colour, decorative quality and flatness of composition; finally, to primitive art periods for the 'animism' that informs his work. But Picasso, Ernst and de Chirico are by far his largest creditors. Take Picasso's so-called Guernica postscripts: *The Weeping Head* or *The Weeping Woman* of 1937 created in the emotional reaction to the destruction of Guernica. The line which interests us here stems from Picasso's *Crucifixion*, 1930. This is a sublimation of Crucifixion imagery, and as such makes no attempt to rival Grünewald's *Crucifixion*, especially the one in Karlsruhe, in the matter of intensity of belief. When Sutherland embarked on his Northampton Crucifixion he was faced with a problem which he could not solve in the intensely Expressionistic manner of Grünewald. The historic image of Christ suffers necessarily when viewed through pantheistic spectacles, even if these are tinted with enthusiasm for the Catholic creed. Picasso was also under Grünewald's influence, but he avoided this schism by the superimposition of Neolithic imagery on fading Christian ideas. Stemming from the Crucifixion the line leads us to the Minotauromachy, to the Lies and Dreams of Franco and the Guernica composition. This Picassoist sequence of ideas, Christian, Neolithic, Mythical, has caught every artist of our time in its snares, and has impressed itself on our age with an urgency and a primary force which no one has been able to escape. Sutherland's *Thorns*, 1945, his study for *Crucifixion*, 1946, his *Thorn-Head*, are so many tributes to it. Sutherland's way led from a pantheistic metamorphism and animism to a religious conception. The thorn suggesting suffering and aggression was, by way of conscious or half-conscious traditional ideas, already the suffering head of Christ, and thus led to the Crucifixion theme in Sutherland's work. De Chirico was the great master of metaphysical space, and to people that space he felt himself impelled to substitute for the real human figure shapes that to him were present though not visible. These expressed for him the enigma of contemporary man more forcibly than it could be expressed by known conventional figures and conventional faces. Here the idea of metamorphosis is brought directly into relationship with the human figure. 'The object which replaces the human figure,' said Sutherland, 'is for the time being a necessity for me. It will not always be so, I feel.' One may ask why a substitute for the human figure at all? The Expressionist, for instance, is content with the distortion of it. 'Because one has to approach the question of rendering the human figure obliquely,' said Sutherland to me. 'To bridge the gap between the reality of the resemblance and the actual thing. What I feel is that the shock, the impact, the surprise of a figure walking or standing in a room can only be preserved by using something in its place. Because these appearances are so familiar that they would not give the surprise that a thing with the realistic elements slightly slipped away gives one. The actual form has become a cliché which one does not react upon in quite the same way. It is still possible to use the actual form. . . . I shall get nearer to using actual form with a slightly different twist to give the beholder the impression of never having seen it before.'

Actually the portraits Sutherland has hitherto painted reveal this tendency. His art is essentially realistic, and that not only when he chooses a likeness or a detail instead of the whole to achieve an effect of surprise (a Surrealist moment), or when he enlarges or emphasizes a detail to achieve a specific expression or to make a discovery, but also when he transforms. Reality in the age of the Quantum theory, of the Einsteinian space-time continuum, of Jungian psychology, of Cybernetics is, however, a reality vastly different from that which was defined by the exclusive law of causality, the mate iality of matter, the mechanical principle in the interpretation of life or by pragmatism.

4

BARBARA HEPWORTH

The Meaning of Abstract Art

Il faut être de son temps.—*Daumier*

No style is timeless. However much an artist may strive to represent eternal values and an ideal beauty, the formal language he uses or invents stamps him as a representative of his own age and of the ideological and other factors which distinguish it. All art history is confirmation of this fact. There is no exception to the natural law of change and evolution. Since art, like nature, is a creative activity producing forms, it follows that it is governed by the same morphological principle, which may be defined as form within change. This approach gives us the scope and the time limit of the problem, and enables us to look at abstract art in a sufficiently objective way.

To-day, only forty years after the first modern experiments in abstract art were made, an abstract artist has been selected to represent England officially abroad.[1] This is a public acknowledgment of an art historic reality. Abstract art has had to face severe opposition, and therefore the very fact of its continued existence may be regarded as proof of its necessity. In any case it is a fact which must influence taste and the general attitude towards artistic values. The term abstract of itself elucidates little. From time to time other terms have been used to replace it, as, for example: constructive, concrete, non-figurative, but all of them leave unanswered the important question of whether an absolutely abstract art is possible, i.e., an art which works with forms or combinations of forms not derived from sensual experience. It is the old philosophical problem of *a priori* knowledge. Picasso said that all abstract art has its roots in reality, but that the traces of reality can be removed one by one. 'Abstract sculptural qualities,' Barbara Hepworth says on the other hand, 'are found in good sculpture of all time, but it is significant that contemporary

[1] Barbara Hepworth at the Venice Biennale, 1950.

sculpture and painting have become abstract in thought and concept.' The whole problem of abstract art is more a problem of
living forces than of logic. The question of abstraction resolves
itself into a question of degree and conception. Geometric forms
seem more abstract than organic forms. Plato developed the
theory that abstract shapes, especially definite geometrical forms,
are beautiful in themselves. They are for him direct imitations of
the eternal forms or ideas, and not imitations of imitations as in
representative art. Even if we take Plato as a starting point, we
find that the 'absolute' freedom of the contemporary artist is only
relative. But however that may be, it is unlikely that our age will
find in Plato's philosophy the ideological basis for the modern
conception of pure design. There are also abstractions in the art
of primitive peoples, but in this case the abstractions have a
magical significance. In the work of a modern abstract artist we
can notice the different stages of a dialectical process, and in
recognizing how certain modern ideas have disintegrated traditional forms, how, after many metamorphoses, they have led to
a synthesis, to a new conception of beauty and significance, we
shall fill the term abstract with a living content.

There is no doubt that scientific thought has made an impact
on modern art. Science dominates our age, and the artist feels the
need to give this scientific age its artistic image. 'If,' says Barbara
Hepworth, 'we had lived in a time when animals, fire-worship,
myth or religion were the deepest emotional aspects of life, sculpture would have taken the form, unconsciously, of a recognizable
god; and the formal abstract relationship in the representation
would have been the conscious way of vitalizing those ideas; but
now these formal relationships have become our thought, our
faith, waking or sleeping—they can be the solution to life and to
living. . . .' And then: 'Contemporary constructive work . . . is an
absolute belief in man, in landscape and in the universal relationship of constructive ideas.' From these words we can deduce that
abstract art is not concerned only with a mechanistic interpretation of life. As science has moved from a more mechanistic to a
more complex way of looking at phenomena, so the artist, at first
intrigued with the mechanical and geometrical relationship of
forms, now stresses more their spiritual value and inner life, and
builds on the unconscious components in his creative efforts. ('As
the sculptural idea is in itself unfettered and unlimited and can

choose its own forms, the vital concept selects the form and substance of its expression quite *unconsciously*.'—Barbara Hepworth.)

Abstract art is the expression of the idealism of a time which is in a state of transition and of crisis. Violent changes are taking place in all spheres of thought and activity. The abstract artist does not rebel against his age but against certain of its shortcomings and tradition-bound errors, and he does so because he believes in the new vistas that constructive scientific thought is opening up for mankind. He accepts them as the next goal to be reached. Barbara Hepworth says: 'In his rebellion he can take either of two courses—he can give way to despair and wildly try to overthrow all those things that seem to stand between the world as it appears to be and the world as it could be—or he can passionately affirm and reaffirm and demonstrate in his plastic medium his faith that this world of ideas exists.' Barbara Hepworth has chosen the latter course, and her work is an acceptance not only of her own time but of herself. Matisse once expressed this same attitude with the words: 'Il faut s'admettre.' And for Barbara Hepworth 'the present moment is the only time'. There is a mighty formal tradition of global extent which supports the abstract artist of to-day from prehistoric times onward. The work of Barbara Hepworth shows that, contrary to the assertions of some psychologists, there are even elements of myth in an abstract work of art. She herself has said: 'At the moment we are building up a new mythology.'

The quotations from Barbara Hepworth used here[1] often date back about thirteen years. It is significant to note that these ideas expressed her style, her inner certainty and direction even before she was able to give them a definite shape. The works she produced in those years, were only steps towards those which, in their transmutation of musical and metaphysical values into plastic values, finally formed a unity of idea and execution. These are masterworks of a new imagery in which the surrounding space is made an active partner of the figure, and without a doubt they win for her a place among the foremost sculptors of our time.

The Phases of Development in Barbara Hepworth's work

Barbara Hepworth's early work was representational, and consisted of portraits, single figures and groups. It was in Italy in

[1] See: *Circle*, London, 1937, and *The Studio*, London, October 1946.

1923-26 that she began to carve directly in wood and stone. At that time great emphasis was laid upon direct carving, especially in England. Eric Gill, the early Epstein, Henry Moore, Gaudier-Brzezka and Skeaping all advocated and practised it. These artists believed in it as the only method, and refused to model and transfer the clay form to wood or stone. Direct carving changed for them their whole outlook on sculpture. The material had its character and imposed that character on the work, sometimes, when the imposition exceeded a certain measure, to the disadvantage of the work as a product of the artist's imagination. But on the whole this direct approach to the final material had a liberating effect and justified itself by its fruitful results. A perfect unity was sought between the idea, the material and the dimension. This unity was manifest in the works of primitive peoples—Neolithic, Archaic Greek, Etruscan, Negro, Pre-Columbian, Aztec, Easter Island sculptures, etc. See in this context Barbara Hepworth's *Head*, 1930. In *Torso*, 1929, the forms are not so much the naturalistic forms of a female body as forms belonging essentially to the wood which embodies them. Up to 1934 her work was inspired exclusively by the human shape; simplified, sometimes so as to verge upon the abstract, it was always easy to recognize whence the inspiration came. From 1934 onwards there is a complete change. She began to be occupied with geometric shapes, but only for a relatively short period. The more organic forms returned, and later on those of the human figure. The titles of her sculptures were now: Conoids, Conicoids, Spheres, Hemispheres, Helicoids, Discs, etc. This purist-geometric thought not only changed, but also, to a certain extent, frustrated her outlook. It was through a long process of inner assimilation that the geometric element became fused with her work and then not as a separate idea, but as an organic part of a whole which could no longer be broken down into its parts by analysis. Barbara Hepworth's development is characterized by the impact of a constructive thought, the realization of that thought in a more or less rational theoretical form, the submerging of it in the unconscious and its reappearance as an integrated, inseparable part of her imagination.

Free forms constitute a further experimental stage in Barbara Hepworth's development. In 1934, abstract free forms appeared in her work for the first time, bringing with them a new version of an old problem, that of the perceptual unity of shapes separated through space; the solution was that no physical continuity was necessary (*Two Forms*, 1935). *Mother and Child* shows another aspect of the same problem. It is an assemblage of two forms, necessarily connected but not carved in one piece. In 1932 Barbara Hepworth made her first pierced work. A new function of space was discovered and she explored its possibilities with unfailing enthusiasm. But she did not and does not now use concavities and holes in the same sense as does Henry Moore. Hers is a classical, a static conception; his is basically organic, nature-bound, romantic. Whereas the hole in a work of Barbara Hepworth pierces straight through a figure, Moore's is inclined to widen and to wind through it. In reducing the mass he often diminishes the figure to a shell covering, as it were, the most important of its messages, the Secret of the Within. Endless new aesthetic possibilities appeared to Barbara Hepworth of exploiting the music and the rhythm of lines created by light and shadow and by the boundaries where form and space meet. The roundness, the unity of the object lies, not as with Maillol, in the convexity, not in seclusion from the outer world, but in the penetration of light and air into the closed form, in the new entity of figure and surrounding space. In works like *Pendour*, 1947-48, Barbara Hepworth attains absolute beauty. Here colour appears as part of sculpture. Colour was used by the old Greeks, by the Egyptians, by the Assyrians and by primitive peoples. With Barbara Hepworth, who is one of the few sculptors who have explored this special field, it is not a question of 'coloured sculpture', of applied colour (she very seldom uses colour on the outside, mostly in the concavities), but of intensifying through colour—white, grey or blue in different shades—the form and the depth required by the volume. This artistic problem occupied her from 1937 onwards. She accorded to colour an organic function similar to that which nature accords to the colouring on the inside of certain flowers. Wood, especially foreign hardwoods like blackwood, lignum-vitae, ivory wood, etc., and stone are the materials she prefers. She does not use either perspex or plaster, cement or metal, and that for the reason that they are not living materials. In 1939-40 we find her producing her first stringed sculptures. The strings give both transparency and form. *Pelagos of* 1945 is a good example of the introduction of this new element. Sometimes the strings have another function; in running together towards a common focal point they suggest a

Goethe in 1832.
Pencil Drawing by C. A. Schwerdgeburth.

Photo Roger Parry

André Malraux, 1951.

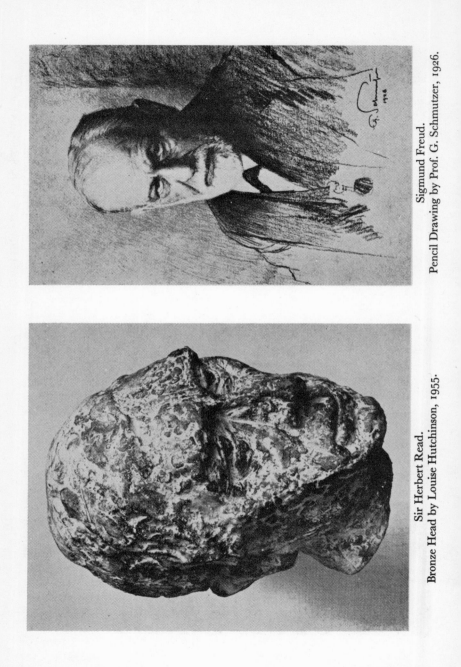

Sir Herbert Read.
Bronze Head by Louise Hutchinson, 1955.

Sigmund Freud.
Pencil Drawing by Prof. G. Schmutzer, 1926.

greater depth than the sculpture itself could convey. Or again they produce an effect of tension, the solid form thrusting in one direction and the strings offering a counter strain in the other. Devices and inventions similar to those in the work of Barbara Hepworth are to be found in the *oeuvre* of Archipenko, Lipschitz, Arp, Brancusi, Giacometti and Moore; taken together they provide a complete compendium of modern abstract sculpture. The question of precedence is thereby not raised.

In 1939 Barbara Hepworth moved from London to Cornwall. The Cornish sea and landscape had a beneficial effect on the cerebral component in her work. Through the influence of nature the constructive-geometrical forms became softer and her whole conception of sculpture more organic. There also she found the inner relationship between sculpture and landscape. Before this change of scene she had been preoccupied with the relationship of sculpture and architecture. In Cornwall Barbara Hepworth's sculptures became more subtle, and some of her works, as, for example, the four recumbent non-figurative compositions made in the competition for the ends of Waterloo Bridge, reveal a beauty which can be enjoyed directly without reference to the principles of abstract art. Of her latest works, *Dyad* in rosewood, with two engraved profiles, the lyrical *Rhythmic Form*, also in rosewood, and *Biolith* in blue Ancaster stone, all of 1949, may be mentioned. In the *Biolith* a face appears on each side of the sculpture, the one male, the other female. Seen from the point of view of construction, there is a hole pierced through the stone, and this forms the eye of the one face and leads through to the other on the opposite side, whilst a deep groove down the middle imparts a spiral movement to the solid mass, forcing the beholder to go round it. This work shows a new approach to the problem of the front view and back view of a sculpture; it eliminates them by emphasizing the unity of two elements, of male and female. In the *Cosdon Head* of 1948, four times life-size in blue marble, the idea of the two faces is anticipated. The most sophisticated work that Barbara Hepworth has yet created, and one that may be regarded as the climax of her achievement hitherto, is the *Biocentric Form* of the year 1950. The interplay of crystal and human organic forms radiate living energy. The richly faceted monolith itself casts a spell over the mind, but in addition, as we contemplate it, we become aware of suggested images—an image of the human figure with trunk and limbs fused, as always in Barbara Hepworth's work, into one volume, and a mythological image similar in form and style to those in Egyptian works, but charged with a different meaning for our contemporary minds. There is a lyrical and at the same time a monumental quality in this *Biocentric Form*, and this dual appeal to our sensibilities arises from the harmony of soft and severe contours which create fascinating and seemingly endless surprises. In *Monolyth-Empyrean*, 1953, Barbara Hepworth created a new version, both powerful and poetic, of the *Biocentric Form*. And *Pastorale*, of the same year, in white Serravezzia marble uses in an exquisite way again, the contrast of angular and rounded forms.

Parallel with her sculptural work, Barbara Hepworth has often devoted whole periods to drawing. These drawings (also small sketches and sometimes even small clay figures) are not working drawings or maquettes serving as memoranda or annotations for sculpture, but exist in their own right, although it goes without saying that they have an ultimate bearing upon her sculptured work. Recently figurative drawings of nudes, group compositions and heads have taken the place of her former drawings of crystal and geometric forms. The surgeon with his assistants at work in the operating theatre, a dramatic theme, occupied a great deal of her attention during 1949, and many drawings and paintings witness to the intensity of her interest. Barbara Hepworth's drawings have some of the quality of fresco. She draws with firm lines, sometimes with, sometimes without shading or cross-hatching, and occasionally she adds colour or a toned ground of chalk or plaster of Paris applied to wood panels. Her drawings suggest that she was inspired by Degas, by Renaissance masters, such as Giotto, by the Pre-Raphaelites, by Braque and others, but every influence is assimilated in the personal experience of the artist. It is of interest to note the tension set up between these representational drawings and the abstract sculptures produced at the same time. We feel that just here is the key to the understanding of her working method, which is that of a constant interchange of outward observation and inner reflection. And behind the visible creation of the plastic artist we divine also the reconciliation of those other opposites, of art and life with their often conflicting exigencies, of nature with her imperious realities and the human spirit with its passionate affirmation of the ideal.

5

BERNARD LEACH

And His Thirty Years in the Service of Ceramic Art

I.

IN the Victoria and Albert Museum there is a cut and planed stoneware bowl in warm grey and rust glaze by Bernard Leach. The simplicity of its form and its vitality made me think of the severe beauty of Romanesque architecture. What source of knowledge and what artistic and ethical conception had inspired this exquisite ceramic work?

Born in Hongkong in 1887 of English parents, and trained as an etcher, Bernard Leach went, in 1909, to Japan. It was the magic of Lafcadio Hearn's books which brought him to this decision. 'I must say at once that there is another side of Japan too.[1] The wealth of its artistic material, of stored Eastern wisdom, gives every visitor the possibility of finding new beauty and knowledge and makes him feel like an explorer.' Among this people, Leach learned his craftsmanship from the representative of the sixth generation of Kenzans in Tokyo. In accordance with custom the head of a school allows his best students to take his name, his palette and glazes. Bernard Leach and his Japanese friend Tomimoto represent the seventh generation of the Kenzan tradition through the certificate of proficiency which they received from their master. Its first representative, Ogata Kenzan (brother of the painter Korin), was famous about 1700 for his use of a wide variety of colours, his fine breadth of calligraphy and his brush-work. Leach stayed in Japan for eleven years and returned there for a year in 1934. From Japan he visited Korea and China. He studied the development of Eastern pottery and held many exhibitions of his works in Japan and Korea.

Japan is known for the value it sets upon ceramics through the

---

[1] This essay is based on a conversation with Leach which took place in St. Ives shortly after the war.

ceremonial drinking of tea, Cha-no-yo, which is regarded as a means of imbuing life with beauty. There Leach learnt to understand the harmony which was achieved under the T'ang dynasty in China through the reinterpretation of Greek and Buddhist influences and their combination with elements within the native framework of Taoist and Confucian concepts. During the greatest period, that of the Sung dynasty, all these different influences were welded together into one. From India these cultural elements came to China and through Korea they reached Japan in the sixth century. 'To-day the supremacy of twelfth-century Chinese pottery is undisputed. Only the best of the Ming can take a place beside it, Korean celadons and Ri porcelain, early Japanese teamaster's ware, early Persian, Hispano-Moresque, German Bellarmines, some Delft and English slip-ware' (especially Thomas and Ralph Toft, Ralph Simpson and William Taylor, whose tradition Leach has taken up in England).

The perfection of old Chinese ceramics came from the Chinese potters' technical skill in the use of natural colours and different textures of clay, the quality of their glazes, their slow baking. There is a living beauty in their shapes. That is why Leach says: 'It is not without reason that important parts of pots should be known as foot, belly, shoulder, neck or lip, or that curve and angle should often be thought of as male or female.' Leach's best works are inspired by this Chinese and Korean art. Not copying but working in its spirit he combines East and West in a new creative impulse.

'The ends of lines are important,' he says, 'the middles take care of themselves. Lines are forces and the points at which they change or cross are significant and call for emphasis. Vertical lines are of growth, horizontal lines are of rest, diagonal lines are of change. Straight line and curve, square and circle, cube and sphere are the potters' polarities. Curves for beauty, angles for strength. A small foot for grace, a broad one for stability. Enduring forms are full of quiet assurance. Overstatement is worse than understatement. Technique is a means to an end. It is no end in itself.'

When I said a few admiring words about the beautiful material of the unglazed parts of his ware, he only smiled: 'The warm brown tone which reminds you of a golden biscuit, the natural voice of the material, is achieved by the combination of a high temperature—we bake our ware between 1,250-1,350 degrees (the temperature for Japanese and Chinese porcelain respectively) —with the composition of clay and the glaze given by wood ashes which are allowed to fall on the ware from the fire in the kiln. We have here a kiln consisting of three chambers, a traditional kind of Eastern kiln on rising ground which was built with the help of one of the most skilled pottery technicians in Japan, the late T. Matsubayashi. Each chamber takes about 700 pieces. We heat it partly with oil, partly with wood. The heat flows from one chamber into the other, the fire is lazy and slow for the "reduced" effects.

'When I was considering introducing the Eastern practice into my own country they said to me: "It takes twenty years to establish a new pottery." They were right. It has taken twenty years before we reached economic security without sacrificing what we started with and believed in. To establish a relationship with new material, native tradition, the public, takes a long time.'

Bernard Leach built his workshop in 1920 at St. Ives, in Cornwall, an artists' colony since the 'nineties, connected with the names of Whistler and Sickert.

'You have noticed that the glaze does not cover the whole form in many of my things and that the natural colour of the body is used as a decorative effect. This also has its origin in early Chinese practice. To prevent the glaze from running over the edge of the ware and sticking to the support they left the lower part uncovered. The Chinese craftsman, who does not distinguish between aesthetics and utility, saw beauty in the necessity and used it. His natural methods resulted in a good colour and texture.

'The colours of my glazes range from grey, grey-green, occasional quiet blues to the iron colours, i.e., from rust to black and variations of these. This colour scheme is limited by the high temperature of the kiln. For the glazes I often use vegetable and wood ashes, and we have done much in England to introduce the knowledge of these ashes as fluxing agents in high temperature glazes.'

So there is no secret about how you reach the choice effects of your ware?

'I have no secrets. When I was in Japan my workshop burnt down one night and with it hundreds of recipes which I had collected with great trouble through many years. I was in despair.

What happened? Potters whom I had learnt from or helped came to my assistance and in a few months I was richer than before. I shall never keep secrets. Later when I found our art students and even masters stealing from each other's notebooks I said to myself: This is a practice which ought to be broken down.'

Your pupil Cardew says that the only secret in pottery lies in integral tradition, in continuity of culture.

'The quality of craft is not unrelated to the general level of a culture. I used to have prejudices against industry and machinery and I have become a little less prejudiced. I think that the machine is of help to humanity. But we have to inspire this external activity through an internal fervour. Things should be done for the sake of the work, for the sake of humanity, not for the sake of economic interests. To give an example: I have started here with a group of ten people who under my leadership work by hand against the background of industry. There is love, pleasure, and co-operation in our work. We have a certain faith about the matter, that the world needs it. If people would plan their activities more with their hearts and not only with their brains, it would be a more peaceful world. The most difficult task to achieve in the experiment is the social one: to create a well-knit group out of a handful of people, some of whom are students, some from the countryside. A high common denominator of belief is requisite. It is rather a question of life including art than of art including life. What we produce jointly is *domestic ware*. It is the product of our common efforts in striving for the best form for objects of daily life. Last year we turned out 17,000 pots. In the current year it will be 17,000 up to 22,000 at the net return of three shillings a piece. This ware is signed with the St. Ives mark, S.I. In addition to it there are *individual pieces*, mostly produced by myself. Decorative tiles, jugs, bowls, plates, vases. They have the additional signature B.L. or the initials of another member of the group besides the usual S.I.'

Bernard Leach's son, David, interrupted our conversation. In the workshop they had just opened the first chamber of the kiln, and the whole group were eagerly awaiting the result of weeks of work. We went down. Carefully the ware was taken from the hot kiln, the glaze and soundness of each article were tested, and then piece by piece it was wrapped in rugs to protect it from the cold wind. I saw in their faces the contentment which individual work gives. I felt that these people were happy because there was a meaning in their life.

When I took my leave, Leach said to me: 'After the war everything is in a melting-pot, in a kiln if you like. There is now a chance for the crafts in England. During the war the government would not recognize craft for itself, only as a branch of industry. Utility regulations had a quite devastating effect on the crafts. Out of 2,000 less than twenty workshops were left, and most of them were led by old people. We are still subject to the Board of Trade. Labour can still be directed. There is no final authority in matters of arts and crafts yet. We don't want any Ministry, we don't want to be subject to politics. But we are hoping that we may have an Arts Commission in the House of Commons in case a vital decision has to be taken to protect our position. Good-bye to you and don't forget: The love of work is the basis, and the only basis, for the larger process of all making.'

2.

> However its form may change, only at a great loss can Asia permit its spirit to die, since the whole of that industrial and decorative art which is the heirloom of ages has been in its keeping, and she must lose with it not only the beauty of things, but the joy of the worker, his individuality of vision, and the whole age-long humanizing of her labour.
>
> *Kakuzo Okakura*

Years have gone by. Due to the efforts of Bernard Leach and others the crafts of England are now organized in The Crafts Centre of Great Britain. The interests of the craftsman are now watched, public support is secured, the standard of the work is a matter of unceasing consideration. The crafts have recovered and are on a slow move upwards. There is no true peace, however, and fatalistically Europe is facing day by day and month by month the cold war with the East. The prospect even of survival in a nuclear age, when the H-bomb is casting its black shadow on the tortured imagination of man, is an object of serious study for outstanding scientists.

Bernard Leach, deeply concerned with the mission which the

spirit of the crafts has to fulfil in an industrial civilization, tries to anchor more securely the convictions to which his entire life has been devoted. In 1952, in the company of Hamada and Dr. Yanagi, he left Europe for Japan to drink anew at the source of Far Eastern wisdom. Only later on did he actually realize the underlying motive which had drawn him back to the East once again. It was 'to rediscover the unknown craftsman in his lair, and to try and learn from living and working with him what we have lost since the Industrial Revolution of wholeness and humility.' Leach, however, did not feel altogether happy about it. In the diary pages which he used to send from Japan to his friends he wrote: 'In Japan I have found the old truth and beauty of crafts dying with the life which gave them birth. The culture of Japan was defeated by the civilization of the West before the war began. . . . Japan has gone headlong into industrialism and lost the ballast of her inheritance. This process is reflected in the modern Japanese craft movement which is nevertheless the most unified and widespread in the world to-day. There are just two or three creative men in it who have managed to bridge the gulf between the East and the West. They are the pioneers—the men of Zen; where they can go others will follow, but it is still only the same drop in the bucket as in the West. It is a leaven of individualism which does not begin to answer the great communal need.' Leach, who felt his responsibilities grow the stronger, took on what he considered his duty and an act of gratitude towards the East, with the typical self-reflecting modesty which is his own: 'I don't know if I have justified my existence as an artist. I think I had a small genuine gift and a strange calling in a great cause—the meeting of East and West. But during the last year I have come to see that the meeting in art and in craft is only a fragment of a far greater vision—of the unity and maturity of mankind—and that my secondary cause is dependent upon the primary. . . . In becoming a convinced Baha'i, the only discarding of slowly gathered convictions has been the replacement of self at the centre of the circle by—"The Other Power"—God; and the result has been strange, for the jig-saw pieces begin to fall into place—seemingly by themselves.' (Quoted from *My Religious Faith*, private print.)

To our surprise we read in the diary pages devoted to Onda—a remote village in the southern island of Kyushu, famous for its pottery tradition which dates back as far as 240 years—that young potters who had come from Koishibara, walking four hours over the mountains to meet Leach in Onda, asked him what he thought of Picasso as a potter? This fame in a far Eastern village must flatter even a master used to so much praise. 'I gave my usual reply,' writes Leach, 'that however gifted as an artist, he simply was not a potter. Potters start from clay—up; he starts from painting—down. His pots are often vital and interesting as creative design, but the "Pic-assiettes" of his thousand imitators, without his birthright, are an international disaster.'

We understand this answer of a man whose great aim has been to bring forth a revival of ceramic art on sound foundations, but we feel also, both in his religious and stylistic development, that his is more a traditionalist outlook; that the young will only with difficulty follow him on his Eastern Odyssey to discover a style, and may not share his doubts as to the inward possibilities of a modern culture; for they believe, with Picasso, that the global tradition of the arts and crafts has imbued them with the courage to seek and to find new means of expression, corresponding to our present-day needs. For any young potter, however, the name of Bernard Leach, standing as it does, for high ethical convictions and a craftsmanship which is masterly in form and quality will remain the great name of that generation which achieved through honest striving and self-sacrifice the Renaissance of the style and the aptitude of a tradition practically as old as mankind. Following generations may safely build upon their work.

3.

In his work *A Potter's Portfolio—A Selection of Fine Pots*, a book which will be the Bible of the modern individual potter and which is one of the most beautiful books produced in England recently, there is a motto by William Morris which reads as follows: '*Every improvement in the standard of work men do is followed swiftly and inevitably by an improvement in the men who do it.*' In support of his formal point of view Leach is in search of the underlying unity in modern thought valid for all crafts, which is no surprise to those who have already witnessed an exact parallel in the pictorial arts. In most forms of art, Leach says, a Classic background has provided a criterion which has held good over a long period (400 years). In ceramics, however, a vague conception has been predominant. No collection either in books or in museums has been based on primarily aesthetic grounds. It has therefore seemed to Bernard Leach important that such a selection should be published in the form of a large book from which the illustrations could be extracted. These reproductions may be framed for the walls of a private room or hung in a studio or school. *'One has to live with fine pots in order to appreciate their character, for they are intimate expressions of peoples and their cultures.'* In his search for the new criterion of style, life and beauty in pottery, Leach has chosen sixty pots from all periods and backgrounds except that of industry. This exception was deliberate. The formal values obtainable by sub-division of labour and responsibility are of a different order of merit from those obtainable by the human hand and tool work which preceded the machine, or by the more conscious artistry of to-day.

In choosing these pots, it was not only personal preference—the preference of a great artist—that was the guiding principle, but also a specific approach to traditional aesthetic values. The last fifty years represent a great leap forward in the creative interpretation of life. The high classics of 1900 are not those of 1950. The eyes of the form-conscious potter still turn to China, but it is the China of the seventh to twelfth centuries, and not of the thirteenth to eighteenth centuries. It is this *'Classic'* period in Chinese pottery *'exhaling gently an elusive meditative spirit of austere nobility'* which Leach puts as the ideal style before the potters of our time, the style with the help of which he might be able to put the lost criterion of beauty into pottery. Only a poet like Leach is conscious that such pots must be seen together with poetry, calligraphy, painting, sculpture and other arts as an expression of a cultural ethos. He is aware of the unity and wholeness of a spiritual orientation which is lacking in our time, and for which we have to strive. The direct relationship of the arts to an all-embracing view of life and its meaning, to philosophy and religion seems clear. Never has there been such a widespread disruption in concepts as in our age. England, which was the birthplace both of industrial and counter-industrial concepts, suffers from Conservatism. 'The English,' Leach says, 'tend to look over their shoulders towards the past and so fail the insistent needs of the present. The workmanship is good, the ideas generally safe and dull. In the background of industry—the factory-made pots are not produced by the whole man—the soul is absent: feeling, intuition, imagination.' The problem which presented itself to Leach was the problem of how to find a new way of life, a work with reward and fulfilment in the effort, even at the cost of a simpler standard of living. This represents the formal and moral quest for the contemporary potter; the aesthetic quest is based on the hope of a reconciliation between the old wisdom of the East and the analytical spirit of the West. It is the question of the relation between inner and outer aspects of feeling, thinking and acting. It is basically a religious problem. The emphasis with Leach lies on the Taoist and Zen-Buddhist conviction of the inner as preceding and determining the outer.

The Western abstract art born out of the scientific age and the organic abstraction of the Far East have to be brought into true relationship.

'The modern craftsman is an individual cut off from the security of a living tradition. He has only disintegrated standards of right thinking and corresponding technique. The greatest danger in the West to-day is the destructive self-consciousness and the intellectualization of ourselves and our art; the overstressed self which stands between our efforts and the quiet integrity of the best Sung pots.'

Leach's world view provides him with the arguments for criticizing modern production. 'In France, Scandinavia and North America there is lacking, whatever the idiom, that degree of vitality which springs from the born character of the author and from a deep race root. The relationship between form, pattern and colour-texture is often strained or artificial, producing an effect of deliberation, instead of the easy flow of nature. Such pots are "made not born". In America the race-root of accumulated understanding is necessarily absent; there has not been time for a tap-root to form and feel its way down in the dark earth to the springs. The wonder is that despite this handicap there have been artists who in their solitary quest have found sustenance and genuine expression.'

This impressive volume of Bernard Leach's, provided with a preface, comments and a formal analysis in the shape of notes on the illustrations—partly printed in Leach's own handwriting— is dedicated to 'the unknown potter'. It is primarily meant for those potters who are struggling to find their way in a difficult period with very little material, moral or aesthetic support from their contemporaries. The illustrations are arranged in three groups—Primitive Pottery—the earliest pieces, about 6,000 years old, from Crete and Egypt, some of them made without wheel or kiln and all of them unglazed. The beauty of such pots has been too long neglected, or simply not perceived, as with all primitive art prior to the advent of Picasso, and the modern artists in France and Germany in the first decade of this century. Pre-Industrial Pottery—the largest group—and Post-Industrial Pottery.

The great problem which arises out of all these thoughts is the question: *What is a good pot?* 'How can we recognize qualities in pots which can be related to values which we already set store by in life?' It is basically a question of whether these can be translated into *'terms of pots'*.

Bernard Leach answers this question in the positive. It is not only possible to him *'but the very justification of art, provided the translation is not literal or didactic'*. Leach explains what he calls *'familiar virtues'*. He attempts to suggest something of the way in which the spirit of a culture and the experience of race flows through the focal consciousness of the individual potter. He defines this awareness of the human background behind pots, which is so essential. Therein he shows himself to be the wise man of whom Confucius said: *'The wise man is he who in his maturity can make natural use of the gifts with which he was born.'*

CONTEMPORARY ENGLISH
SCULPTURE

Recent Trends and Their Origin

T HERE occurs rhythmically in the sphere of modern culture
a change of taste which reveals, whenever a new solution of
formal problems is embarked on by each generation, that
that change is dictated more by opposition to the previous trend
than by the exploration of its inherent possibilities. These changes
are very frequent and short-lived in contrast to the long periods
which are known to us by the familiar names of styles like Romanesque, Gothic, High Renaissance or Baroque. We have to bear
in mind also that all these styles were developed within the framework of one and the same system of thought, that is the Christian
world-view in its marriage to Greek ideas—marriage with all its
history of attraction, of struggle, attempts to divorce, of ageing
and re-attraction. To exemplify our thesis the Baroque style was
initiated in opposition to the static High Renaissance style, inasmuch as it laid stress on the dynamic element. It was able to
mature into a style because it expressed a need of the time, the
idea, that is to say, of the militant and finally the triumphant
church. Although having developed in opposition, the Baroque
is, formally seen, a direct continuation of the Renaissance style. It
might therefore be conceivable that the different stylistic trends in
our contemporary development, which we distinguish so clearly
in the belief that they represent essential values, will reveal themselves in historic perspective, as shades only of one great attempt
—the attempt, namely, to create a contemporary style, the
adequate expression of an age dominated by scientific and techno-
logical realities. Even these, however, are ever changing and
developing. Metaphysical notions are coming back into the

world-view of the modern physicist. All such facts have their reflections in art; not so much in the theoretical way of the artist's knowing and understanding, say, the principle of relativity or the hypothesis of 'continuous creation', and acting accordingly in his work, as in the sense of an urgency which is the main intellectual trend of a time, and for which the Germans have found the notion of *Zeitgeist*. In the last fifty years we have witnessed in the arts the impact of a purely rationalistic spirit; but as a fine instrument always seeks to return to equilibrium, we find also the diametrically opposite trend, towards the roots of knowledge, towards a conscious amalgamation of primary values of perception, towards the fundamentals in art by the emphasis on the unconscious. We speak of metaphysical, significant, symbolic tendencies in approaching the mystery of life, a method which is more primary than the cerebral one. Is it not quite obvious that a time which has witnessed nuclear research, Gestalt-psychology, the discovery of the soul of the primitives, should also find in art the problems of transparency, super-imposition, and multi-valence in the visual approach? To see an object only from one viewpoint, a purely rational convention based on optical vision, is set against the representation of an object as if seen simultaneously from different angles and sides. This leads to the conception of the inner volume as being complemental to the outer volume, to the dissolution of the so-called 'closed form' into an 'open form'. These elements were invented and explored for the first time by the Cubists but were later developed, changed and fertilized. The intrusion of the surrounding space into a volume led to the question of representing space in a way which was basically more architectural than sculptural. Henry Moore is representative of the opening up of the closed form. The present generation of young English sculptors are the followers of those pioneers on the continent who took the last step in the dissolution of the closed form. Just as the young English sculptors developed their tendency—and we have the feeling that we are here confronted with a definite school, although they are all individually independent of each other—in opposition to Henry Moore, they are also—in the same sense as the Baroque was a traditional continuation of the High Renaissance style—based on him. The new phase in English sculpture is the phase of the open form on its way towards an architectural and constructive conception of space surrounding figures or objects, taking up movement not in a sculptural sense but as a reality (mobiles), and with an emphasis on lower animal forms, i.e., lower biological organizations. (Trend to the fundamentals of life.) In contrast to Moore the human figure has been practically abandoned. This, however, is not the whole story. In Moore's sketch books many of the ideas, now flourishing among the young English sculptors, were foreshadowed, awaiting further exploration in his sculptured work. Proof of this may be seen already in his *Double Standing Figure of* 1950. In Moore there was also a strong Surrealist (Max Ernst) and animist trend. The main influences on the young English sculptors did not, however, come from him, but from Giacometti, Calder, Richier, and, significantly enough, also from the realm of painting, from Klee, Miró, Masson, Michaud, Sutherland. The frontiers between the different arts are blurred in our age. Leonardo's arguments from his *Paragone* have lost their meaning for the time being. Even philosophy and literature have played their part in this movement. There is a straight ideological line between the Insect forms in Reg Butler's work, certain ideas of Masson, Matta, Michaud, Klee, Ensor (*The Insect Family*, a self-portrait) and Franz Kafka's short story, *The Metamorphosis*. Hans Sedlmayr speaks of a regression from humanism to lower animal organizations in contemporary art. But not only does contemporary sculpture try to express within its limits what apparently does not, in the strictest sense, fall within the objectives of sculpture; it must also be noted, at the same time, that there has been another significant development in contemporary sculpture in the opposite direction. Marini, Manzú, Greco. The Italian sculptors belong to a more sensuous tradition than their more rationally-minded English colleagues. There the Catholic South; here the Puritan North.

The new vision of reality used as a new means of expression forged iron, wire, corrugated iron, the contrast of heavy and light metals in mobiles, to mention only a few. They all have their history. To indicate the main line of influences *in the sphere of the closed form* (and among those so influenced we have to include Moore) we must name Brancusi, Modigliani, Arp's '*configurations et concretions*', Picasso's large heads at the Spanish pavilion in Paris, 1937, or his *Figure Throwing Stone*, March 8, 1931, with all their primitivist elements from Cycladic, Pre-Columbian, Palaeolithic cultures, the impact of Negro sculpture, Etruscan, Aztec, Early

Chinese, Egyptian, etc. *In the sphere of the exploded, the dissolved, the hollow form*, the sources of influence are: Picasso's Mandolin Construction in Wood, 1914; Sculpture in Painted Iron; Face, 1918; Guitar, 1926 (sackcloth with string, pasted paper, oil-paint, nails); the iron wire Construction, 1928; ditto, 1931 (produced with the assistance of Gargallo); the small, emaciated, elongated bronze figures of 1931, based upon archaic models and anticipating Giacometti; also *Une Anatomie*, 1933, suggesting the sculptural metamorphoses of Henry Moore. Picasso's *Projet d'une sculpture en fil de fer*, 1928, leads directly to Reg Butler. Lipchitz' Composition, 1927, uses the dynamic outline in bronze as an offset to the compact stylized volume of his Reclining Women with Guitar, 1928. Boccioni in the Futurist manifesto for sculpture emphasized the inside of the volume and called for consideration of the space surrounding a sculpture. (Example: *Sviluppo di una bottiglia nella spazio*, 1912—The Development, the Unrolling of a Bottle in Space.) Holes appeared in Archipenko's sculptures even before 1920. Tatlin used the new materials, cement, iron bars, corrugated sheet iron even during the First World War (Composition, 1917); he followed Meduniezky and other Russians. Gabo's and Pevsner's Constructive Realism broke up the closed volume by means of engineering devices. In the twenties C. Moholy-Nagy propagated the Russian methods in Germany. Gonzales' work in wrought iron, which technique he taught Picasso, must also be mentioned here. Vantongerloo, a doctrinaire Cubist in the beginning, tried to solve, in a manner more architectural than sculptural, the relationship of space—also the surrounding space and the time sequence—which he finally expressed through the dynamic of a line stiffened in metal. His 'Construction in Wood', 1931, illustrates his statement of 1932: '*Les volumes, les uns par rapport aux autres, nous impliquent la notion de l'espace, et la distance des volumes, les uns des autres, nous impliquent la notion du temps.*'

The next step leads up to Giacometti. Before we deal with him, let us add a few more words about Henry Moore in his rôle as inspirer and pacemaker of the younger generation of English sculptors. Among these there are already such mature personalities as Reg Butler, with Kenneth Armitage following (an individual solution of the human figure—Etruscan, Germaine Richier —and a dynamic use of the space); Eduardo Paolozzi (main influence Giacometti, Miró, Michaux, Dubuffet—emphasis on the study of objects in the Natural History Museum, similar to Klee's study in the aquarium of Naples), and Lynn Chadwick (main inspiration Calder). Bernard Meadows, like Butler a former assistant of Moore's, is trying to rid himself of the influence of the master through avoiding the human figure. William Turnbull, whose work is characterized by Giacometti's architectural space constructions, has recently returned to the human figure under the influence of Marino Marini. The same is true of Armitage. Geoffrey Clarke's wrought iron forms are derived from Calder, Butler, and the primitives. He is a good craftsman also in the field of other techniques such as ceramic tiles, lithographs, etc. Robert Adams is the only one of the young *avant-garde* English sculptors who still seems preoccupied with static Cubist shapes. The works of Henry Moore, which have influenced these artists in their new endeavours, are his stringed figures (themselves influenced by Giacometti and the primitives), 'The Helmet', Ideas for Metal Sculptures, 1938 (following Picasso, Rodchenko, Tatlin; de Chirico's principle of the substitution of the human figure by animated objects), Sculptural Object in Landscape, 1939, Two Women, drawing, 1939 (Collection Sir Kenneth Clark), Ideas for Metal Sculptures, 1948. There is a drawing by Moore from 1935 (Pen and water-colours, Collection Paul E. Bradshaw) based upon the principle of Cubist collage but 'animated' in the sense of Miró's and Klee's complex pictures. It may have stood as god-father to similar works, collages, etc., by Paolozzi.

When studying a genuine composite object, 'The Property of a Dead Man'—placed over his grave—bamboo sticks, string and iron, from British New Guinea, or Max Ernst's 'Object' (1919-20, *carde, fer, fil*) we meet here *outside the field of art* (in the first case obviously; in the latter, when taking into consideration the Surrealist programme) the predecessors of the trend predominant in recent English sculpture. Other examples can be looked for in the applied arts of primitive peoples.

Masson expresses some important principles in his generous aphoristic manner which certainly created tendencies. '*Ne pas séparer: l'inanimé de l'animé, l'homme des éléments et des règnes, le conscient de l'inconscient.*' This is the principle of metamorphosis. '*Il n'y a rien que soit en repos . . . Peindre des forces; carrière ouverte.*' This is the principle of the dynamic line replacing the static volume. '*Contrairement à l'habitude européenne de se placer devant les choses—*

conception scénique et policée de monde—il s'agirait d'une vision diffuse. Je ne suis pas devant ceci ou cela, je ne suis pas devant la nature, j'en fais partie.' A Heraclitean principle, newly formulated in modern physics and in contemporary philosophy by Bergson, Heidegger, Jaspers and the Existentialists. It is Giacometti's philosophic approach. *'Qu'il ne soit plus question d'objet dans l'espace. C'est l'objet qui deviendra espace.'* This is the sculpture of Cubism, of Futurism and of Moore. *'Un espace devenue actif, fleurissant, murissant, s'evanouissant. Le contraire de l'espace—limite. Un espace agissant où les corps ne serait que des trajectoires.'* This is Giacometti. Masson himself has made animated dynamic forged iron sculptures (Praying Mantis, 1942).

Henri Michaux (influence on Paolozzi) represents in a degenerated form the Klee notion: *'Dessinez sans intention particulière, griffonez machinalement, il apparat presque toujours sur le papier des visages.'* This formulates the principles of *Animism and Surrealist Automatism.* His influence may be said to be dangerous from the formal point of view. *Calder* solved the problem of movement and dynamics in sculpture through a decision which reminds one of Columbus' egg. Not in the line of the later Michelangelo, the Baroque, Rodin, the Futurists, but by abandoning the human figure and by taking over movement into sculpture directly through moving objects. His Mobiles are often reminiscent of stylized renderings of trees with trunks and branches and leaves shivering in the wind. Kites playing on a tense line, Chinese paper flowers unfolding and moving under water, weather vanes evoke similar impressions. *'Chaque élément pouvant bouger, remuer, osciller, aller et venir dans ses relations avec les autres éléments de son univers'* (Calder). This was the principle. The way to it was opened up by the use of new materials, like wire. Chadwick, on the basis of this principle of Calder's, achieved new but far less sensitive and playful solutions. His works are rather Stabiles —a term used by Arp in connection with Calder, whose work also includes Stabiles—and semi-Mobiles.

Let us now look at Giacometti's *'Palais de Quatre Heures'*, in its different versions (1932-33), or at *'Projet pour une Place'*, 1930, with its *'objets mobiles et muets'*. There is an important sculptural aspect to be propounded, space and figure in their relationship, and also a psychological situation. The latter is indicated by Giacometti's preoccupation with Surrealist ideas and his introvert nature, creating an art which lies between painting and sculpture, theatre decoration, architecture and literature. He had difficulties in rendering a figure in the traditional classic or romantic manner. '*Les figures n'étaient jamais pour moi une masse compacte, mais comme une construction transparente. . . . Impossible de saisir l'ensemble d'une figure.*' He was trying to formulate a new vision *de la realité*. This seems to go back to a strictly personal experience; deep unconscious reasons are at its roots, but, strangely enough, it found followers and might be considered as one of those cases, where the personal sensation expresses something inherent in the time, namely, the longing of the sculptor to be given his place in an architectural framework. Through his experience, Giacometti broke through the hitherto classical notion of sculpture. '*Il me manquait,*' he said, '*ce que je ressentais pour l'ensemble, une structure.*' And so he made '*des cages avec une construction libre à l'intérieure*' (*Squelette dans l'espace*). A similar tendency, however different in 'style', is obvious already in the Baroque. To the two elements, the figure and the space surrounding it, was added a third—the movement.

To the figure: When Giacometti tried to make a head, it '*devenait pour moi un objet totalement inconnu et sans dimensions*'. During the work '*les sculptures devenaient de plus en plus petites*'. An unconscious tendency to get rid of the volume; but also of the likeness, of the human being. (*Longues et minces figures.*) This process led to objects like '*Oiseau Squelette*', '*Epine dorsale*' (See Paolozzi.) The images he was striving for were accomplished in his brain. *Tout achevé à mon esprit* (Introvert).

To the space: He had only to try '*à les reproduire dans l'espace, sans me demander ce qu'elles pouvaient signifier . . .*' '*Je ne sais pourquoi elle s'est peuplée de l'épine, etc. . . .*' There is a statue *de femme, dans laquelle je decouvre ma mère*. And: '*je ne puis rien dire de l'objet sur une planchette qui est rouge. Je m'identifie avec lui.*' (Unconscious Solipsist imagery.) In the middle of the composition stands *l'échaffaudage d'une tour*. (Butler, Turnbull, Clarke.) A fine matchlike construction accomplishes the cage of inner experiences. Concave-convex forms ('*Projet pour une place*') help to realize it. In his painting, too, dreamlike pictures of nearly transparent Gothic or Etruscan elongated, emaciated figures and faces: something else seems to be important behind, beyond them. Perhaps the image of a future mankind overcrowding the earth and starving to death. The individual is dissolved, becoming impersonal like all the passers-by in the streets of a metropolis: ants. Giacometti represents them in an anonymous movement neither from nor towards each other. He found the sculptural expression for the dehumanizing power of the industrial centre. All this has become the world of some of the young English sculptors, more or less transformed, more or less formalized, mannered.

In recent biological research work certain particles' before entering the body, were charged with radioactive energy to enable the scientist to trace their way through the different organs. If artistic ideas could materialize in colour, every original contribution having its specific shade, what an exciting colour stream it would give to follow the flow of ideas in the intellectual and artistic becoming of a time! The ways of material movements in the body are a mystery and how much more mysterious and untraceable seem the movements of ideas. We follow them, as far as they allow it, with the interest of scientists wishing to find out the psychological reasons for their movements and the results which they finally give as patterns. The tracing of such a pattern has been the chief aim of this study.

Part Four

THE METAMORPHOSIS OF VALUES

I

GOETHE'S SUCCESSION

WE cannot, by thinking, by the writing of a book, by
working out an idea, alter the course of things immediately. It is, however, not as though we had merely
drawn figures in the sand, some activity undertaken for the sheer
sake of escaping from the restless ego. But just as it evolved from
an inner necessity, so too will it be in harmony with an external
necessity. We build a basis on which to interpret our doubts and
fears and undo our errors, in order to set out into active life again
with new faith and new strength.

1. *The Dehumanization of Life*

> The most important thing is always the con-
> temporary element, because it is most purely
> reflected in ourselves, as we are in it.
>
> *Goethe*

If one wished to describe the present state of mankind in a
parable, nothing could be more appropriate than one that we all
know, here given in somewhat changed form: 'And they went up
over all the countries, and rested in all the borders; very grievous
were they, before them there were no such creatures as they,
neither after them shall be such. They covered the face of the
whole earth, so that the land was darkened; and they did change
every thing of the land; and there remained not any healthy thing,
either tree or herb of the field, through all the countries of the
world.' Individual human beings, classes, nations, prey upon each
other and all mankind insatiably goes on digging into the bowels
of Nature. They can regard Nature only as something to be relent-
lessly exploited. Everyday life is imbued with a soulless spirit of

production in which work is robbed of its creative meaning and man's soul withers. The cause of this state is the dehumanization of all our conditions. We feel the inevitability of the catastrophes to which such a state of mind must lead, catastrophes in which we shall all be involved, with or against our will. There is hardly any historical parallel to such an enslavement and humiliation of man—not merely of one class—such an impoverishment of soul and mind. We say this in spite of a certain admiration, mixed with anxiety for the results of scientific and technical progress. The problem is not a new one. Nor is it the same as that older, indeed everlasting problem, the unchangeability of human nature; it is really the problem of evil, arising out of this nature, unrestrained by any humane considerations, conditioned only by greed and fear, egoism and destructive urges, evil that is steadily increasing, at an appalling speed, until now, through science, which has opened up a source of unlimited energy to an over-populated earth, it has become a menace to civilization and even to the essence of life itself. This is probably the reason—and this is something that we, whose childhood lies beyond the First World War, are only really beginning to realize to-day—why we drank in with a holy zeal the melancholy poison of the last generation's poetry; for in that way we set ourselves, like the poets, outside that development, which we instinctively rejected even before we were capable of analysing it intellectually. So we undermined the resources of health, which shoot up, fresh and vigorous, in every child as in every young tree. There is a line of Rilke's the melody of which surrounded us like incense. Now the music of it has fled and all that remains is the bare skeleton of the words, pallid as bones in moonlight: 'Who has no house yet will never build one now.'[1] In those days we still had the strength to experience the beauty of it in spite of its truth. But the baneful development was steadily going on. The ground loosened up by melancholy we then manured with scepticism, morbid doubts and an urge towards the dissolution of all traditional values. We were still strong enough. The threads linking us to hope and confidence, as to an activity that ennobles all things, the threads linking us to creation, had not yet snapped. Through the deafening roar of the machines we continually heard the still, small voice of our own inner being, and the miracle of life gleamed indestruc-

[1] 'Wer jetzt kein Haus hat, baut sich keines mehr.'

tibly as through a veil of smoke. But in difficult moments the
accusation was beginning to loom up: It is the poets' and writers'
fault that we are so wretched. Was it really their fault that the
whole of life was developing in a direction so hostile to life? Of
course not! We loved them, after all; and it was our own life in
them, in Baudelaire and Verlaine, Hamsun and Jacobsen, Multa-
tuli, Maeterlinck, Dostoevsky and Rilke. Their melancholy was
the atmosphere we breathed, their revolt was what armed us for
the fray. We still had the courage to reject Stefan George's
pessimistic vision of the future. 'Why cheat them with delusions,'
he said, 'the end of time has set in. For sheer horror men have
lost the strength to live. They lie in their thousands in the streets
and throughout the country, incapable of resisting the thought of
doom. . . There seems to be a plague raging among us, and no
remedy avails. . . . Even now some of us are turning aside towards
those sombre acres and lauding madness, others are shutting
themselves up in their cottages, full of sorrow and hate . . .' Was
there no way out? Oh yes, there was! The mere awareness of it
was enough—the changing of the conditions of life, the removal
of economic exploitation, the classless society! This gave the
youth of Europe their one slogan between the two World Wars;
and they reached out for it as for deliverance. And what the young
so easily overlooked in their eagerness to make everything different and better was the bloody revolutions, the steely dictator-
ships, that narrow gateway through which mankind had to pass in
order to be saved. And saved from what? From the baneful
consequences of a materialistic, heartless spirtt, by a system that
elevated materialism, mechanistic science, the state and the
machine to the rank of a divinity? In those days we read in
Goethe that *only the understrappers* would *come to the top again*,
that only *the mob* would become *the despot to the mob*. Liberty and
equality *can be enjoyed only in the surgings of madness. Man is not born to
be free.* When Goethe saw all relationships, even those of friendship, destroyed by the *baneful, disembodied party-spirit* and took up
arms against every generalizing slogan, saying: *What is the general?
The particular case. Humanity? That is an abstraction. From time
immemorial there have only been human beings and there always will only
be human beings*—then youth protested. *Never in my life did I care to
set myself up in hostile, futile opposition to the sweeping tide of the many
or of the dominant principle*, Goethe wrote, and we refused to take

it seriously. That was not 'reality'; those were the thoughts of an aristocrat in his ivory tower. But the narrow-minded, banal philosophy of Engels in 'Anti-Dühring' was the gospel for this generation that had been betrayed by its fathers. After all, they had nothing to lose but their chains—as the fine phrase went. They were drunk with the romanticism of the originator of an unromantic economico-political movement. The passages at the beginning of Marx's *Capital* about life being transformed as though by a curse, into dead money—that was no mere poetry, that seemed to be the truth and the key to the future. Only the inexorable reality even before the Second World War, and then the complete disillusionment of the post-war period, brought us on to new tracks. Suddenly we saw that we were, so to speak, surrounded by electrically 'live' prison-bars, delivered up to a process of being enslaved, a process slow but relentless as clock-work, a process that filled eyes, mouth and ears with ashes, making us insensible to life's true values. The defensive process began to be a necessity in the fight for survival. The first step was to exert the last shreds of our courage in facing life to fight off the fears and nihilism of the immediate generation of writers and thinkers, Weininger, Kafka, Kierkegaard, Heidegger, Sartre. Their thoughts settled on our lips and hands like sticky cobwebs. Hopelessness, disease and obscurantism, sucked out our warm blood, our very life. In league with them came the depth-psychologists, whose burrowings into the mysteries of the personality conjured up a second reign of medieval superstition. Was there nothing healthy left? Was there no way to escape from this world-rejecting melancholy, this idea born of the Christian martyr's ideal of passive suffering, except by plunging into the abysses that Nature intended to remain in darkness? There was art—modern art. The artist himself, in the eyes of the young enthusiasts, had taken the place of the Christian Saint and martyr. Van Gogh, Gauguin, Cézanne, Munch. In the eyes of the revolutionary he had dethroned God and put himself in God's place; his creative acts had made him 'absolutely free'. This God-likeness, this *non serviam*, however, looked very miserable. The artist, after all, was commercialized, like everything else, and instead of being a creator he had become—with a few exceptions —a producer of 'works of art' no longer rooted in any common cultural necessity. He flooded the world with his images, which he brought forth from the arsenals of paranoiac self-analysis, the mechanical beauty of machines, the dehumanized imagination of abstraction. All this was infected, and yet it was supposed to be in harmony with delight in creativeness, the bliss of creating, that basic urge which Goethe was the last man in Europe to experience as a unity. *Religion, art and science satisfy man's threefold need: for prayer, for creation and for vision (Schauen); all three are one in the beginning and in the end, although distinct at the centre.* But Goethe knew very precisely what the cause of the intellectual decline was; he knew too that only in decadent epochs do writers and artists become introverted and self-preoccupied, while in the great progressive epochs the creative spirit is concerned with the external world. And without wishing to anticipate, we may ask: Did Goethe find a way out different from that of those morbid outsiders, those self-tormenting solipsists, Kafka, Hesse, Verlaine, Bang, Rilke? The answer is: Certainly he did, and inevitably so, his nature being what it was. That is actually the theme of this essay. Yet, a ray of light may be cast into the darkness we are compelled to describe, even at this stage, by the following quotation: *The man whose state of mind is a wavering one in wavering times increases the evil, extending it further and further. But he who firmly stands by the inner meaning forms the world to his mind.*[1]

The inner meaning is the very essence of life. *Ah yes! the eternally working principle of things moves us incomprehensibly, as though at random for our own welfare, in one thing or another, to counsel, to decision, and to achievement. And we are as it were borne to our goal. To feel this is the highest happiness there is; not to demand it is only our duty: and to await it expectantly is life's loveliest consolation.*[2]

In 1813, in troubled times, the sixty-four-year-old poet wrote in a visitors' book: *I believed, and now I believe all the more, and however strangely things may go, or however badly, I shall remain in the order of the*

---

[1] 'Denn der Mensch, der zur schwankenden Zeit auch schwankend gesinnt ist,
Der vermehret das Übel und breitet es weiter und weiter.
Aber wer fest auf dem Sinne beharrt, der bildet die Welt sich.'

[2] 'Jawohl! das ewig Wirkende bewegt
Uns unbegreiflich, dieses oder jenes,
Als wie von ungefähr zu unserm Wohl,
Zum Rate, zur Entscheidung, zum Vollbringen,
Und wie getragen werden wir am Ziel.
Dies zu empfinden, ist das höchste Glück,
Es nicht zu fordern, ist bescheidne Pflicht,
Es zu erwarten, schöner Trost im Leben.'

faithful. Gloomy though it often was, and dark, in anxiety and distress, in imminent danger, all at once everything brightened again![1]

Let us return to our own time. Does not the sun rise every day? Is not morning followed by midday and evening? Are there not still birth and love and death? We worked out a new formula, putting our time into quarantine. There was, we said, a world of human beings, surrounding us on all sides, hemming us in, and there was a world of creation, from which we were kept away by these same human beings with their present senseless bustling, their ant-like whirl of activity. So there was a dualism, with only a faint notion of a possibility of bridging it. And where was this possibility? Not yet in the consciousness, but in the vital force in each of us, which was beginning to assert itself in self-defence. One could 'feel' what was wrong, but one could neither grasp nor change it. And one could not 'shell' one's life out of the encasing whole. And then came the inevitable.

It was the study of scientific works that first showed the full extent of the human error from which we are all suffering and took the life out of dialectical materialism, which was in fact only a variation of the same intellectual disease under which our life was languishing. Before one can conquer one's enemies, one must know them. There were two certainties, negative, admittedly, but solid as two pillars. The writers who had alienated us from life were to blame, the idealists were to blame, and so were the religious dogmatists of a beyond, who had weakened our will to action to such an extent that it broke down in the clash with reality. They were as much to blame as mechanistic science, which robbed life of joy, or as industrialism running amok in its spirit of competition. Where now was there a way to get out of the dark labyrinth of the present so that good geniuses might inspire us with new strength so that we might once more feel goodness and confidence in ourselves and in the future, like Faust at the beginning of the second part of the tragedy? *Life's pulses beat now with fresh life, gently saluting an ethereal dawn. You, Earth, were constant in this past night too, and at my feet breathe refreshed and new, beginning to*

[1] 'Ich habe geglaubt, nun glaub' ich erst recht,
    Und geht es auch wunderlich, geht as auch schlecht,
    Ich bleibe beim gläubigen Orden:
    So düster es oft und so dunkel es war,
    In drängenden Nöten, in naher Gefahr,
    Auf einmal ist's lichter geworden!'

*surround me even now with delight, starting and stirring a vigorous resolve
ever to strive towards the highest life there is.*[1]

So long as any of us can still experience such a thing, so long as
it is still possible for a tree to burst out suddenly in manifold
beauty and the affirmation of life to bud again in the heart—we
are not lost. But before we come to a new blossoming of those
human values that we can take for granted we must hoe, plough,
fertilize and prune with loving care. Literature to-day, true
literature, is this ploughing, this hoeing, this pruning. For this
reason too we must first lay bare the philosophic and scientific
roots of our human failure, before we arrive at the disturbing
ethical consequences. And even on the way we shall have a
glimpse of the greatness of that mind in the understanding and
imitation of which the present-day world can find support and
guidance—Goethe, one of the most significant intellectual
phenomena in the history of European man. Nietzsche called him
'the event without a succession among the Germans'. Yet in
many marked minds of the present day he has been the initial
cause of a slow organic process of regeneration.

2. *The Guilt of Philosophy*

To investigate what is, and not what suits us.
Goethe

In the Eleatic School of Philosophy in Greece we find the seed
of that dualism that has disintegrated Western thought like an incurable splitting of the mind. It was then, about two thousand
five hundred years ago, that Xenophanes became mistrustful of
the human senses as a source of knowledge. The only compass
given to man, the senses with which he can orient himself in the
world, was regarded as of dubious reliability. Parmenides speaks
of two sources of human knowledge, and in Plato the process is

[1] 'Des Lebens Pulse schlagen frisch lebendig,
Ätherische Dämmerung milde zu begrüssen.
Du, Erde, warst auch diese Nacht beständig
Und atmest neu erquickt zu meinen Füssen,
Beginnest schon mit Lust mich zu umgeben,
Du regst und rührst ein kräftiges Beschliessen,
Zum höchsten Dasein immerfort zu streben.'

organized into a system. There is a phenomenal world and an ideal world. The things of this world, which are perceived by our senses, have no genuine existence. They are always changing, but never exist. What we perceive by means of the senses is like shadows in a cavern, cast on the walls by a light to which our backs are turned. Since then the philosophers have not been concerned with what Nature has to say to man, but they have constructed systems dealing with the question of the relation between human experience and this world of appearances. The intellect became completely darkened when Platonism was joined by Christian philosophy, which, with its contempt for the world of the senses and its belief in a beyond, was actually a popularized form of Platonism. It turned out to be heavier-laden with destiny than Platonic philosophy itself. The fathers of the Church used it to gain control over Western man's emotional life. Aristotle on the other hand put the main emphasis on Nature as an integral form of being, on reality as the sum of all perceptible phenomena. Only in the human mind, he taught, not outside it, can ideas lead an independent existence. Aristotle was an obstacle to Christian philosophy, which therefore reinterpreted him as intending to have said that the human mind was not supposed to seek creative ideas in reality—for these were God's revelation to man—but only to confirm them. Augustine made the unbridgeable dualism of God and man a matter of dogma: 'Unwaveringly we will believe that the thinking soul is not of the same nature as God, for God permits of no such communion, but that the soul can receive illumination through partaking of the divine nature.'

Thomas Aquinas, in his attempt to curb all critical thinking, bound up revelation and reason so closely that the highest truths given to man in revelation and human knowledge have a joint frontier where they merge into each other, i.e., at the stage where revelation, descending to man, and reason, mounting to God, meet—or in other words, where the doctrine of salvation and human knowledge meet.

When European man began to seek the truth according to his own resources (Bacon of Verulam, Descartes), Western thought was already so infected that nothing appeared but ever new variations of the Platonic-Christian pattern. Although Bacon did lay stress on the external phenomenal world, which was new, the idea that man deciphered from it, the living and effective force in it, was for him only subjective, existing only as a notion and not in reality (*sic!*). So European man went blindly groping on. Descartes, again, decreed that only human thought had the force to produce convictions. *Cogito ergo sum*. Not 'I live, therefore I am,' but 'I am, because I reason.' As the perfect idea of God could not come into existence in an imperfect being, he goes on thinking, it must have been deposited in him. (*Sic!*) Spinoza in his Ethics tried to sum up the total of all knowledge according to a rational system based on mathematical principles. An idea arising out of a sense-perception is to him adequate. Scarcely a hundred years after Spinoza, Hume tried to trace the source of knowledge, again, only in perception. Life and thought remained split, every time. Between God and man, man and Nature, body and soul, idea and perception, there is a chasm. In Hume the perceptions are linked, not because there is any natural necessity but because reason has become accustomed to bringing things into relation; hence ideas are mere habits of thinking. Kant united all these philosophic streams in one mighty river. He recognizes truths that are produced by a pure thought-process and he denies experience the capacity to arrive at equally necessary truths. Hume's influence, furthermore, becomes apparent in the fact that the ideas do not originate in experience, but that thought adds them, as it were, to experience. So the world of experience is subjective, produced within, not objective, perceived by the subject in the external world. The mind is incapable of knowing anything about things *an sich*, in themselves. Man is not concerned with things but with the impression that they make on him. Religious concepts also play a part. If things in themselves are beyond the reach of human knowledge, how could the idea of God and the other Christian notions come into the sphere of what can be comprehended by reason? Rudolf Steiner, in his attempt, written in 1897, to give a philosophic view of Goethe, traces the antithesis between the Christian-idealistic world view current in the time when Goethe was growing to maturity and Goethe's own intellectual attitude, which evolved organically out of his own being. Steiner's other Goethe-essays cannot be dealt with here. In spite of building up his own development on ideas of Goethe's, Steiner did from the very beginning feel at variance with Goethe on essential points. The quasi-religious movement that he founded, the Anthroposophy of the Goetheanum at Dornach, has little to do with Goethe, whom we see as a symbol of European man.[1] Steiner's indubitable merit remains the fact that, with Carus[2] as his point of departure he made the first systematic attempt to apply Goethe's thought to our time therapeutically.

Goethe, who had a subtle sense of living creativeness in Nature itself, was impervious to the Platonic distinction between ideal and experience. He felt himself one with Nature; he did not confront it mistrustfully, as something alien. *I noticed that the old controversy was being renewed as to how much our personality and how much the external world contribute to our spiritual existence. I had never distinguished between the two. . . . It is by the strokes of the pendulum that time is ruled*, Goethe says, *and what rules the moral and scientific world is the alternating movement between idea and experience.* However, the idea in Goethe's sense is something different from what it is for Kant. *Kant*, Goethe said, *regards the subjective perceptive faculty itself as the object, sharply, although not quite correctly, isolating the point where subjective and objective coincide.* He reports of his intercourse with Kantians: *Although they did listen to me, they could not answer nor in any way advance the discussion. More than once it happened to me that one or the other confessed, with smiling admiration: That was, admittedly, an analogy of Kantian conception, but a strange one.* The anthropologist Dr. J. C. August Heinroth, a contemporary of Goethe's, perfectly summed up the nature of Goethe's way of thinking. Goethe noted: *Herr Dr. Heinroth speaks favourably of my nature, work and*

---

[1] Goethe felt himself to be a symbol. He wrote to Frau von Stein: *God uses me as He did His saints of old, and I do not know how it comes to me. You know how symbolic my life is.* As an old man, four months before his death, his experience of himself was quite impersonal, typical and historical: *If I may express myself with old-time familiarity, I confess frankly that in my great age everything seems more and more a matter of history. Whether something belongs to past time, in remote realms, or is going on quite near to me in space at the present moment, it is all the same, indeed I even feel myself more and more as history.* (Letter to Wilhelm von Humboldt.)

[2] (C. G. Carus, 1789-1869), a younger contemporary of Goethe's, doctor, anthropologist, writer and painter, had a deep understanding of the poet, whom he knew personally. Many of his most important scientific works owe their first impulse to ideas of Goethe's. Carus is regarded as the founder of modern psychology. 'The key to the understanding of the nature of the conscious life of the psyche lies in the realm of the unconscious.' Compare with Goethe's: *The best in man is formless. I believe everything that genius does as genius happens unconsciously.—Man cannot stay long in the conscious state; he has to plunge back into the unconscious, for that is where his living roots are.* Carus was a pioneer in his essays, 'Göthe, Towards a Closer Understanding,' 1843; 'Goethe, his significance for our time and for times to come', 1863; and in his letters on Goethe's *Faust.*

influence, indeed he describes my mode of procedure as a peculiar one, saying that my faculty for thinking functions objectively (gegenständlich). By this he means that my thinking does not separate itself from its objects and that the elements of the objects, the views, are absorbed into it and utterly permeated by it, so that my beholding is itself a kind of thinking, my thinking itself a kind of beholding (Anschauen).

These words give us only a glimpse of how new Goethe's conception in fact was. It can only be seen clearly from a significant selection of dicta from his poetic and scientific works, as well as from letters, conversations, notes and epigrams, as contrasted with our own errors. The most outstanding thing Steiner did in contributing to a revised view of Goethe was to point to the importance of his scientific thought. Here too he followed in Carus's footsteps. Steiner says: 'Nobody can dive into the depths of Goethe's art if he does not know Goethe's observations of Nature.' In his studies of Nature, from the very beginning, Goethe experienced quite directly the fact that the world of ideas is nothing other than the creative, active force in Nature, which man perceives through his senses and his thought. *The primal phenomena are not abstractions but fundamentally living entities, ceaselessly in an inner process of creation.* So the fatal dualism between God the Creator and creation itself was, for him, non-existent. *What would a God be who only gave a push from outside, making the universe spin like a hoop round the tip of his finger?*[1]

Man and creation were to be comprehended as a unity: *Everything that is in the object is in the subject.* Goethe was definitely hostile to philosophers and theologians whenever they crossed his path. *Recently, in a pretty apostolically Capuchinish declamation of the Zürich prophet's, I came across the senseless words: 'Everything that has life lives by something outside itself,' or something to that effect. That is the sort of stuff such a converter of the heathen will dash off, and when he revises what he has written his guardian angel does not even tug at his sleeve.——You consider the Gospel . . . the most divine truth. Not even a clear and distinct voice from heaven could convince me that water burns and fire quenches, that a woman can conceive without a man or that a dead man can rise and live again. On the contrary, I consider this a great blasphemy against the greatness of God and his revelations in Nature. . . . He who will deny that Nature is divine revelation might as well deny all revelation and be done*

---

[1] 'Was wär' ein Gott, der nur von aussen stiesse,
Im Kreis das All am Finger laufen liesse?'

with it. . . . Jacobi[1] on the Divine gave me no pleasure. How could I welcome the book of a friend whom I love so sincerely, when I found it stating the thesis that Nature conceals God? With my pure, deep, inborn and acquired way of seeing things, which has taught me to see God in Nature and Nature in God, so that this way of thinking forms the basis of my whole existence, must not such a curious, one-sidedly narrow statement for ever put a distance between me, in mind, and this noblest of men, whose heart I honoured and loved? . . . God chastised you with metaphysics, a thorn in your flesh; me he blessed with physics. I take my stand on the atheist's[2] reverence for God and leave to you all you call and may call religion. You put your trust in faith, I mine in direct vision.

Schauen, a word for which there is no exact English equivalent, which we may however call 'direct vision', was Goethe's great contribution to healthier thinking in the scientific and philosophic realms. In 1801 he wrote to Jacobi: *If philosophy is predominantly concerned with separating, then I cannot very well get on with it and can indeed say that it has done me some harm, by disturbing me in my natural course of development. But if it unites, or rather, if it exalts and assures our original feeling that we are one with Nature and transforms that into a deep, peaceful vision, with the continual syncrisis (union) and diacrisis (splitting) which we feel as divine life, then I welcome it, even though it is not permissible for us to feel such a thing.* And Goethe speaks of a natural state of philosophy. *It always seems to me that if one part can never reach the spirit from outside by entering in, the other will hardly reach objects by coming out from inside, and that therefore one always does well to remain in the natural state of philosophy and to make the best possible use of its unseparated existence, until some day the philosophers agree as to how what they have, after all, separated, may be united again.* From Italy Goethe wrote enthusiastically: *It is indescribable how happy my way of beholding the world makes me and how much I learn every day! And how almost no form of life is an enigma to me! The fact of it is, everything speaks to me and emerges into the light of day for me.* And in 1831, to Boisserée: *Direct vision of things is for me everything. Words count less than ever.* Direct vision abandons itself to phenomena until they reveal their meaning. Together with this goes something else, something quite foreign to most modern scientists, as a result of which they have alienated science from life and life from

[1] F. H. Jacobi, philosopher, 1743-1819.
[2] Spinoza, whose pantheism, with its conception of the unity of God and the world, meant a great deal to Goethe.

human beings. *One cannot get to know anything except what one loves, and the more profound and more complete the knowledge is to become, so much stronger, more intense and more alive must be the love, nay, passion.* That is the human element that Goethe was thoroughly proud of having introduced into thought and research: *that I introduced the subject, the receptive, perceptive organ, into physics.* Sciene, he said (1822), had made the tremendous mistake of setting itself in place of Nature. For Goethe *everything that we call invention or discovery, in the higher sense, is the significant application of an original sense of truth, which, having long been quietly coming to perfection, unexpectedly, with the speed of lightning, leads to fruitful understanding* (Erkenntnis). *It is a revelation from within that develops in the external sphere. . . . It is a synthesis of world and mind.* Besides the human element in Goethe's *Schauen* there is an artistic element; one may indeed say that no thinker's and scientist's work can be beneficial unless he has a higher kind of vision and the fertility of spirit that is proper to genius. As Goethe says: *Anyone who faithfully follows the course of a higher knowledge* (Erkenntnis) *and intuitive understanding* (Einsicht) *cannot fail to notice that experience and learning* (Wissen) *can progress and be enriched, but that thinking and real understanding do not become more complete in anything like the same measure. This has a quite natural cause: learning is infinite and accessible to anyone who looks around at all curiously, but contemplation, thought and combination are something confined within a certain circle of the human faculties, in such a manner that perception* (Erkennen) *of the phenomena confronting us in the universe, from the fixed star to the smallest form of microscopic life, can become ever more distinct and detailed, while real intuitive understanding of the nature of these things is impeded by its own nature, and to such an extent that not only individuals but whole centuries move in a perpetual circle from error to truth and from truth to error.* In this idea of *Schauen*, therefore, the religious, artistic and scientific elements are preserved as a unity, the justification for which lies in man's integral personality. So Goethe's philosophy eliminates any further dualism. If Nature, the Eternally Creative, the Idea, God, or whatever it may be called, wanted to conceal itself, it could not be 'beheld' (angeschaut). And here we may perhaps quote Goethe's profoundest conviction: *The highest of all things would be to understand that everything concrete is already theory. . . . It is essential not to try to go behind phenomena; they themselves are the doctrine.* Or again, Goethe sums up the identity of man and creation by saying that *Nature proceeds according to ideas, in the same way that man pursues an idea in everything that he sets about.*

This sense of unity is also expressed in Goethe's poetry: *If the eye were not sunny it could never glimpse the sun. If God's own strength did not lie in us, how could the divine delight us?*[1] We find this notion of identity in Indian philosophy, too; only there it is bound up with passivity and a denial of life. This too was a youthful phase undergone by those of us who are now in our forties. A wave of Asiatic passivity and negation of life, emanating from Brahmanism, Buddhism, and Taoism, linked up with Christianity and European pessimism had a paralysing effect.

Why is Goethe's unity of man and creation so important to us? What does it mean? It is the natural, naturally conditioned communion between man and creation, man, not only apparently but really one with it. If we felt that, how could we feel fear of death or fear of the historical evolution of things, since we would necessarily regard them morphologically, i.e., historically and as conditioned by their evolving form,[2] not subjectively and moralizingly. We then could not fail to have confidence in the eternal powers. And does that not mean ultimately, freedom? Seeing Nature as something perpetually distinct from himself, the forces of Nature as something alien, hostile, man feels that he is subject to determination and hence unfree. But if he experiences the forces of Nature as Goethe did, as vibrations of the same spirit that works within himself, then he feels the untrammelled carefreeness of the child—real freedom. As Goethe puts it: *Those who come to understand my writings and, indeed, what I stand for as a whole, will have to admit that they have attained a certain inner freedom* (1831, to Chancellor von Müller). In Goethe's juvenile essay on Nature, which, even though it may not have been directly his own work, yet definitely represents his views at that time, we find: *We are enclosed in it, incapable of extracting ourselves from it.* For Goethe that

---

[1] 'Wär nicht das Auge sonnenhaft,
    Die Sonne könnt' es nie erblicken.
    Läg' nicht in uns des Gottes eigne Kraft,
    Wie könnt' uns Göttliches entzücken?'

[2] Morphology was a new science founded by Goethe, new not as a subject, but as to approach and method. It is the doctrine of the form, formation and transformation of organic bodies. From it there later developed a theory of *Gestalt*, the science of the law of forms and their development within the scope of object and meaning, its method being to arrive at pictorially integral entities by means of comparative experience.

was not a cause for despair. On the contrary: *It has put me in and it will lead me out again. I entrust myself to it. It may have its way with me, for it will not hate its own handiwork.*

In order to arrive at this truly-felt unity of man and creation, which is alien to the dissociated man of the present day, even though he may appreciate it purely intellectually, man must ponder this question meditatively. The result will be man's humility in creation, his reverence for Nature and the significance of life. His stifled power of appreciating the beautiful will begin to revive. Dr. Alexis Carrel, the author of *L'homme, cet inconnu*, concludes his book with the words: 'Nous devons libérer l'homme du cosmos créé par le génie des physiciens et des astronomes, de ce cosmos dans lequel il a été confermé depuis la Renaissance. Malgré sa beauté et sa grandeur, le monde de la matière inerte est trop étroit pour lui. De même que notre milieu économique et social, il n'est pas fait à notre mésure. Nous ne pouvons pas adhérer au dogme de sa réalité exclusive. Nous savons que nous n'y sommes pas entièrement confinés, que nous nous étendons dans d'autres dimensions que celles du continuum physique. L'homme est à la fois un objet matériel, un être vivant, un foyer d'activités mentales. Sa présence dans l'immensité morte des espaces interstellaires est totalement négligeable. Cependant, il est loin d'être un étranger dans ce prodigieux royaume de la matière. Son esprit s'y meut facilement à l'aide des abstractions mathématiques. Mais il préfère contempler la surface de la terre, les montagnes, les rivières, l'océan. Il est fait à la mesure des arbres, des plantes et des animaux. Il se plait en leur compagnie. Il est lié plus intimement encore aux oeuvres d'art, aux monuments, aux merveilles mécaniques de la cité nouvelle, au petit groupe de ses amis, à ceux qu'il aime. Il s'étend, au delà de l'espace et du temps, dans un autre monde. Et de ce monde, qui est lui-même, il peut, s'il en a la volonté, parcourir les cycles infinis. Le cycle de la Beauté, que contemplent les savants, les artistes, et les poètes. Le cycle de l'Amour, inspirateur du sacrifice, de l'héroisme, de renoncement. Le cycle de la Grâce, suprème récompense de ceux qui ont cherché avec passion le principe de toutes choses. *Tel est notre Univers.*'

These are fine words, the words of a humanist. They express a modern biologist's wish-dream. But how is it to be realized? Carrel has nothing to suggest. And we have grown so tired of words! For in this age of printer's ink and propaganda even well-meant words have been prostituted as never before.[1] Goethe knew and showed us the answer in his life; but the scientist of our own times has no ear to hear.[2]

What the scientist generally wants from Nature is to decipher her, control her and use her for his own purposes. *Nature and art are too great*, Goethe wrote to Zelter,[3] *to be used for any ends.* And again: *The attitude that a living being comes into the world for certain purposes, and that its form is determined to those ends by a purposive primal force, has hindered us in the philosophic consideration of natural things for several centuries now and is still hindering us, although some individuals have been vigorous in combating this attitude. . . . It is, if one may so express it, a trivial way of seeing things, and it is trivial precisely because, like all trivial things, human nature finds it comfortable and adequate.* And then, very decisively: *Every creature its own purpose.* The modern scientist has no respect for Nature, he knows no limitations. What a fine sense Goethe had for the limits that Nature sets where man is concerned. *Man is not born to solve the problems of the universe, but, instead, to try to find where the problem arises and then to keep within the limits of the comprehensible. In Nature there is the accessible and the inaccessible. These should be carefully distinguished and borne in mind—with reverence.—Faced with primal phenomena we feel a kind of awe amounting to fear. Sensual men take refuge in astonishment. But the next moment the busy pandar intellect comes along, trying, in its well-known way, to convey the noblest and the basest in one.—The highest that man can attain is astonishment, and when the primal phenomenon astonishes him, he should be content. It cannot yield him anything loftier, and it is not for him to seek further beyond this; here is the boundary-line. But the sight of the primal phenomenon generally is not enough for human beings; they think there must be some way of going on from there, and they are like*

[1] Goethe once said: *I should like to give up talking altogether. I should like to speak as Nature does, merely in signs.*

[2] Exceptions only confirm the rule. When Albert Einstein spoke of his 'religiosité cosmique', qui ne connaît ni dogmes ni Dieu qui seraient conçus à l'image de l'homme', he raised the question: 'Comment la religiosité cosmique peut-elle se communiquer d'homme à homme, puisqu'elle ne conduit à aucune idée formelle de Dieu ni à aucune théorie? Il me semble que c'est précisément la fonction capitale de l'art et de la science d'éveiller et de maintenir vivant ce sentiment parmi ceux qui sont susceptibles de le recueillir. . . . La plus belle chose que nous puissions éprouver c'est le côté mystérieux de la vie. C'est le sentiment profond qui se trouve au berceau de l'art et de la science véritables.'

[3] Intimate friend of Goethe's old age, Berlin composer. Their correspondence is of great beauty and profundity.

children who, when they have looked into a mirror, immediately turn it round to see what is on the other side. The feeling of happiness that so many of us felt when we first heard of the uncertainty principle in modern physics, meaning, in fact, that the modern scientist has a glimpse of the limitations to his own knowledge and must put up with it, can only be measured by the fear pervading this time, as a result of science's lack of reverence. Which of us does not feel dismay? That explains why André Gide wrote in his Journals: 'Seuls les conversations avec Goethe (Eckermann) parviennent à distraire un peu ma pensée de l'angoisse' (24 June, 1940). Gide keeps coming back to Goethe. Even in the first volume of his Journals (1889-1912) Goethe is quoted, more fully than between 1923-31 and, significantly, most of all in the Journals 1939-42. It should not surprise us to find him writing: 'La grande influence que peut-être j'ai vraiment subie, c'est celle de Goethe.' In the foreword to the seventh edition of his book *Goethe's Lebenskunst*, Dr. Wilhelm Bode says: 'A Munich psychiatrist once wrote telling me that he prescribed this book for his patients.' In a new attempt to give an inward portrait of Goethe, in his *A Study of Goethe*, 1947, which is agreeably free from the German sentimentalism of Bode and the biographer Bielschowsky, Professor Barker Fairley writes, in the foreword: 'The introspectiveness that he (young Goethe) endured and finally mastered must not be regarded as the mark of a bygone day, but rather as the forerunner of an age not yet terminated in which introspectiveness was to be one of the characteristic trends. The special appeal in our time of abnormally introverted figures like Hölderlin, Rilke, Kierkegaard, Kafka and others may serve to remind us how near we still are, whether we like it or not, to Werther and to Tasso. To this extent Goethe's problem is our problem or part of our problem; we cannot afford to ignore it.' There are words towards the end of Professor Fairley's book which seem to me to confirm my own ideas; for here is the conjecture 'Whether he may not prove to have a wider and a more immediate bearing on the betterment of the world,' a conjecture that Carus answered in the affirmative only a few decades after Goethe's death.

The mature Goethe, who has achieved inner balance after a hard struggle, was in very decisive opposition to everything diseased, decadent, nihilistic and pessimistic. He avoided it as though it were a plague. The great secret of his personality is the capacity to array the elements of life, strength and creativity against the destructive forces in his own psyche and in his environment and so always to maintain inner harmony. So he conquered time with eternity and personal fate with the idea of necessity, accepting reality and not letting himself be tricked by any illusions. He lived in reality, and for him reality was the whole; not only the 'difficult' present, but the whole of creation. His defensive attitude to Kleist is well known and has often been made the subject of reproach. But any age fighting for its own balance, must reject the world conception of the Kafkas, Sartres, Hesses, and Rilkes as Goethe did Kleist's. *What is not your own you must leave alone. What disturbs your inner being you must not tolerate. If it forces its way in, we must be valiant.*[1]

It is a matter of recovering health. Our generation which was brought up only on things nihilistic and disharmonious, melancholic, tragic, schizophrenic or paranoiac, and which learnt to recognize truth and value only in such things, must first of all learn to understand the health and beauty of man as Goethe conceived of him. What is at stake is the classic and the healthy, as opposed to all that is romantic and dislocated. Goethe specifically referred to romanticism as diseased. What is at stake, what must be achieved, is the affirmation of life and meaningful activity, which leads to such an affirmation. *Longing vanishes*, Goethe says, *in work and action. . . . Where there is enough to be done, no room is left for aimless contemplation. For we are dependent on life and not on contemplation. . . . The intellect is incapable of doing anything towards healing mental disease, the mind cannot do much, a great deal can be done by time, and resolute activity can do everything. . . . For the efficient man this world is not mute—so why need he go roaming out into eternity?* And in the West-Eastern Divan Goethe speaks of the *daily observance of difficult service. And now let there be a sacred bequest to fraternal will and memory. Daily observance of difficult service—there is no need of any other revelation. If in the flame of every lamp you can recognize, in awe, the reflected glory of a higher light, then no ill fate will ever forbid you to honour God's throne in the morning. There is our life's imperial seal, for us*

[1] *Was Euch nicht angehört,*
   Müsset Ihr meiden.
   Was Euch das Innre stört,
   Dürft Ihr nicht leiden.
   Dringt es gewaltig ein,
   Müssen wir tüchtig sein.

and angels a sheer mirror of God, and even what can only stammer forth praise of the Highest is assembled there in the circle of the circles.[1]

Ever and again Goethe attacks narcissism and introversion. *Man has really been set into the midst of a real universe and endowed with such organs that he can recognize and produce the real and, incidentally, the possible. All healthy human beings are filled with the conviction of their own existence and of the existence of all things around them. Yet there is also a blind spot in the brain, i.e. a place where no object is mirrored, just as in the eye itself there is a point that does not see. If man becomes particularly aware of this and concentrates on it, he becomes a prey to a sickness of the mind, has forebodings here of things of another world which are actually non-things without either content or limit, empty realms of darkness that frighten him who cannot tear himself free, haunting him worse even than spectres. . . . My medium is the plastic! he exclaims. I have tried only to make the world and Nature clear. And now these fellows come, raise a dust, show me things now in the distance, now oppressively close at hand, like ombres chinoises—the devil take it!* (1826). Goethe admits that without a pathological interest he could not succeed in working out tragic situations. *And so I have tended to avoid them rather than seek them out. . . . Admittedly I do not know myself well enough to know whether I could write a genuine tragedy, but the mere thought of setting about it does dismay me and I am almost convinced that I might destroy myself in the mere attempt.*'

'It is from Rome, out of the midst of a deeply rich and magnificent life,' so Chancellor von Müller reports, 'that the first serious maxim on renunciation dates, something that Goethe practised throughout the whole of his later life, finding in it the only sure guarantee of inner peace and equilibrium.' So renunciation stands beside productivity and belief in the eternity of life—*I am eternal, for I am*, which one may compare with the rationalist's *cogito ergo*

---

[1] *Und nun sei ein heiliges Vermächtnis*
Brüderlichem Wollen und Gedächtnis.
Schwerer Dienste tägliche Bewahrung
Sonst bedarf es keiner Offenbarung.

. . . . . .

Werdet ihr in jeder Lampe Brennen
Fromm den Abglanz höhern Lichts erkennen,
Soll euch nie ein Missgeschick verwehren
Gottes Thron am Morgen zu verehren.
Da ist unsers Daseins Kaisersiegel,
Uns und Engeln reiner Gottesspiegel,
Und was nur am Lob des Höchsten stammelt,
Ist in Kreis um Kreisen dort versammelt.

sum—and in the Mothers. *The Mothers! Mothers! How strange it sounds.* With the intellect alone one cannot come near the miracle of life, one can engender only homunculi, artificial mannikins bred in test-tubes. *The intellect (Verstand) cannot reach right up to her* (Nature). *Man must be capable of rising to the highest level of reason in order to touch the hem of the divinity that is revealed in primal phenomena. . . . The divinity is at work in all that is animate, but not in the inanimate; it is in all that is evolving and undergoing transformation, but not in what has reached completion and rigidity. So the mind (Vernunft) too, in its inclination towards the divine, has to deal only with what is evolving and alive; the intellect is concerned with what is complete and rigid, and with making use of that.* Modern scientists still do not seem inclined to believe this. There is evidence of that in the mathematical formulae of even a humanist thinker such as Erwin Schrödinger, whose book *What is Life?* has, significantly enough, quotations from Goethe at the head of three of the seven chapters.

For Goethe life was always the great miracle, which he regarded with reverence. He once asked himself: *Who knows whether man as a whole may not be a throw of the dice aimed at something higher?* Hence, too, came his conviction of the personality's being constantly renewed, always changing. *I had to give up my life in order to be.* And the celebrated lines: *And so long as you have not this Die-and-become! you are only a dismal visitor upon this gloomy earth.*[1]

The aged Goethe was preoccupied with an idea, related to Aristotle's entelechy, of life-forces becoming embodied in man at his birth, their nature being activity, they themselves eternal. *Existence (das Sein) is eternal! No being can crumble into nothingness.* This leads us on to an understanding of the full implications of what Goethe meant when he said to Eckermann: *If I remain ceaselessly active to the end of my days, Nature is under an obligation to allot me another form of existence, when the present one is no longer capable of containing my spirit.* And: *I do not doubt the continuance of our existence. May it then be that He who is eternally living will not refuse us new forms of activity, analogous to those in which we have been tested.* Yet in all this, if it was to receive blessing, love had to have a part, the Eternal-Feminine. As Carus wrote in his Faust letters: 'That love which is

[1] *Und solang du das nicht hast,*
dieses Stirb und werde!
Bist du nur ein trüber Gast
auf der dunklen Erde.

symbolized in genuine, perfect femininity is the one and only means of guiding mankind to all that is lofty; and in particular to a living comprehension of the blissful ideas of beauty, goodness and truth.' Steeped in this love, Goethe found the expression for his highest conception of mankind. Of them he said: *Those comprehensive individuals whom one might in a prouder sense call the creative ones, are in the highest sense productive; for since they always take their point of departure from ideas, they are always expressing the unity of the whole.*

After having dwelt on the unity of philosophy and science for such a long time, we now come to the question as to how far art and science form a unity. Our own time has separated these intellectual realms so definitely, that their possible unity strikes us as improbable and even, indeed, as undesirable.

Goethe's journey to Italy in 1786, that decisive event in his life, brought all his spiritual resources to full bloom, maturing his classical views on art and Nature. Goethe's mind flowered freely and luxuriantly in the sunshine and culture of the South, and the secret of an integral creative principle in art and Nature was the crowning of his ideas. *The great works of art are at the same time the greatest works of Nature produced by men according to true and natural laws. Everything arbitrary and illusory collapses. There is necessity! There is God! . . . I have the surmise that the Greeks acted according to the laws by which Nature herself acts; and I am on the track of them.* (Goethe was at that time intensely preoccupied with the metamorphosis of plants.) Of the artist's style he said that it was *based on the deepest fundaments of knowledge, on the nature of things in so far as we are permitted to perceive it in visible and tangible forms.* The analytical method of science and modern art—in contrast to the idea of *Gestalt*—naturally proceeds quite differently; it refuses to recognize this kind of perceptual knowledge. Goethe knew that in order to comprehend the processes of life in art and Nature one must have a different kind of vision from that by means of which the manifestations of inorganic and mechanical Nature can be perceived.

Here now more detailed attention must be paid to the conception of *Gestaltung* and *Gestalt* in Goethe's thought. There are already indications that they will only come to fulfilment again in a future science and society. As early as in his botanical studies, when he discovered a fundamental form, the *Urpflanze*, Goethe said: *It means becoming aware of form, with which Nature is always, as it were, only playing and, in playing, bringing forth life in all its multiplicity.* Form, pattern, *Gestalt*, is to him something like an element. He does not dissect it or break it up, as for instance into atoms, for then life would escape. *Gestalt* is a primal manifestation of life. Lavater, who in his *Physiognomic Fragments for the Advancement of the Knowledge and Love of Mankind*, 1775-78, claimed to decipher the character of the soul from the forms of the body, was a symbolist. Goethe, however, was even then regarding external form for its own sake, setting out to perceive its laws and formative energy. *Gestalt* is nothing rigid, for it is alive; but it is subject to metamorphoses. And Goethe uttered a warning: *The idea of metamorphosis is an extremely venerable, but at the same time extremely dangerous gift from above. It leads into formlessness, dissolving and destroying knowledge (Wissen). It is like the vis centrifuga and would become lost in infinity, if it had not been endowed with a counterbalance: I mean the urge towards specification, the tough faculty of persistence in everything that has ever attained to a state of reality—a vis centripeta against which, in its profoundest depths, no externality can prevail.* The formative process, *Gestaltung*, that brings forth *Gestalten*, i.e., living, changing, self-propagating, self-sufficient and self-contained forms, is the really creative process of life. Analysis, mechanical or calculated measuring and weighing, splitting and dissecting, may indeed annihilate life, but they cannot bring forth life. As Goethe wrote to Zelter: *No one will realize that the highest and sole operation of Nature and art is Gestaltung, and that the Gestalt is the specification in order that each thing may become, be and remain a particular and significant entity.* Those who offend against the law of *Gestaltung*, those who do not take it into consideration, offend against the most fundamental law of Nature, and their activity must ultimately turn out to be hostile to life.

In 1911 the doctor and psychologist Georg Groddeck wrote in his essay 'Hin zur Gottnatur' ('Towards Divine Nature): 'Goethe, a man at one with Nature, will for centuries to come be what Homer has been for centuries past. . . . Goethe understood the great secret of life and tried to live his own life in accordance with it, to merge his separate existence in the great life of Nature. This is the reason, and this alone, why we feel him to be at once strange and familiar, cold and remote, though brimming over with energy and passion. The sole foundation of art is this power of losing one's separateness, of feeling oneself at the same time a whole and yet a part of something far greater. This power we have lost, but Goethe had it. He is a miracle in modern history even greater than Leonardo, who alone of all the moderns can claim kinship with him. . . . A work of art is a work of Nature, even as the tree. There you have a devastating criticism of modern art, and though Goethe certainly did not intend the implication, the soundness of the criticism is not thereby affected. For centuries past our greatest writers have ceased to look to the natural work for inspiration, and have limited themselves to the study of themselves and their neighbours, hoping to understand the secrets of men's souls and make their poetry out of these. . . . The great writers Heine, Victor Hugo, Musset, Verlaine, Baudelaire, Nietzsche, all show the same psychological tendencies, the same incapacity to step outside their own and their neighbours' affairs. . . . Goethe is in himself a proof that neither in drama nor in epic or lyric poetry need there be individual characters, for no one surely would maintain that Faust had a personality, or Egmont, Klärchen or Gretchen . . . they are types, or, if you like, representatives of mankind . . . Shakespeare's people, on the other hand, are all definite individuals, sharply delineated.'

'Could but the vain European who has for so long looked upon himself as the lord of Nature be brought to know that though the world truly is round, he does not stand at its centre, then would life again be worthy and the world once more seem fair.'

3. The Guilt of Science

Only what is fruitful is true.—*Goethe*

Nature becomes mute when put to torture.—*Goethe*

From criticism of philosophy let us now pass on to criticism of science. Its general outlines appear nowadays in every considerable work on sociology and psychology, in biography and even in art history. If here we refer specifically to Professor A. N. Whitehead's lectures, delivered in 1925 at Harvard University and published under the title 'Science and the Modern World', it is only for the reason that they give a full and dignified statement of the development of science, its nature and aims. It is a great book, not because it suggests ways out of our dilemma—it could not achieve a really revolutionary view of things, since Whitehead was a Platonist—but for the lucidity with which the problems are apprehended and the defects laid bare. Whitehead's book has that seriousness and discipline which is proper to a scientist with a philosophic training. What is particularly interesting to us here is that every critical argument adduced by Whitehead was fully stated by Goethe one hundred and fifty years earlier. So in dealing with each problem we shall add Goethe's point of view parenthetically, in order to simplify comparison. Certainly Whitehead did not take into consideration Goethe's scientific thought; and indeed rarely any scientist has. In a passage wherein he criticizes the ideological basis on which scientists place their ultimate principles, he adds: 'No alternative system of organizing the pursuit of scientific truth has been suggested. It is not only reigning but it is without a rival.' To this we may be allowed to retort—no! Goethe had a scientific attitude and method, he had a philosophic view and a way of life that, even if they do not amount to a 'system', yet contain, as a living tree contains all botany, all the basic ideas from which a future human science can take its bearings. Where Whitehead advances on to positive, new ground, saying: 'My point is that a further stage of provisional realism is required, in which the scientific scheme is recast and founded upon the ultimate concept of organism,' Goethe retained the concept of *Gestaltung*—form within change. The physicist L. L. Whyte in his book *The Next Development in Man* has sketched out the basic scheme of a system of unitary thought, from which he looks for a renewal of human conditions. Among the thinkers whom he quotes as representatives of his idea in various epochs, he sees Goethe as the unitary man of the eighteenth century. Of him Whyte says: 'All that is universal in him is characteristic of the periods which still lie ahead. . . . Goethe stands beyond the range of personal or literary criticism because, like Socrates and Jesus, he unhesitatingly followed a vision of life which bore within it the germ of centuries to come. Like them he dared to live his vision, not in isolation but in the world of man, and to live it out to the end. The vast difference between him and them, which makes the comparison bewildering . . . arises from the fact that they heralded the dissociated man whom we know, while he foretells a unitary man who is not yet recognized.' In Whyte's eyes Goethe overcame the misleading antithesis of free will and necessity, and he recognized the formative principle as universal. 'His life was unitary in that it reveals no general or permanent conflict . . . no neurosis of dissociation, no fanaticism, or moral intolerance or anger. . . . He never allowed the dualities of his nature to harden into a dualism. . . . Goethe's thought . . . was of a unitary form, not because he decided that was the right way to think, but because a process of that form dominated his life and person without the distortions which mark dissociated man. . . . His general approach to experience offers the first mature example of historical, as opposed to analytical reason. . . . Goethe's resentment of Newton was an indication of what was to come. . . .'

'The sixteenth century of our era,' Whitehead says, 'saw the disruption of Western Christianity and the rise of modern science. . . . The new mentality (resulting from this) is more important even than the new science and the new technology. It has altered the metaphysical presuppositions and the imaginative contents of our minds.' *Earlier centuries had their ideas in the form of imaginative vision, ours has its ideas in the form of conceptions,* Goethe said. *The great ideas of life were then seen as Gestalten, as gods. . . . Then productive power was greater, to-day destructive power or the art of dissection. . . .* The process took three hundred years to develop the catastrophic symptoms which we to-day can hardly control any longer. The individual consequences Goethe saw as follows: *How tame and feeble life has become in these last few miserable centuries! Where do we ever now meet with a nature true and without guile?* And the general consequences: *I see the time coming when God will take no more pleasure in it* (mankind) *and will have to destroy everything yet once again to make way for rejuvenated creation. I am quite sure that everything is prepared and time and the hour are already ordained, somewhere in the remote future, when this epoch of rejuvenation is to begin.* Goethe does not speak of decline and fall, but of a rejuvenated creation, an epoch of rejuvenation. Whitehead also has optimistic confidence, not only in man, who can renew himself inwardly and rise again, but in the rhythm in which ideas reproduce themselves. 'General climates of opinion persist for periods of about two to three generations, that is to say, for periods of sixty to a hundred years. There are also shorter waves of thought, which play on the surface of the tidal movement.' How much more profoundly Goethe seems to have seen this question than the Platonist! He knew that *moral epochs change just as do the seasons of the year. . . . Everything undergoes transformation, rising and sinking, and we cannot hold it fast any more than we can the sun, moon and stars; and yet these things are not mere natural events. They slip through our fingers, by our own fault or some other fault, by accident or fate, but they change, and we can never be sure of them.*

What, then, is the spiritual cause of our misery? Whitehead says: 'Thought is abstract; and the intolerant use of abstractions is the major vice of the intellect.' Mathematics, which were so alien to Goethe—*It is an undeniable truth that, however purely and safely mathematics can be handled in itself, in the field of experience it instantly and at every step becomes fraught with danger and may lead one into error, just like every other maxim put into practice, nay more, may make the error enormous and so pave the way for its own future shame*—according to Whitehead provided 'the background of imaginative thought with which the men of science approached the observation of Nature. Galileo produced formulae, Descartes produced formulae, Huyghens produced formulae, Newton produced formulae.' Whitehead sees the seventeenth century as 'the century of genius'. Francis Bacon, Harvey, Kepler, Galileo, Descartes, Pascal, Huyghens, Boyle, Newton, Locke, Spinoza, Leibniz are only some of the names. Goethe suffered deeply from the consequences of their genius. *Several men of this kind dominate science, which is a sort of immense guild, always . . . becoming worse the more one neglects individual vision (Schauen) and direct thought.* Vision and direct thought kept Goethe from slipping into the wake of mathematical and one-sided analytical research. He had an altogether different conception of research: *Here, first and foremost, let us admit and pronounce the fact that we . . . are in the region where metaphysics and natural history overlap, that is to say, where the serious, faithful researcher most loves to linger.* As a poet, in Faust's metaphorical descent to the Mothers, those fundamental productive forces of the universe, Goethe approached a sphere in which he had learnt: *The capacity to shudder in awe is the best part of man's make-up. However the world may make him suffer for his feeling, he is deeply moved by his sense of what is vast and incomprehensible.*[1]

---

[1] *Das Schaudern ist der Menschheit bestes Teil;*
   Wie auch die Welt ihm das Gefühl verteure,
   Ergriffen fühlt er tief das Ungeheure.

Which will prove right—Goethe or the seventeenth century? This question may sound ironical, but we are faced with a cultural decline that leaves modern man with a grave responsibility. As Whitehead says: 'We are now so used to the materialistic way of looking at things, which has been rooted in our literature by the genius of the seventeenth century, that it is with some difficulty that we understand the possibility of another mode of approach to the problem of Nature. . . . Having regard to this triumph can we wonder that scientists placed their ultimate principles upon a materialistic basis and thereafter ceased to worry about philosophy?' But how did these scientists see Nature? 'Nature was a dull affair, soundless, scentless, colourless; merely the hurrying of material, endlessly, unceasingly. However you disguise it, this was the practical outcome of the characteristic scientific philosophy which closed the seventeenth century.' (Whitehead). Goethe's Nature is different. It is according to *her great iron laws that we must all complete the circle of our existence.—Everything that separates us from Nature is falsification.—Nature is always in the right, and the faults and errors are always man's.—When man's healthy nature works as a whole, when he feels himself in the universe as part of a great, beautiful, noble whole, when harmonious enjoyment gives him a sense of pure, free ecstasy, then if the universe could be aware of itself it would achieve its goal, would jubilate, admiring the peak of its own evolution and being.*

'This triumph of materialism,' Whitehead continues, 'was chiefly in the sciences of dynamics, physics and chemistry.' In the eighteenth century 'the notion of the mechanical explanation of all the processes of Nature finally hardened into a dogma of science.' Could philosophy, Whitehead wonders, help us out of this dilemma? Scarcely, he thinks. 'The idealistic school, as hitherto developed, has been too much divorced from the scientific outlook.' Goethe, however, knew that idealistic philosophy built up with materialistic science into a solid intellectual structure not only would not offer a solution but would merely bring about double confusion. But there has to be a way out, all the same. For 'a civilization which cannot burst through its current abstractions is doomed to sterility after a very limited period of progress.' Whitehead indicates a way out: 'The point before us is that this scientific field of thought is *now*, in the twentieth century, too narrow for the concrete facts which are before it for analysis.

This is true even in physics, and is more especially urgent in the biological sciences. . . .' We must take a very definite stand as regards this 'now'. For just as surely as man has been in a state of melancholy ever since the Renaissance, so surely too did Goethe recognize the evil in a too narrow conception of science. It is not that the concrete facts in the twentieth century have proved the narrowness of the scientific field of thought, but that science's whole attitude was false from the very start. *No one would believe,* Goethe said, *how much there is in science . . . that is either dead or fatal . . . and indeed on the whole it seems to me that scientific people are activated rather by a sophistic than by a truth-loving spirit. . . . There is much that we would know better if we did not try to know it exactly.* And against this kind of 'exactness', and against the specialization of science: *This sort of treatment always seemed to be a kind of mosaic, in which one puts one finished stone beside the other, using thousands of details in order to produce the appearance of a picture; and this is more or less the reason why the demand seems to me odious.* It is in Goethe too that we find the pronouncement that, metaphorically speaking, unfurls the problem of a *human* science: *Both microscopes and telescopes shift man's actual standpoint.* He often went so far as to be indignant. *And the living man is in the right. He has a knavish right to be worse than those who lived before us. . . . The increase in mechanization worries and frightens me.—Everything is now ultra, everything is everlastingly transcendental, in thought as in action. Nobody knows himself now, nobody comprehends the element in which he lives and moves and has his being. . . . Young men are stirred up too early and then swept away in the maelstrom of the age. Wealth and speed are what the world admires and what everybody strives for. Railways, express-mails, steamships and every possible kind of facility for communication are what the civilized world is out for, to become over-civilized and so to persist in mediocrity. And another result of the aspiration of the masses is that an average culture becomes general. This is the goal towards which the Bible societies, the Lancastrian teaching-method and all that sort of thing is striving. It is, in fact, the century for the capable, for quick-thinking, practical people who, being equipped with a certain adroitness, feel their superiority over the many, although they themselves are not gifted for what is highest. Let us keep as much as possible to the mode of thought in which we grew up. With, perhaps, a few others, we shall be the last of an epoch that will not soon come again.*

The Platonist Whitehead comes to the aid of the mathematician Whitehead. The idealistic humanist is aroused, and behind the conception of biology he discovers man, even, indeed, man as artist: 'The mechanism of God and the mechanism of matter were the monstrous issues of limited metaphysics and clear logical intellect. . . . It is in literature that the concrete outlook of humanity receives its expression.' In the romantic movement in literature he sees the 'conscious reaction against the mentality of the eighteenth century.' Here, however, we shall devote our attention to Goethe who saw in world-rejection, in the melancholy and distortion of romanticism a danger at least equal to materialism and idealism. It is Goethe's philosophy, the secret of his positive mind, rooted so deep in reality, always regaining its equilibrium and affirming life, that offers us a way out. For Whitehead romanticism and idealism are 'representative of the intuitive refusal seriously to accept the abstract materialism of science.' 'English poetic literature is a witness to the discord between the aesthetic intuitions of mankind and the mechanism of science. . . . The nature-poetry of the romantic revival was a protest on behalf of the organic view of Nature, and also a protest against the exclusion of *value* from the essence of matter of fact.' This romantic literature gives him a chance to sketch out a provisional guiding-line for the future. 'I am giving the outline of what I consider to be the essentials of an objectivist philosophy adapted to the requirement of science and to the concrete experience of mankind. . . . I hold that the ultimate appeal is to *naive* experience and that is why I lay such stress on the evidence of poetry. My point is that in our sense-experience we know away from and beyond our own personality.'

How was it possible, we may ask, reading this, that no scientist harkened to Goethe's voice, that no scientist could comprehend the profound human wisdom revealed in his kind of vision, his *Schauen*, nor believe in his warning against rationalism? *Consciousness is no adequate weapon, indeed it is sometimes dangerous to him who wields it*.

The nineteenth century produced only that advance of materialistic science and technology, that 'quick, conscious and expected' evolution that has brought us to the brink of the abyss. Nature, to which Goethe built altars, was plundered to the limit. 'Science, conceived not so much in its principles as in its results, was an obvious storehouse of ideas for utilization.' The industrial revolution began in England. By 1840—eight years after Goethe's death

—biology and chemistry were established on an atomic basis, and the last twenty years of the nineteenth century, the years of greatest material prosperity and greatest social misery, are described by Whitehead as 'one of the dullest stages of thought since the time of the First Crusade.' Society's attitude to art, religion and morality was merely negative. What remained were the nineteenth-century slogans: Struggle for existence, competition, class-warfare, commercial antagonism between nations, military warfare. We have gone still further. Through the discovery of the splitting of the atom we have seen immature mankind penetrate into the inmost secrets of matter. Every sensitive person was seized with horror when the atom bomb was used to end the Second World War, in which respect for life had already reached a very low level. Here we stand on the threshold where the irreverence of soulless twentieth-century man, who believes only in uniformity, mass-production and power, goes so far that soon we shall only be able to talk in terms of ancient allegories, the Flood, the Tower of Babel, the Apocalypse, the Last Judgement. Nature is a living being and will shake off mankind. It will be able to defend itself against the fatal analytic rhythm of science and technology, as against a foreign body or a plague. The earth is already mutinying here and there, threatening to starve man out.

Goethe had a profound reverence for life and for man. Goethe still had a sense of meaningful function, for the creative productivity of labour and the highest productivity of all, that of genius. That is continually apparent in his writing. For instance, in *Wilhelm Meister's Years of Travel* he makes youth, scientifically trained in its professions, go through three stages of reverence in order to become maturely established in its humanity. I say 'humanity' and not 'morality', since Goethe's insistence on reverence for life is a 'natural' and not merely a social demand and he would have rejected any social or moral attitude as too narrow. Goethe to Lavater: *Your little bit of morality alone will not enable you to take a great view of the universe!* Since no religion, so far, had solved the ultimate problem for him—*what else are the thousandfold religions but thousandfold utterances of the healing power that is meant for the intellectual wounds dealt us by Nature?*—they must go through them all. *The general, the natural religion really has no need of belief!* An 'invisible church' is created, out of the three stages of reverence. The first stage is that of the pagan and ethnic religions, that is, reverence for what is above us and stronger than ourselves; the second stage, the philosophic, is that of reverence for what is equal to us; and the third, the Christian, is that of reverence for what is beneath us, for whatever is afflicted by misery, suffering and death. But only all three stages together produce reverence for ourselves, which is reverence for the divine in ourselves. Man must be productive, Goethe demands, because productivity and fertility is the essence of Nature. *To be active is man's first duty.—How can one learn to know oneself? Never by contemplation, but always through action. Try to do your duty and you will instantly know what you are worth.* And because even genius is only a vibration in the harmony of the whole, he says: *Every productivity of the highest kind, every great thought that produces fruits, is in nobody's power. Those are things for man to consider as . . . unhoped for gifts. It is related to the daimonic principle, which overwhelms and does as it likes with him, and he yields himself up to it all unawares, believing meanwhile that he is acting spontaneously.*

Such ideas of Goethe's had a great influence on Albert Schweitzer's philosophy of life and mode of action—one of the few real, vigorous attempts that anyone has made at present to extricate himself from our ignoble conditions. Schweitzer has a definite view of Goethe's nature. In his book *Culture and Ethics*, preceded by *The Decline and Reconstruction of Culture*—a work clearly aimed against Spengler's, even its title showing, in its polarity, how deeply Schweitzer's thought is imbued with Goethe's spirit—Schweitzer begins by stating Goethe's reverence for the reality of Nature and contrasts it with Descartes and the ethical belief in progress. 'His greatness is that he dared to stick to what is elementary in an age of abstract and speculative thought. . . . For him it was an inner necessity to find a place in natural philosophy for his view of activity. The conviction that *effective action (Wirken)* gives the only real satisfaction in life and that there, then, lies the mysterious sense of existence, is something that Goethe expresses above all in *Faust*. Then comes Schweitzer's criticism of the age: 'The full significance of Goethe's *Weltanschauung*, with its penetration of reality, remained hidden from his contemporaries. They had no appreciation of any knowledge of the universe and of life that could not be reduced to a system but obstinately stuck fast in facts. They kept to optimism and ethics.'

Let us return to Whitehead. He believes that 'we are entering upon an age of reconstruction in religion, in science and in political thought. Such ages, if they are to avoid mere ignorant oscillation between extremes, must see truth in its ultimate depth. There can be no vision of this depth of truth apart from a philosophy which takes full account of those ultimate abstractions, whose inter-connections it is the business of mathematics to explore.' There speaks the mathematician coming to the aid of the Platonist. Goethe's idea of the fullness and unity of life is the answer here. Whitehead feels the inadequacy and so turns to life itself. He wants it to give him the answer—organic life, the organism, not matter. First he gives the following definition: 'The organism is a unit of emergent value, a real fusion of the character of eternal objects, emerging for its own sake.' We have already mentioned Goethe's *Gestalt*-philosophy. Now we come to the question whether Whitehead's definition implants reverence for life in the soul of modern man. He appeals to the creative spirit: 'The other side of the evolutionary machinery, the neglected side, is expressed by the word creativeness. . . .' 'The clash (of opinions) is a sign that there are wider truths and finer perspectives within which a reconciliation of a deeper religion and a more subtle science will be found.' And Goethe in his appeal to posterity speaks of a *pure, living feeling that there is something imperishable, and that even if it is not immediately recognized, yet ultimately not only the minority, but the majority will rejoice in it.*

How was it that our decline could go so far? Whitehead states that it is in consequence of the crisis in religion: 'During many generations, there has been a gradual decay of religious influence in European civilization. . . . Religion is the vision of something which stands beyond, behind and within, the passing flux of immediate things. . . . It is the expression of one type of fundamental experience of mankind. Whitehead demands that religious thought develops into an increasing accuracy of expression, disengaged from adventitious imagery, and claims that the interaction between religion and science is the great factor in promoting this development. . . . The fact of the religious vision, and its history of persistent expansion, is our one ground for optimism. . . . The vision claims nothing but worship; and worship is a surrender to the claim for assimilation, urged with the motive force of mutual love.' Goethe's conception of religious feeling forms *a priori* a unity with art and science; it is the way that leads man through life, from his innate love to reverence, to astonishment and to action—not a mere rectification of dogma by science and the worship of a vision lying beyond or behind the passing flux of immediate things.

The world has become very sombre. The scientists admit it themselves. 'The Western world is now suffering from the limited moral outlook of the three previous generations.' (Whitehead.) Goethe would not regard it as a problem of morality. The fiend of technique rages on. Inevitably one thinks of Goethe's ballad about the sorcerer's apprentice who set the mechanical forces in motion and then could not bring them to a stop, because he lacked the wisdom. *Master, I am in great extremity. The spirits that I conjured up I cannot now get rid of.*[1]

'The progressiveness in detail,' Whitehead says, 'only adds to the danger produced by the feebleness of co-ordination.' Goethe knew that it was no mere question of co-ordinating the specialized branches of science, of technology and social evolution, but one of a false spiritual attitude. 'The soul cries aloud for release into change. . . . In the most advanced industrial countries, art was treated as a frivolity. . . The fertilization of the soul is the reason for the necessity of art.' So far Whitehead. But how is art to break through the antagonism to the spiritual in our time, for which science, technology and material greed are to blame? And can that possibly be done by modern art, which in many of its aspects shows the ailments of its time and which in its highest achievements must be said to aim at quite a different adventure of the spirit than that suggested by the Classical conception? Whitehead concludes on a dubious note: 'It may be that civilization will never recover from the bad climate which enveloped the introduction of machinery.' Here, in the conditional, he restates Spengler's thesis of the decline of the West.

In spite of the reserve with which Whitehead's Platonism is here treated, it is to be wished that this book could have been as widely known on the Continent as Spengler's work, which merely further undermined spiritual energies already shattered by the First World War and drove the Germans, with their taste for the wordy and obscure, into the arms of an utterly brutal dictatorship.

[1] *Herr, die Not ist gross!*
Die ich rief, die Geister,
Werd' ich nun nicht los.

How cynical Spengler's basic thought actually is, becomes apparent in his later work, *Man and Technique*. His greatest failing is his reluctance to subject himself to any voluntary intellectual discipline, a discipline that often becomes sheer beauty in Whitehead. It was not only the morphological method that Spengler took over from Goethe, but also the dynamic idea of *becoming*, not merely *being*, a living idea in the minds of all Europe's greatest thinkers since Heraclitus. But he made a negative use of it, while Goethe in his instinctive wisdom never lost sight of the process as a whole, the rise and fall and rise again. In its essence it is analogous to the feminine and masculine principles in Chinese thought, Yin and Yang, the one always waxing as the other wanes, or to the old Jewish allegory of the wheel, every point of which must always begin to rise again the instant that it has reached the lowest level. This in spite of the fact that the motto to Spengler's work is taken from Goethe and that in it we are always running into wisdom of Goethe's, his exact sensual imagination, his objective thinking, from all of which there grew the immediate inner certainty that Nature had a destiny and not merely a causality. *Everything transient's only a symbol* . . .[1]

Spengler remains only a man of great erudition; he is not a sage, as Goethe was. He mistakenly sees in Faust the evolution of Titanic man—much like Nietzsche's Superman, who is ultimately traceable back to Faust too—whereby Spengler identifies Faust with Goethe, with German, Germanic and so on, an error that has done a great deal of harm, while Carus, for instance, quite clearly recognized the daimonic nature of Faust's character and uttered a warning against identifying Faust with Goethe. The result is that in Spengler's work we are always stumbling over a wrong conception of the 'Faustian'. He speaks of an Apollonian, Magical and Faustian spiritual life, of Faustian and Apollonian experience of Nature, of Faustian physics, of which the dogma is force—a particularly dangerous formulation, since in Spengler's work it coincides with the most brutal nationalistic instincts of prey—of Faustian thought in money, etc. Now all this Spenglerian Goetheanism has led us a long way from Goethe. Spengler's *Kultur-philosophie* sees machines becoming ever more 'mystical'; he regards the engineer as an 'initiate and priest', and finally he laments the fact that the white race was not clever enough to keep

[1] *Alles Vergängliche ist nur ein Gleichnis* . . .

the secret of technique to itself in order to dominate the coloured world by this means.

No time seems to have needed Goethe as much as ours, and in none have so many attempts been made to bring him nearer to us. Even though Emil Ludwig's biography again conjures up for us the image of the Olympian, the 'human' hero, that is perhaps no bad thing in a time that has lost respect for spiritual greatness. His work is written with a freshness that, although it avoids the depths of Goethe's problems, does bring the man Goethe nearer to us— much nearer than, say, Friedrich Gundolf, whose merit, compared with the older biographers, lay in crystallizing those ideas of Goethe's which were the driving forces of his life. Naturally it is impossible here to discuss all the more important writings on Goethe, such as those of Simmel, Brandes, Cassirer, Leisegang, and Bahr. They have little to do with our thesis. Inevitably Thomas Mann took up the challenge of Goethe in several essays. He has also worked out several important themes suggested by Goethe in *Dichtung und Wahrheit*, for instance the Joseph cycle, and so created a literary Goethe tradition. He also makes Goethe his basis in novels—*Lotte in Weimar, Dr. Faustus*. There is one other attempt that must be mentioned here, with yet one more reminder that an arbitrary interpretation of Goethe cannot show us what we are looking for, namely an understanding of Goethean man, who has experienced the laws of *polarity*—that all manifestations of life are expressed in two opposite conditions that form an inseparable unity: soul and body, dark and light, life and death, man and woman, 'to heaven exulting, grieved to very death,' meditation and action—of *intensification* (*Steigerung*)—that there is an ever-striving ascent going on in Nature—and of the *wholeness* of all manifestations of life; and who proclaimed the moral code of the balanced and free human being in the words: *Only he deserves liberty—or life, who must conquer it anew each day*. A novel meaning was given to the Greek ἄνθρωπος μετρον ἀπαντων, *man the measure of all things*, the only slogan we have to set against religious dogmas, which wrongly base morality in the transcendental instead of in the human sphere and so deprive morality of its vital force. *Man the measure of all things*—that seems to us to be the only wisdom with which we can defend ourselves against the menacing dehumanization of science, of economic and social life, the devaluation of man and his soul. *Man the measure of all things* means that everything should be measured up against the human, that everything that takes no account of man is inhuman and hence harmful.

The last attempt at an un-Goethean interpretation of Goethe that we shall mention here is by Werner Deubel, a disciple of the German philosopher and graphologist Ludwig Klages; with Steiner and Carus as his basis, he claims to see the fulfilment and systematic completion of Goethe's *Weltanschauung* in Klages's philosophy. Deubel believes he has discovered contradictions in Goethe, which he traces back to Goethe's ideas of the Christian-idealistic view of the world having been mixed with other, spontaneous ideas of his own. He cannot accept the harmonizing law of balance, which forges polar, ever-renewed opposites into a living whole, but splits Goethe into two parts and, taking sides with the one, concludes that German romanticism, sombre, melancholy, Catholic romanticism, with its attempt to 'liberate itself from the clutches of the Logos-philosophy'—the characteristic of this being dualism: mind-God/Nature, law/chaos, moral freedom/fate, consciousness and will/unconscious body-soul, etc.—follows in Goethe's footsteps but collapses under the attack of mechanistic materialism and German idealism. Now we know enough about Goethe's attitude to romanticism. The next revolt, in Deubel's view, came through Nietzsche, in whose posthumous writings were found the words: 'My ancestors: Heraclitus, Empedocles, Spinoza, Goethe!' But the mature Goethe rejected the Dionysiac principle and would have felt Nietzsche as much an antipode to himself as Klages, who, although he takes as his starting point certain ideas of Goethe's, Carus's and Bachofen's, goes to the other extreme and grants full validity only to the unconscious soul.[1] On the contrary, Goethe knew the key to the riddle was balancing the unconscious with the conscious. *What would all culture be if we did not seek to overcome our natural urges?*

Certainly Goethe did use the symbol of the Mothers, which became the *leitmotiv* of Bachofen's life work.[2] Certainly Goethe did very definitely point to the unconscious, and found a distinguished pupil in Carus. But our modern, exaggerated, de-

---

[1] Ludwig Klages, *The Mind as the Soul's Adversary, Of Cosmogonic Eros, Goethe as Psychologist.*

[2] J. J. Bachofen: *Das Mutterrecht.*

railed depth-psychological self-torment and romantic-nihilistic delight in the underworld must be offset by the mature, harmonious man rooted in creation and in a life of activity, the man who dams up passion with control and renunciation, in whose soul both sun and moon shine, the one bright, the other mysteriously gleaming; in whom dreaming does not displace waking, in whose mind poetry sings and laborious research has its dwelling and everything urges on to the great work. His ideas, matured by contact with reality, are deepened by Orphic wisdom: *Daimon—the law in which you once began is that in which you must exist*; *Tyche (the accidental element, chance)—You do not remain solitary, you form yourself in social activity. Eros—Many a heart floats away into generality, but the loftiest heart always dedicates itself to one*; *Ananke (necessity): There again it is, as the stars willed, condition and law and every will is all one volition, because we are meant to do it so, and face to face with this will all wanton wilfulness falls silent*;[1] and finally Elpis (hope), without which there is no life.

Goethe knew the art of learning from mistakes and suffering, and in doing so he experienced the law of, what he called, *succession*; for knowledge lies only in relating the new to the old and so rising to a higher stage of wisdom. His life was a perpetual striving to become better and nobler, and in this he endured. *What counts in the end is holding out and outlasting the others.*

The harmonization of polarities is Goethe's great human bequest to us. It is the ground on which his classicism grew, in all its healthiness. 'It may truly be said,' Carus, the doctor, wrote about the mature Goethe, 'that all the energies of the mind were present in equally high degree and in most beautiful harmony and that even his imagination, so lively and so creative, was restrained and kept in check by the dominance of the intellect. This was particularly so where the physical was concerned: no system, no function, had the upper hand; all worked together for the maintenance of a grand equilibrium.' He describes him as a 'beautifully and powerfully organized' human being. Only the later Goethe literature has revealed how consciously, austerely and intensely he himself built up that organization, dominating

[1] *Da ist's denn wieder, wie die Sterne wollten,*
 Bedingung und Gesetz und aller Wille
 Ist nur ein Wollen, weil wir eben sollten,
 Und vor dem Willen schweigt die Willkür stille—

Nature, the body, with his mind and controlling his mode of life by his will.[1] That is doubtless why in *Wilhelm Meister's Apprenticeship* he portrayed the youth who believed he only needed to reach out for the treasures of this world and they would instantly be his. He thought he need not make any sacrifice for the sake of beauty, love, wealth, enjoyment, happiness and greatness, neither in the form of freedom nor in that of independence, not in effort, work or patience. He wanted to be master of everything and everybody, and was not even master of himself. Is there a better portrait of all our disillusioned idealists, of all the discontented who are riddled by inferiority complexes, hatred and envy and of a humanity that, in its attempts to overcome the frustrations of Christian philosophy and of science, goes stumbling from one extreme to the other? For Nietzsche was an extremist, and so was Marx. The extreme always has devastating consequences. That is why Goethe acknowledged the liberal spirit as the truly human spirit.

In order to arrive at a contemporary understanding of Goethe we must not only consider the calamities of our situation and seek the answers in him; we must see the personality of Goethe as a representative of the human race, in a sense much wider than was possible for Emerson in his time. So, too, it seems to me that Carus's view of Goethe, in spite of being fragmentary, is that which does him most justice. Carus was the first to point to Goethe's significance for the future, because even in 1850 he contrasted Goethe's personality with the quite distinct symptoms of that disease of our conditions that causes us so much suffering to-day. Should anyone succeed in combining the profundity of Carus's view of Goethe, and the poetic warmth that raises his third letter on Faust to the rank of a work of art, with a lucid grasp of our problems, he would undoubtedly make Goethe a fertile inspiration for our time.

---

[1] I often suffer from complaints of the intestines, but the mental will and the energies of the upper part of the body keep me going. The mind must not give way to the body! For instance, I work better when the barometer is high than when it is low; and since I now know this, when the barometer is low I try to cancel out the disadvantageous effects by greater efforts, and I succeed.

2

THE CULTURAL PSYCHOLOGY OF
SIGMUND FREUD

Psychoanalysis Then and Now

The passions gave mankind knowledge of reason.
Marquis de Vauvenargues

SOME weeks before his death Sigmund Freud completed in exile his book on Moses and Monotheism. He made an attempt to establish Moses' Egyptian origin, already suggested by various authors, by way of psychoanalytical speculation, and clarified as the source of monotheism an esoteric and suppressed doctrine. With this book, Sigmund Freud completed his life's work. To a career accomplished and to a personality finally set apart by death, a new attitude is adopted by posterity. The achievement, separated from the man, and thus detached from the latent danger hidden in the power of the creator, begins an independent existence of its own. It is rounded off on all sides, and can surprise us no more by any collapse, or revaluation, or unforeseen radiation. Its life manifests itself in the form of a homogeneous emanation, a kind of regular breathing. The personality of the author must also crystallize in becoming thus detached from his work. There should be greater willingness to accord more charitable recognition to the human factor in it; and in cases where it is crowned by a significant production, by a far from ordinary accomplishment which even in the last moments forced from existence 'a piece of newly-blazed scientific ground', we might expect it to be duly honoured. Newspapers and periodicals had much to say on the occasion of Freud's death; they were far more favourable than critical; they weighed up merit and overestimation, and indeed, spared no words; yet, even so, they did not take into account the fact that an intellectual Titan was gone from us, leaving us his legacy—one of those Titans of whom legend recounts, marvelling, that they fought triumphantly with the gods. When reading Freud's obituaries, I was constantly reminded of Mark Antony's two-edged words over Caesar's coffin, with their unmistakable import that if Caesar was righteous and honest, why then was he murdered? and with their unforgettable refrain: 'Yet Brutus is an honourable man.' In other words, Mark Antony's speech over Caesar's dead body was no more a judgment of Caesar than the public obituary notices were of Sigmund Freud. The tragic conflicts in present-day man, on which Freud has done so much to enlighten us, have cast their shadow on his death. His ideas were vigorously attacked during his lifetime. They would certainly have been killed by the hostile onslaughts, deliberate misinterpretation and prudish misunderstanding if it were at all possible to kill truth. A great contemporary has stated: 'It is precisely that courage to speak the truth which constitutes the ethical character of analytical depth psychology.'[1] This courage was therefore destined to be opposed. We must admit that hostile criticism has to be considered the criterion of an idea's worth or worthlessness. We are rightly suspicious of one that immediately gains universal favour. Nonetheless, the first ten years of the solitary battle for recognition fought by the founder of the revolutionizing doctrine of the activities of the unconscious mind must have been very hard ones, and we can read in words he wrote when already sixty-nine years of age how bitterly he paid back certain hostile attacks: 'There is no excuse for this excess of arrogance and shameless mockery of logic, nor for the crudeness and bad taste of the attacks.'

The attitude to psychoanalysis has changed slowly. It is perhaps noteworthy that America was the country where Freud first won full recognition (1909). Only after this date did Central and Western Europe follow suit. Hostility became indiscriminate admiration. Freud became the fashionable psychologist, just as Schopenhauer, in his time, had been the fashionable philosopher. Such a change always involves a popularization which distorts the truth, and which can for a time obscure the value of scientific work, though not render it less. If this state of affairs made Schopenhauer 'the pessimist', it turned Freud into the apostle of 'sexualism'. As a further consequence, an acute crisis in psycho-

[1] Thomas Mann: *Freud und die Zukunft*, 1936, in *Adel der Geistes*, Stockholm, 1945.

analysis was proclaimed, particularly in matters concerning Freud's pupils and their scientific works.

In some quarters, the practice of psychoanalysis was forbidden, in others the new scientific discoveries were either ignored or rejected as 'veterinary psychology', just as Darwinism was once labelled 'veterinary philosophy'. On the whole, however, much light is thrown on the basic concepts of psychoanalysis by the relationship to Darwin. In his *Autobiographical Study*, Freud writes: 'Darwin's then modern doctrine attracted me powerfully, since it promised a most excellent method of promoting comprehension of the world'; and elsewhere: 'The fact that ontogeny is a repetition of phylogeny must also be applicable to mental life.' C. G. Jung's notion of archtypes is an adaptation of this idea. It was certainly not at random that H. G. Wells averred that Sigmund Freud's name was as important in the history of human thought as that of Charles Darwin.

Nothing could be more contradictory than the various experts' assessments of Freud's depth psychology. One calls it 'a philosophy of no prospects,' because it affirms the roots of our being to lie in wishes that can be neither satisfied nor suppressed; while another sees the effects of its teaching in 'a future for humanity freed from anxiety and hate, and ripened into peace.' To some, Freud is a romantic, one who awakened symbolism to new life; to others his theory is the direct continuation of the philosophy of enlightenment, 'replacing the astral explanation of certain phenomena by human motivation, and defending the primacy of the intellect'. A third group regard him as a kind of centaur, a rational irrationalist, thus creating an 'ambivalent' concept which Freud himself used analogously in psychoanalysis itself.

The perspective with the most human appeal to our critical faculties is that of time that has just passed. Objects assume their proper contexts and dimensions, overestimation and condemnation give place to a more objective, impersonal attitude; personal bias no longer decides the issue. Time has a salutary influence on the assessment of a work's innate value. In these days, when psychoanalytical terms and concepts are a contemporary cultural heritage, and analytical viewpoints have made a kind of *pénétration pacifique* into psychology and philosophy, we can look with more equanimity on the reproaches levelled at the psychoanalysts. While developing their science, they were accused of claiming to give a universal explanation of the personality's basic elements, and a full interpretation of all its aspirations and errors. This charge is groundless. Freud himself parried it when he wrote:

> Only seldom can this science by itself solve a problem; but it seems called to make important contributions to the most dissimilar spheres of knowledge. That practical province of psychoanalysis stretches as far as that of psychology, which it powerfully and effectively complements.

It was further maintained that the psychoanalytical terms (complex, libido, repression, the subconscious, and so on) did not correspond to reality: that they were merely assumptions, constructions—briefly, a working hypothesis, and above all products of Freud's fertile imagination. Freud defended himself thus:

> Our opponents saw in psychoanalysis a product of my speculative imagination, and would not believe in the long, patient, wholly pioneer work which went to build it.

This latter charge involves a far more dangerous one, stemming from Wundt's physiological psychology: that psychoanalysis ignores the biological causes of mental activity. 'Psychoanalysis does justice to the human sexual function, in that it follows every detail of the significance, recognized by many poets and a number of philosophers, but never by science, which this function has in mental and practical life,' writes Freud; and elsewhere: 'having completed the work of psychoanalysis, we must look for the connection with biology, and be content if even at this stage it seems ensured in one or another essential point.' This brings us to the most important objection to psychoanalysis, the one concerning 'pansexualism'—as if Freud had 'sexualized' the entire mental life of man. It is this charge of a gross, anti-cultural materialization that is brought against him. Let us hear how Freud himself meant the term *libido* to be understood:

> These love instincts are called in psychoanalysis, *a potiori* and according to their origin, sexual instincts. Most 'educated' persons have felt the name to be an insult, and avenged themselves by hurling the reproach of 'pansexualism' at psychoanalysis. He who considers sexuality as something shameful and debasing for human nature is welcome to use the more exalted terms 'Eros' and 'eroti-

cism'. I could from the first have done so myself, thus saving myself much opposition. But I did not wish to do so, for I prefer not to make concessions to timid natures. There is no knowing where such a line may not lead: first one gives way over words, and then gradually in facts. I cannot see any merit in feeling ashamed of sexuality: the Greek word Eros, which would soften the shame, is after all only the translation of our word love; and finally, he who knows how to wait needs make no concessions.

Thomas Mann defended Freud on this point:

In this doctrine there is an element of mental approach which confines its anti-intellectualism to knowledge without letting it encroach on will. And this very intellectualism is bound up with the idea whose predominance in his work has aroused the most violent opposition, since Christian bias has accustomed us to look at it in terms of impurity or sin—the idea of sex. When Freud describes the death and destruction wish as the living man's endeavour to revert to the passivity of the lifeless state, and over this 'Backwards!' inscribes sex as the real life wish to which alone all inner tendency to higher development, union and perfection is bound, he gives to sexuality a strain of revolutionary intellectuality which Christianity would be far from allowing it.

How totally different, in our view, is this scientific body of thought, which seeks to plumb the foundations of our sympathetic and antipathetic emotional currents, and to transfer them to cultural phenomena by a brilliant inductive method. But a new objection arises: Freud's problem is reputedly clinical, while the way of solving it is psychological. Now, can a method evolved for the curing of pathological conditions also, under any circumstances, be used for normal mental activities? The value of the pathological as a path and a means to knowledge is widely accepted. Bergson pointed out that many of the most important contributions to this world were made by persons of neurotic temperament; and Nietzsche stated that 'no deep knowledge is accessible without experience of sickness, and all higher health must have undergone sickness.' Insight into the mechanism of the neurotic state has led Freud to trace out that of our mental faculties. 'Psychoanalysis,' he writes, 'is a striving towards a new and more thorough knowledge of the mind, which is equally indispensable to an understanding of the normal psyche.'

Despite all hostility, even Freud's opponents have had to admit that his work forms a turning-point in the history of psychology. He has thrown a bridge between the normal and the abnormal, and explored the innermost regions of the mind. The dynamic feature in his psychology, i.e., reference to the libidinal factor in mental conflicts and the conception of all human mental activity under the unifying aspect of motive, has been of crucial importance to our knowledge of the human mind. It is strange that his work should not culminate in these findings but should, in the truest sense of the word, only begin with them, to develop into the inspired fabric which sought to fathom the 'human, all too human' in a new way by a further tracing of the higher and complicated from the lower and primitive.

The Panorama of Psychoanalysis

Culture is awareness of the psychological
André Malraux

When psychoanalysis left the pathological sphere where it was born and applied its knowledge to the normal mind, it was already possible to discern its next step, from the individual psyche to an understanding of cultural phenomena as the forms in which the collective mind expressed itself.

In 1880 a Viennese doctor, Josef Breuer, cured a young girl of hysteria by means of hypnosis. Her pathological symptoms disappeared after she had talked, while hypnotized, about the forgotten cause which first produced the symptoms—that is to say, after it had penetrated into the conscious sphere. Breuer communicated this surprising fact to his younger colleague, Freud, who had himself been contemplating hypnotism and suggestion while working with the pyscho-pathologists Charcot and Bernheim. For the moment, Freud considered hypnosis irrelevant, having learnt from the case histories that the question was one of an only *apparent* forgetting, which deceived the patient's conscious mind. He looked for a method of proving that it was 'the repression' of an event irreconcilable with the affected subject which had taken a physical form and sought an outlet in hysteria or obsession. This led him to the associative method. The 'free associations' expressed by the patient were interpreted by the doctor via the repressed complexes. The method was not simple, since the same force which caused the repression resisted the return to the conscious mind of what had been repressed. Freud discovered that these repressed fancies came without exception from the sphere of sex. 'I was not prepared for this result, I did not expect it at all; I had quite unsuspectingly set about the investigation of neurotics.' The unconscious mind of the neurotics was revealed. In normal cases the method was first used to interpret lapses and faulty actions of everyday life, and it was proved 'that these phenomena are not fortuitous: they can be physiologically explained, are fully significant and interpretable, and ultimately go back to checked and repressed feelings and intentions.' The next object of study, i.e., the dream, also a phenomenon of normal mental life, provided further data concerning the psychic mechanism. The manifest dream content, which remains in the waking mind as recollection, hides more deep-lying phantasies, the latent dream thoughts. The interaction between these two is provided by the dream-work and its censor. The function of the dream is to protect sleep and provide the wish fulfilment impossible in reality. A secondary adjustment gives a logical stamp to the entire dream content. The study of these courses reacted upon medical methods. 'He who understands the dream can also penetrate the psychic mechanism of neuroses and psychoses.'

The complicated mental processes which could hardly be studied in cultural man, and only with difficulty in neurotics, were found to be most easily accessible in the child. Research into the mental life of children led to the epoch-making discovery of infantile sexuality, whose first stage was established as auto-eroticism (with the child's own body as object), while in the second its satisfaction was transferred to other objects (the parents). Here appear the first conflicts in the child mind, known as the Oedipus complex, the Electra complex, etc.

The sexual instincts of infancy subsequently influence the character. This attaches an important task to upbringing, the main item on whose programme at present is, as Freud once ironically put it, 'to retard the sexual development and hasten the dominion of religion.'

Between the first sexual impressions during the ages from three to four and the process of puberty, there is a latent period when the mind is filled with daydreams and fanciful images. The apparently vanished instinctual urges of childhood are for a long time active under the surface in the adult. And if the former infantile instinct is satisfied neither by a sex life nor by sublimation, it seeks its own points of eruption. One of the most important decrees of psycho-analysis is sublimation, the deflection of the instincts from the sexual sphere to a higher object in keeping with the cultural level of the individual. In his speculative writings, Freud has deepened and expanded the results of his mental analysis. This gave rise to his metapsychology, which distinguishes in the human mind an Id, an Ego and a Superego, with their complicated interrelations. The Id is the source of life, the animal life; it is primitive and irrational, the dark inaccessible part of our personality. The little we know of it has been learnt from the study of the dream-work and the neurotic symptoms. (The child is defined as an Id, with a potential Ego.) The activity of the Superego is reflected in humanity's progress towards civilization, and in the 'conscience' of the individual. The Ego, the conscious portion of the Id, 'is modified by the proximity and influence of 'he outside world, and is so constituted as to receive and resist stimulus, as a small lump of living substance surrounds itself with a layer of shell.' If we supplement these concepts with those of the two life forces, i.e., the instinct of self-preservation and of preservation of the species, pitted against the silently working death and destruction wish, and if instinct is quite generally taken to imply vital elasticity, we see with surprise how a world view grows out of a simple therapy. Such were the lines Freud's genius followed. What the individual mind stages in dreams and neuroses is similarly present in the mind of the whole of humanity, and finds expression in culture. The same conflicts on which the neurotic founders, and which the normal individual works all his life to subdue, break through in religion, myth and art with mighty manifestations of the strong instinctual urges which are unrealizable in practical cultural life.

Unlike dreams and neuroses, which are asocial, these creations of the mind have a social context: they offer protection, comfort and satisfaction to every individual; and therefore culture has adopted them as a precious human asset. There is no doubt that they correspond in structure to certain dreams which recur to different people with the same or similar significance, and which obviously derive from the instinctual urges and complexes of the earlier infantile mental life. Dreams of the love relationship with the mother/father and hate towards the father/mother have found their symbolic expression in the Antique stories of Oedipus and Electra.

Some people spend their lives almost entirely in the realms of the imagination. Their phantasies are strong and structural, and continue to appeal to the senses of posterity. Humanity's eternal longing finds its purest expression in works of art. Here the conflicts are hidden in a more complicated and dexterous way. A high degree of satisfaction is imparted by a work of art when it gives concrete form to a repressed and yet coveted situation as faithfully as possible, and at the same time can find so successful a disguise that the ruling forces in the conscious mind are not offended. 'This fulfilment without battle with the censor is felt as a purifying of the soul from the slag of passion. Aristotle himself described the effect of tragedy as purification—catharsis.'

As well as in art, the cultural man found a vent for repressions in the joke (Freud: *Wit and its Relation to the Unconscious*). The most important guide for repressed feelings is symbolism. Freud therefore called it the favourite language of the unconscious. In early ages, when the method of thinking in comprehensible abstract terms was in its infancy, thought was couched in symbols. Symbolism also forms the quintessence of cult rituals, religious myths, sagas and heroic epics. In the dream, our ability to express relationships in logical terms is lowered, and we return to the infantile level of thought.

In the early epochs of human culture, all conceptions connected with emotions found their expression in religion. Myth and cult are inconceivable without religious tendency. Religion is the mightiest and foremost guardian of all cultural accessions. It is one of life's great fabrics of compromise. By clearing the way for a higher civilization, it satisfies the unattainable and repressed instinctual feelings of the individual. 'Since the unconscious has contributed to the birth of all mental and cultural concepts, in religion and custom, in speech and law, we must know how it functions before we can possibly understand these things fully.' In this age, psychoanalysis extends its influence into every sphere of thought. Philology and psychology, philosophy and biology, evolutionism and cultural history, art, literature and pedagogics, all owe as much to psychoanalysis as do sociology and the psychography of the creative personality.

The Mirror of Our Age

> What is of importance to me is man's own
> progress.
>
> *André Gide*

In his well-known essay *Man and Culture*, Johan Huizinga writes: 'Certainly, no one could call the culture of our age healthy. But opinions differ even as to which are the pathological or actually critical symptoms—not to mention the question of remedies.' As a scholar of cultural history, Huizinga has also to include in his record of modern phenomena the contemporary distrust of culture, and is forced to the honest question: 'Do we really know just what we mean when we talk of culture?' His attempt to define culture and to discover means for its cure leaves us unmoved, however. The wound is too deep or—to keep to the same metaphor—the trouble too alarming to be allayed by aesthetico-ethical prescriptions. Can the masses be educated to culture—when we ourselves do not know what it is? But Huizinga hastens to add:

> We have only to substitute for the vague term *culture* the precise Italian *civiltà* to get an answer. *Civilitas* is the general condition of an ordered State, and the personal conduct of each individual as a civilized, free and responsible *civis*, *polites*. Thus would the political, the State, be acknowledged as the frame of culture, but only insofar as this *civilitas* really were *humana*, insofar as it embraced mankind, and as this *civilitas humana* (Dante: *Monarchia*) effectuated the peaceful communal life and well-intentioned mutual understanding of the many and the heterogeneous.

How often have we not heard variations on this theme, intoxicated and stupefied ourselves with them, and yet not cured the sickness of our age? The people must be educated to culture! Huizinga says: 'Only the ethical adherence to a *summum bonum* makes the people into bearers of culture.' How is this possible?

The beginnings of a cure could be ensured under the rule of a genuine, deep, pure and living faith. From a genuine faith we could penetrate to the foundations of our spiritual life and achieve that restriction and simplification of culture which we consider indispensable.

We agree—and find ourselves back where we started. Our ears ring with the terrible '*j'accuse!*' as much as our hearts are troubled by the tormenting question: Why is our situation so confused? Why are we not helped by the pious, honest, burning wish which fires so many of us? 'A fervent longing for peace, freedom and humanity is passing through the world.' To my mind, those sceptics are far nearer the truth who say with Anatole France:

> Universal peace will one day become reality, not because mankind has become better (that we cannot hope for), but because a new scheme of things, a new science, new economic exigencies will impose upon it a state of peace, as once the same conditions of existence led it into a state of warfare and kept it there. (*Sur la pierre blanche.*)[1]

While the Dutch humanist vainly tries to find in history the guiding-lines for the future, the psychologist Sigmund Freud seeks a cure in man's innermost self. Freud, too, recognized that our culture was sick. When applied to our cultural situation, the neurotic principle—which is the pathological result of a repression—yielded the surprising diagnosis that this situation is comparable with a repression neurosis. To Freud, our culture is 'a thoroughly unstable, thoroughly labile pseudo-perfection and pseudo-harmony, akin to that condition in which a neurotic without the will to recover adjusts himself to and reconciles himself with his symptoms.' This is why we feel so discontented in civilization; indeed, in our heart of hearts we distrust it. Freud tries to analyse the causes of this discontent. His experience that emotional life is conservative is very useful to him here. He speaks of the principle of conservation, of inertia, in the realm of the psyche. This is one of the reasons why men obstinately cling to ideas and associations that have long proved their inability to solve our critical situation. The essential question is: Why is it so difficult for man to be happy? The fault lies in Nature's supremacy, the frailty of our own bodies, and the shortcomings of the institutions regulating human relationships in family, State and communal life. We must submit to the first two causes, but the

[1] This was also Kant's opinion. In his study on 'Perpetual Peace', published in 1795, he insisted that ethical arguments should not be advanced in its favour.

third challenges us to act. Why cannot the institutions we have ourselves created be a protection and a blessing to us all? Since we have been so unsuccessful in making them so, we have to ask whether they, too, are not part and parcel of insubordinate Nature. We have often heard that so-called culture is responsible for most of our wretchedness, and that we would be happier if we abolished it and returned to primitive conditions. But this gets us nowhere, since we do not know if the men of former times felt themselves to be happier, nor how much of any such feeling was due to their cultural conditions. Psychoanalysis, proceeding from its conviction that the essence of happiness is, in all cases, to be found in satisfaction of the instincts, ascribes our lack of ease to the fact that progress has not increased the degree of satisfaction which human beings expect from life. Man's growing mastery over Nature did not *ipso facto* guarantee him happiness. Now if, with Freud, we take culture to denote the sum of accomplishment and living standards distinguishing our life from that of our more animal forebears and serving the dual ends of protecting man from Nature and of regulating human relationships, and if we see how science and technique have given physical shape to humanity's fairy-tale aspirations (Icarus, the seven-league boots, the magic carpet, and so on), we must with all the more sorrow observe that modern man does not feel happy in his 'likeness to the gods'.

We come closer to the heart of the question if we realize the remedy required by this untenable situation. Some say that it is only necessary to change our conditions of life, and everything will then improve. Others maintain that a moral advance is unthinkable without first bettering the individual. These statements embody two different ethical attitudes towards the surrounding world; one is social and political, the other subjective and individualist. Freud writes:

> Life as it is imposed on us is difficult, it brings us too many sufferings, disappointments, insoluble tasks. We must have anodynes to bear it. There are perhaps only three such: powerful distractions, which make us think little of our misery, substitutes for satisfaction which decrease it, intoxicants which render us insensible to it. Something of this kind is essential.

The most concrete and effective of these means is the last-mentioned: it changes the chemistry of our body, and renders it insensible to pain. From a more exalted point of view, it is to be deplored, since it wastes vast quantities of energy which could be used to improve the lot of mankind. Another method of controlling our instinctual life is to kill, and not merely deaden, the instincts. This is what the medieval sages taught, and it was adopted by Yoga. But thereby 'life was sacrificed.' Another similar method is to keep the instincts in check and resign oneself to the consequent loss of happiness. The active principle here is provided by the higher mental powers which have submitted themselves to the dictates of reality. Another technique is to change the direction of the libido, and here sublimation of the instincts comes to our aid. We get furthest if we can learn how to enhance the pleasure obtained from imaginative and intellectual work. Thus, the artist feels satisfaction in his creation, the scholar in the solution of problems. We may also mention the aesthetic attitude to life, which seeks happiness in the pleasure given by beauty, whether found in human beings, Nature, artistic or scientific solutions. It offers no protection from threatened suffering, but can lighten many burdens. Work's value to the economy of the libido has an importance that has not yet been fully appreciated.

'No other technique of living binds the individual so firmly to reality as the stressing of work, which at least integrates him securely with a portion of reality, in the human community. The possibility of projecting a powerful conglomeration of libidinal components— narcissistic, aggressive, and even erotic—into the sphere of a profession and its attendant human relationships gives work a value as great as is its indispensability as a foundation and justification of existence in society.'

The most radical method sees the sole enemy to happiness in reality itself. The hermit turns away from this world. But we can also seek to refashion it by substituting for its most intolerable sides others corresponding to our own wishes. He who takes this desperate path to happiness will, says Freud, as a rule achieve nothing. He finally loses his reason. Yet there seems to be one method which most nearly reaches the goal—the one centred on love, and looking for all its satisfaction in loving and being loved. 'The weak side of this technique of living is obvious; otherwise it would not occur to anyone to abandon this path to happiness for any other. Never are we so vulnerable to suffering as when we love, never more helplessly unhappy than when we have lost the beloved object or its love.' As a final living technique, we might mention refuge in nervous maladies, 'the achievement of pleasure by chronic poisoning or the desperate condition of psychosis.'

Where is the boundary-line between the individual and society? When does his interest end and its intervention commence? Are not their goals in many respects diametrically opposed, and is a reconciliation at all possible? There is one way of life which makes the transition from one to the other, and beneficently tries to cater for both—i.e., when the individual, as a member of human society, uses scientifically directed technique to come to grips with Nature and subdue it to the human will. All are then working together for the happiness of all. This is the method Freud himself adopted when he rejected the one that, 'springing from the cowardice of the intellect, seeks to lower the value of life and falsely distorts the picture of the real world.' Now if, without being able to prevent humanity's unconditional surrender to life's suffering, an attitude of this kind tries to impose itself on all men alike, to the detriment of free selection and adaptation in the struggle for happiness and protection from tribulation, then a religious venture is the solution. We shall return to this important cultural sphere later.

In *Totem and Taboo*, where Freud penetrates the obscurity of our earliest history, and where he analyses the evolution from the first family to the next step in communal life, the fraternal groups, he shows that social good (the security of communal life) had to be paid for by a restriction in the libidinal sphere (the taboo on incest). It is obvious that modern communal life also demands sacrifices from the individual, and that much of humanity's struggle clashes over the task of finding a suitable compromise between these individual demands and the claims of the cultural group. It is the problem of our destiny whether this compromise can be reached by giving a fixed conformation to culture, or whether the conflict is insoluble. Freud always firmly dissociates himself from the assumption that culture is synonymous with a perfecting process, that it constitutes the path to perfection laid down for mankind. Connected with this is his refusal to recognize any difference between culture and civilization; and therefore he does not consider the freedom of the individual to be, in itself, yet another cultural value. If 'the desire for freedom' is a revolt against an existing injustice, it may help to further culture; but if it is a relic of the original asocial personality that was not held in check by culture, it can pave the way to an antagonism to culture. Freud analyses problems of social psychology by regarding them as analogous with the instinctual life of the individual. He finds rational sources for the emergence of law and the battle for justice, the parts Eros and Ananche play in the life of the people, the struggle between 'good' and 'evil', and lifts them above the attitude of *credo quia absurdum*. To give but one realistic example: the commandment 'Thou shalt love thy neighbour as thyself,' whereby culture seeks to inter-unite members of society both libidinally and otherwise, raises the gravest difficulties. Why? Apart from very personal relationships, it demands that love also be extended to the stranger who, as must honestly be admitted, is generally not only unworthy of love but may rather deserve hostility and even our hate, since he does not display the least love or consideration for us. Indeed, he does not hesitate to harm us if it benefits him, or if he finds pleasure in so doing. If the commandment had read: 'Thou shalt love thy neighbour as thy neighbour loveth thee,' it would seem wiser and more acceptable. The exhortation to 'love thy enemies' raises even greater difficulties. Freud argues thus: As long as the incontestable conflicts between 'good' and 'evil' remain in force, obedience to these exalted ethical commands must injure cultural intentions, since evil is directly encouraged.

> The often denied reality behind all this is that man is not a gentle, lovable being. . . . He must also reckon a considerable number of aggressive leanings among the instincts bestowed on him. As a result his neighbour is, for him, not merely a possible helper and a sexual object, but also a temptation to satisfy his own aggressiveness, to exploit the other's labour without compensation, to use him sexually without his consent, to seize his belongings, humiliate him, cause him suffering, martyrize and kill him.

Now, if the epithet evil could be originally applied to those factors which curbed man from satisfying his own instincts, and only later, in a transferred sense, to those rendering communal life more difficult, the above remarks together form a single but many-faceted picture of human life, in which dark and light, love and hate, life and death, all have an equal share. Who, after all the present experiences of life and history, is bold enough to challenge the maxim '*homo homini lupus*'? asks Freud; and must we not admit that, despite all exertions, this effort to put love towards our neighbour into effect has not led to much?

We all reach the point when we have to relinquish as illusions the hopes we pinned in our youth to our fellow-men, and must learn how much their ill-will has complicated and embittered our lives. It would be wrong in so doing to reproach culture with wishing to exclude struggle and competition from human activities. These things are assuredly indispensable, but difference of interests is not necessarily enmity; it is only misused to cause it.

The Communists, so Freud polemizes, claim to have found the means of deliverance from evil: according to them, man is un-equivocally good and well-disposed to his neighbour, but the system of private property has spoilt his nature. Possession gives him power, tempting him thereby to abuse his neighbour. Freud is not concerned with criticizing the economic system; but he finds the psychological premises of Communism to be empty illusions. Property is only the tool—and not the strongest, at that—of the human lust for aggression. He also opposes the claim that 'all men are equal', since 'nature, by the utterly different qualities and mental gifts of the individual, has committed an injustice against which there is no appeal.' It is fitting in this context to mention Freud's social leanings, which he voices more than once in his books.

The dramatic image of the ambivalent conflict, the eternal battle between Eros and the death wish, leads us on to the thesis that this conflict flares up as soon as man is confronted with the task of living in a community. Is there never to be an end to this battle, in which Freud sees human life as a planet rotating on its own axis while it circles round a central body? The opposition between the original instincts of love and death allows a final reconciliation in the individual 'such as we also hope one day to see in culture.' The Superego in a cultural epoch rests on the impression which great leading personalities, men of prodigious mental strength, leave after them. The ideals concerning human relationships are summarized as an ethical code, which is to be regarded as a therapeutic means. The bright spot in the assessment of our present situation is that, unlikely as it appears at first sight, men's estimation of values is unreservedly guided by their desire for happiness, and thus embodies an attempt to support their illusions by reasoning.

The question of human fate is whether and how far mankind's cultural development can gain control over the disturbances in community life due to the human instincts of aggression and destruction. In this respect the present time is perhaps particularly interesting. Mankind has now gained so much power over the forces of Nature that it can with their help eradicate itself to the last man. Men know this; hence much of their present unrest, their unhappiness, their anxiety feelings. And now it may be expected that the other of the two 'heavenly powers', the eternal Eros, shall endeavour to play his part in the struggle with his similarly immortal antagonist.

Can we hope for this? And what attitude is to be expected from the great human masses that, as has been so forcibly brought home to our age, are so easily influenced? The further implications of the question are even more intriguing. In our innermost doubts, we are wont to turn not to the public but to its most subtle antithesis, the writers—as men in Antiquity turned to the seers, to the oracle. What answer do we get from those writers whom we look upon as our contemporaries? Do they try to recognize the unconscious powers to be able to control them, as did Freud, or do they side with those powers which unreservedly undermine the attempts to civilize *homo sapiens*? 'Zarathustra,' says Nietzsche, 'the first psychologist of good, is by that same token a friend of evil.' Of the true meaning of man's actions, to which he assigns value, he says: 'Actions are something quite different from what we think they are.' N. S. Leskov tells us: 'A man's character cannot be judged from his well-considered deeds—only spontaneous actions reveal it.' These are the only ones he sets store by. What a feast of uninhibited emotions Montherlant offers us in his works! One recalls with horror a scene where a kind of blood wedding is celebrated, when a Frenchman in the war shoots his first German in the face. What elevating end is intended by Joyce's 'internal monologues' of unbridled lewdness? In André Gide's *Les caves du Vatican*, Lafcadio says: 'I live unconsciously. I have murdered as in a dream, a nightmare, in which I roam aimlessly ever since.' This attitude to life is also typified in a dialogue from Joseph Conrad, where one speaker says that there is only one remedy, only one thing which can cure us from being ourselves; and the other replies that, strictly speaking, the question is not how one is cured but how one can live. Gide's '*acte gratuit*' is a spontaneous action of the inner, hidden, real Ego (Id) that frees itself from the society-made chains of the outer, artificial Ego. The ideas of D. H. Lawrence or of Mauriac have similar foundations—save that the former finally rebels; the latter never ceased to glorify the Catholic Church. But should there come a writer who was more deeply moved by the sickness of the time than by the conflicts of his own soul, who forebore to serve his own subjective idiosyncrasies and threw himself into one scale to send up the other containing the new vision of man's relationship to the Universe, then modern man would honour him, as much as Antique man esteemed Homer, and his truth would be 'the revelation of a modern irrationalism which unequivocally resists every abuse.' So much for the writers.

Now, asks Freud, what does the massed group do, how does it become able decisively to exert influence on the mind of the individual, and what are the mental changes which it enforces on him? Freud proceeds from Le Bon's *Psychology of the Masses*, where the main characteristics of the individual absorbed into the group are given as obliteration of the conscious personality, rule of the unconscious personality, the standardization of thoughts and feelings by suggestion and contamination, and the tendency to put the suggested ideas into effect without delay. The individual has become an automaton without will. Le Bon draws a parallel between the group mind and the mental life of primitive man and children. The group is impulsive, unstable and readily excitable. It is uncritical and thinks in pictures; its emotions are always simple and effusive. He who would affect the group needs no logical foundations for his arguments: he must exaggerate and say the same thing over and over again. As the group has no knowledge of doubt, it is intolerant and believes in authority. It wants to be mastered and kept down, and wishes to fear its master. The individual inhibitions disappear; all cruel, brutal, destructive instincts, the dormant residue of a more primitive age, are aroused. For the group, the most contradictory ideas can exist side by side and be reconciled with one another, without any conflict arising from their logical incompatibility. The group has never known the thirst for truth; it craves illusions. It is a docile herd that cannot live without a master. He, in his turn, must be swayed by a strong faith and possess an inspiring will. Le Bon has less to say about the leader personality. His mysterious, irresistible power, which Le Bon calls prestige, is the dominion which an individual or an idea exerts over the group.

A more modern work, José Ortega y Gasset's *La rebelion de las Massas* (The Revolt of the Masses) goes more topically into these problems. Yet far greater importance must be ascribed to Freud's study of group psychology, since, by laying bare 'the roots', he has shown us how eventually to neutralize the danger of abuse by the masses. First of all, he distinguishes between groups of a short-lived kind (as Le Bon's) and the more stable group formations. He also speaks of natural, homogeneous groups, consisting of similar individuals, and non-homogeneous, artificial groups, i.e., those which also need some external force to keep them together: that is to say, primitive and highly-organized formations. Here, the problems can, of course, only be indicated; our concern in this essay is to piece them into a unified picture of our cultural epoch. In his book, *The Group Mind*, William McDougall has given the following features to the highly-organized groups: continuity of existence, the individual's conception of the mission of the group, the group's position *vis-à-vis* another one, tradition, established customs and institutions, and finally a hierarchic gradation in the achievements of the individual members. Freud found that neither Le Bon nor McDougall had investigated any of the relations, accepted as a matter of course, between group and leader and between the individual members themselves; and, further, that neither author had actually added anything new to what was already known. Above all, Freud introduced the term 'libido' into group psychology (*Group Psychology and the Analysis of the Ego*), and tried to establish the emotional relations determining the essence of the group mind. He tested the basic principles primarily on two highly-organized artificial group formations: the Church and the army. Both have a common overlord, who has the same feelings towards all the individuals under him. Christ expressly emphasized His equal love to all men. It may be objected that, in the army, the concepts of fatherland, national honour and common danger have more weight. But we need only think of great generals such as Caesar, Wallenstein or Napoleon, to be convinced of the importance of the emotional relation. Disregard of the libidinal factor in the army leads, in great danger, to panic and loss of spirits. The emotional bonds between the individual soldiers themselves also constitute an important factor. As regards schism in the religious group, the rôle played by fear in the army is assumed by the ruthless and hostile impulses towards other persons who were originally all bound together by Christ's equal love for all. Intolerance to those outside the community exists both in religious and other group formations; as, for example, the socialistic ones of our own times.

The leader and the leading ideas may also be negative. Hate can unite just as well as love (Freud speaks of a common source of love and hate). The psychoanalytical term 'identification' throws further light on the relation between group and leader, in that Freud explains that the group consists of a number of individuals who see their ideal Ego in one and the same person, and who have consequently identified themselves in their Egos with one another. If this explains the lack of independence and initiative in the group individual and the stereotyped nature of his reaction, we still need an explanation for the return of his mental capacity to an earlier, more primitive plane. In his book, *Instincts of the Herd in Peace and War*, Wilfred Trotter describes the herd instinct of the group. For Freud, this instinct is by no means unaccountable: it must have its history. And he discovers it to be the resurrection and continuance of the original herd in its typical form: the overstrong individual in the midst of a band of followers. This explains suggestibility. In conformity with this, group psychology is the oldest human psychology. Now, what influence does the group exert on what is going on around us? The most terrible manifestation of group psychology is without doubt war. Freud attributes this in part to the desire to destroy, and does not forget to mention that no animal species turns so furiously on its own kind as does man. The anxiety feelings which can be noticed in our times also express a sense of guilt; it is the conscience, which springs from the Superego. The disappointment felt by cultured Europeans at the outbreak of so bloody an event as the First World War is ascribed by Freud to the collision of an illusion with reality, which shattered it. Men have not sunk as deep as was feared, just because they have by no means risen to the heights expected of them. (On the topic of War and Death.)

'For the moment, the nations obey their passions far more than their interests. They use their interests at most to rationalize their passions; they intrude their interests to enable them to find grounds for their passions. In these grievous circumstances, it may be that only a later development will be able to make any change.'

Once again, perhaps, this hope calls forth our doubt—a doubt fostered by bitter experience. Has not Freud himself discovered the ambivalence of the feelings—hate rising from love, the endless conflict between love and the destruction wish?

Einstein writes in his correspondence with Freud:

> You show with irresistible clarity how the instincts of aggression and destruction are inseparably bound up in the human soul with those of love and the will to live. But from your authoritative representations there also clearly emerges the burning wish to attain the noble goal of man's deliverance from the horrors of war, both within and outside himself. This supreme desire has been expressed by all those who, raised above their epoch and their nation, have been venerated as leaders in spiritual and moral spheres. All minds are at one on this point, from Jesus Christ Himself to Goethe and Kant.

Yet Einstein has to admit that these men, however much revered, had little influence on the political course. Freud has taught us to distrust illusions, however much this fearful perspective robs life of hope; and we have to ask ourselves whether Freud himself has seen an escape out of chaos, and if there exists for him any salvation from perpetually recurring destruction. In *The Future of an Illusion*, a work amongst the finest in the modern German style, and comparable to Plato's dialogues not solely by virtue of its formal quality, Freud attacks the problem of culture, the world of faith and struggle in its entirety. The single notes ring out as in a well-co-ordinated orchestra: question and answer, theme and response in a symphonic whole. There grows up before us a new man who, freed from the shapes of his own world of imagination, dares to take the step out of bloody chaos into a better future. Freud has not only freed his generation from a hypocritical sexual code, he has revealed to modern man the deep meaning in the old legend of Achilles, who was only vulnerable at the spot where his mother held him fast when she dipped him into the Styx. Freud is a mentor to those just taking the step from youth to manhood.

Let us proceed from the view that every culture rests on the urge to work and the denial of instincts. The oldest of the suppressed instincts are incest, cannibalism and murder. Two of them are still practised. They form the innermost kernel of an antagonism to culture. While cannibalism seems normally unthinkable, the strength of the incestuous instincts is implicit in their prohibition, and murder is committed—more, ordained by our culture in certain conditions. Freud concludes from this that other wish-fulfilments now fully recognized will come to be regarded as unthinkable as that of cannibalism. He opposes the assumption that the human mind has undergone no change since its first beginnings and, in contrast to the progress made by science and technology, should still be the same as at the start of history.

The strengthening of the Superego is a very valuable cultural asset. Antagonism to culture is sown in certain classes because they further culture by their work but have no share in its benefits. As long as these classes remain frustrated to this extent, this culture will contain a permanent measure of discontent which will lead to dangerous revolts. The antagonism to culture in these classes is so immediately striking as to overshadow the more latent antagonism in the more privileged classes. It is unnecessary to point out that a culture which leaves to many of its possessors dissatisfied, and which incites them to revolt, neither has nor deserves any prospect of permanence.

The moral level of the cultural man is not his only intellectual asset. There is also the wealth of ideals (i.e., the veneration of pre-eminent values, towards which he should put forth all his strength) and the creations of art, together with the satisfaction to be gained from these two. Perhaps the most weighty part of a culture's spiritual content is made up of its religious conceptions. Freud asks what constitutes the particular value of these conceptions. 'Life is difficult for the individual as for mankind in its entirety.' Its privations come from culture, from other men, and finally from Nature, whose influence is felt as a destiny. Culture assumes the defence of mankind against destiny by giving them comfort and by satisfying their thirst for knowledge. This it does by conceptions which have developed throughout countless generations, and which the individual would never be capable of finding on his own. The first step towards the humanization of Nature left man admittedly defenceless, but no longer helplessly paralysed. This situation has an infantile prototype; the little child feels itself equally helpless against its parents, whom it has cause to fear (especially its father), but of whose protection it is sure. Primitive man did not translate the forces of nature quite simply into human beings, but he gave them a father character, made them into gods. The first realization that natural phenomena were bound by laws caused the human features to fade, 'but man's helplessness remained, and with it their father longings, and the gods.' The gods retain their threefold task; to banish fear of Nature, to reconcile man with the cruelty of fate, particularly as manifested in death, and to redress the suffering and privation inflicted on mankind by community life. This situation soon shifted. The gods intervene in Nature only on isolated occasions, by miracles; fate seems inexorable (the Greeks had a foreboding that the Moira was stronger than the gods); all the more does morality become their province. It now becomes a godlike task to level out the inadequacies and injurious features of culture; the cultural laws themselves have divine origin ascribed to them. To render human infirmity more tolerable, life is subordinated to a higher aim: evolution becomes the manifestation of a superior intelligence, which finally turns everything to good. A kindly providence watches over every man; death is not extinction. The same moral laws which our culture has set up also prevail as evolution; all good actions are finally rewarded, all evil is punished —if not in this world, then after death. Thus, all the fears, sufferings and tribulations of life are destined to be wiped out.

Religious conceptions are now regarded as dogma, as statements of the facts and conditions of outer and inner reality; and they demand that men shall believe in them. How can we be convinced of their truth? To prove the earth is round, science gives us Foucault's pendulum experiments, the curvature of the horizon, the possibility of circumnavigating the world. The religious tenets base their claims on the fact that our first ancestors believed in them, that proofs have been handed down to us from prehistory and that, in any case, we *may* not question their validity. 'Our forefathers,' polemizes Freud, 'who backed up their great predecessors' criticism with psychological proof' which sought to solve these problems, were far more ignorant than we are; they believed in things which we to-day could not possibly accept. The proofs they left behind are embodied in writings which themselves bear all the signs of unreliability: they are contradictory, overelaborated, falsified. We therefore find that 'those very utterances of our cultural epoch which might have swayed us most, which aimed at elucidating the riddle of the world and reconciling us with life's sufferings, are those with the weakest foundations.'

The analytical exposition of religious concepts shows that they are not distilled from experience or form the result of thought, but are illusions, fulfilments of humanity's oldest, strongest, most clamorous wishes. The secret of their strength lies in the strength of those wishes. When Freud adds that 'illusion' is not the same as 'delusion', nor need it necessarily be a delusion, he defines an illusion as derived from human wishes. Since the religious concepts are illusions and unprovable, none should be forced to regard them as true. 'As none can be forced to belief, so none can be forced to non-belief.' Freud goes further: 'Ignorance is ignorance.' Science seems to us the only way which can lead us to a knowledge of the reality outside ourselves. Intuition and preoccupation with self can only tell us about our mental life, but can never enlighten us on those questions which religious doctrines have taken upon themselves to answer. When it was objected that psychoanalytical cultural research had gone to the trouble of depriving mankind of 'a valuable wish fulfilment, and sought to replace it with intellectual fare,' Freud rejoined that 'there was more danger to culture in maintaining the present attitude to religion than by dispersing it.' According to him, psychoanalysis is a method of research, an unbiased instrument, rather like the calculation of the infinitesimal. It is conscious that

religion has been of great service to humanity, has done much to suppress the asocial instincts, but not enough. It has had time to show what it can achieve. If it had been able to make the bulk of mankind happy, comfort them and reconcile them with life, make them bearers of culture, it would not occur to anyone to make any change in the present state of affairs. But what do we see instead? That an alarmingly large number of men are dissatisfied with culture, are unhappy in it, feel it as a yoke which they must shake off; that men either exert themselves to the utmost to change this culture, or go so far in their antagonism that they quite simply repudiate culture and control of the instincts. Here the objection might be raised that this situation has arisen precisely because religion has lost some of its influence over human groups, above all as a result of the lamentable effects of scientific progress. . . . It is doubtful if men were substantially happier in the days when religion ruled supreme than we are now; they were certainly not more moral. They always knew how to make the religious decrees into something merely external and according to the letter, and thereby nullifying their intentions. . . . Men sinned, and then made a sacrifice or did penance —and so were free to sin afresh. Russian inwardness has reached the conclusion that sin is essential to human enjoyment of the full bliss of the divine grace—that is to say, is fundamentally an action pleasing to God.

In all ages, immorality has found no less support in religion than has morality. If religion can show no better results as regards man's happiness, devotion to culture and moral conduct, the question again arises whether we do not overestimate its necessity to mankind, and if we are wise in founding our cultural claims on it.

'The more humanity is introduced to the treasures of our knowledge, the more does it turn away from religion, first from its outward, repelling guise, but afterwards from its fundamental principles. . . . Culture has little to fear from the educated and intellectual worker.' As regards the uneducated mass, there are only two possibilities. 'Either the most stringent suppression of these dangerous groups, the most careful preclusion from all opportunity of spiritual revival, or else a thorough revision of the relationship between culture and religion.' Freud does not only demand that cultural laws shall be traced back to social exigencies; by way of example, he also proves in *Totem and Taboo* that the ban on murder springs from the repression of a definite historical fact, patricide, and ordains that 'the consequences of the repression should be replaced by the results of rational scientific work. Our task of reconciling man with culture would thereby receive a far-reaching solution.'

The only way in which man can control his instinctual life is by his intelligence. 'Is it to be expected that people who are forcefully commanded not to think should be able to attain the psychological ideal, i.e., the supremacy of the intellect?' Man will assuredly find himself in a difficult situation; he will no longer be the centre of creation, no longer the object of a kindly providence's tender cares. 'But, surely infantilism is destined to be overcome? Man cannot remain a child for ever; he must eventually enter the "hostile world". This could be called education to reality. Do I now need to disclose that the sole purpose of my book is to draw attention to the need for this development?' And Freud continues in a truly Goethean spirit:

> Something is already gained if man knows he has to rely on his own powers. He then learns to use them properly. Mankind is not wholly without aids: since the days after the Flood, science has taught him much, and it will continue to grow in strength. What pleasure can he get from visions of a great estate on the moon, whose returns have as yet been glimpsed by none? As an honest small-holder on this earth, he will know how to make a living from the plot he tills. By relinquishing other-worldly expectations and concentrating all his enfranchised powers on this earthly life, he can in all likelihood reach the stage where life becomes tolerable for all, and culture no longer oppresses any man.

Let us take leave of Freud with the valedictory words he addresses to his imagined opponent: 'The supremacy of the intellect undoubtedly lies in a remote distance, remote but by no means infinite. And when men can foresee that, within human limits and as far as external reality permits, it sets the same goal for itself as you expect to have realized by God, the goal of human love and mitigation of suffering, then we should be able to say that our antagonism is only transient and not irreconcilable. We hope for the same things, but you are more impatient, importunate and— why should I not say it?—more selfish than I and my kind. You would have bliss commence immediately after death; you demand the impossible of it and will not forego the claims of the private individual.' . . . Perhaps our god *logos* is not signally omnipotent and can only fulfil a small part of what his precursors have promised.

'We believe, however, it will be possible for scientific work to experience something of the reality of the world; science has given us proof in numerous results that it is not an illusion. It is reproached with having taught us so little and with leaving so incomparably much more still obscure. But such detractors forget how young it is, how laborious were its first steps, and how infinitely little time has elapsed since the human intellect was acute enough for its tasks. Do not we all err in basing our judgments on too short a period of time? We should take an example from the geologists. The changes in scientific opinions are development—they are progress, not subversion.'

3

PROBLEMS OF LIVING ART CRITICISM

The True Critic is the Patroclus of Art

> The more aesthetics applies itself to trends
> of art, the more it becomes incapable of its
> true task, that of discovering the quality of a
> work of art.
>
> *Max Liebermann:* DIE PHANTASIE IN DER MALEREI

THE questions to be touched on in this essay do not refer to
the entire sphere of the critical approach to and assessment
of art, but confine themselves to a criticism of modern art
—what in France is called *la critique de l'art* as against *l'histoire de
l'art*.

What is implied by the title: On the problems of *living* art criticism? That a theoretical treatment of this subject is only of value
when it is able to affect life, an analysis meaningful only when it
finally leads to a new synthesis; likewise, criticism is only critical
when, with other necessary ingredients, it contains an evaluation
of the purely pictorial elements of the work of art. This question
has appeared to the author as a *living* problem also, because both
art-lovers and artists have a living interest in it, the former to
intensify their awareness of art, the latter because they demand
correct interpretation of their work. If the artist were to question
whether art criticism is justified at all, what interest it serves and
what its aims are, this would seem to strike less at the necessity of
art criticism itself than at the present existence of a gulf between
artists and art critics, at a decadence in art criticism. It is in fact the
protest against the type of critic who is defined as 'a gentleman
who takes ink and paper and writes what he pleases'. The very
nature of the problem that gives such great significance to the
word *living*, implies not a limitation but an extension. The produc-

tive contact of the critic with living art is of such importance
because the art life we experience provides our only means of
learning how artistic creativeness actually takes place, how the
mind of the artist works, how traditional values are given new,
unexpected shapes—briefly, because, from life, we glean experiences by which we can test the truth of theories and hypotheses.
It necessarily follows that living art criticism must seek contact
not only with the work of art and its impression on present-day
people, but also with the artist, the living author of the work.
And how else can the breadth of a personality be more truly
judged than by direct contact with it? The thought that this
might render the critic's judgment less 'objective' does not out-
weigh the advantages accruing from such contact between artist
and critic. If the artist's judgment proves more correct, it can
hardly harm the critical attitude of the critic. On the other hand,
a critic of sound judgment, knowledge and instinct can mean
much for the artist. The direct contact between artist and critic
also makes possible a critical confrontation of the intentions of the
artist with the work in which he has realized them. Art historians
have gone to infinite pains to reconstruct little-known details of
the lives of great artists, not only from an interest in their person,
but also because they know how much time and environment
affect creativeness. The careers of great artists stimulate succeed-
ing generations of artists and have a moral effect on all those who,
in the lives of these artists, would see a high endeavour towards an
exalted goal, thus obtaining a close view of the daily struggle for
poetry and beauty and the will to enrich art with new values.
There is another, even greater purpose than this biographical and
moral one, which could be outlined as follows. The art critic has
approximately the same relation to the work of art as the naturalist
to Nature. If Nature could provide a being who could answer her
students' eager questions as freely as the artist willingly communi-
cates with the beholder, who will deny that the naturalist could
rejoice in results which he might otherwise never reach? We are
deeply grateful for the conversations with great artists which have
come down to us, and for each line in which they themselves embody their thoughts and their feelings. Modern art scholars
should recognize the great worth of the accounts of the lives of
modern artists resulting from direct contact with the subjects.
The art critic is dependent on the problems which encounter the

artist in his work, as is clearly proved by the mass of faulty interpretations and confusing definitions and concepts generated by modern stylistic trends. Only living contact with the artist can establish unequivocally what he had in mind. It would therefore be an inspiring task to write the lives of a whole generation of artists, and by discussions, conversations, correspondence and personal observation lay the foundations for an assessment of present-day art which would surely be far more stable than any incidental comment, and of infinite importance to historical perspective.

For the art critic, the requirement of living contact with the artist is necessarily linked with a revision of the concept of tradition. The custom in art history is to start at the beginnings of art as we know them and work forward to our own times. The creative artist does not see tradition as something impersonal and linear. He experiences it more concentrically, from the starting-point of his own creative will—the formative will of the present, our own age. The line of vision is thus reversed; from the present to the past. Thus the artist finds anchorage in life itself and can dispense with a fruitless journey in the wake of his predecessors, following the track of art 'development' through one art epoch after another. Only in the sphere of technique, can the idea of development be fully accepted. There is no mechanical logic in creativeness, however; often the development proceeds by leaps and bounds; it follows its own innate urge divorced from that of chronology and causality. It is difficult to speak in art of a development to something higher. Our present day has taken impulses from primitive peoples and ages even in the technical sense. And when twentieth-century city-dwellers find sources of inner life in the art of the primitives, we can hardly speak of development in the ordinary sense.

Every critical question can penetrate to the essentials of the problems of art. An art critic whose mind has a unifying tendency, the innermost ramifications of whose ideas form a world view, has a surer and more steady grip on his task than one who merely allows himself to float on the changing moods of the moment, or whose limited personal register cannot admit anything in the living generation which is greater than or different from himself. Sentimental criticism and that prompted by resentment, the criticism of unsuccessful artists, and that which is dictated by art-political reasoning—cultivated by cliques, groups, partisanship due to other than purely artistic reasons, such as humanitarian, social, class-conscious, and so on—are harmful to art criticism as such. An obvious question arising in this connection is whether there can be any absolute and objective art criticism. It has to be answered in the negative. Just as there is no absolute truth accessible to man's mind, so also is there no objective attitude to a work of art. The most paradoxical consequences could be deduced from this statement, and, indeed, these are often verified in practice. They can, however, be avoided by not regarding as criticism one which does not display certain significant elements. What are these elements, and what must the critic do to make his subjective judgment valid? The first question concerns the substance of the criticism, the second that of the critic.

In his foreword to *La vie littéraire*, Anatole France upheld the standpoint of subjective criticism as the only possible one:

> Objective criticism is no more possible than is objective art, and all those who pride themselves on having put anything other than themselves into their work are victims of the most deceptive philosophy. The truth is that one can never get away from oneself . . . we are shut up in our personality as in a permanent prison. The most we can do, it seems to me, is to accept this bitter state of affairs cheerfully, and admit that we are speaking of ourselves every time we have not the strength to keep silent.

The battle between the subjective and the objective approach in art criticism is a manifestation of the battle for liberal principles in art, in the sense that no absolute laws of beauty and taste, having a restrictive influence upon artistic creativeness or approach are now recognized. The notion of the existence of absolute beauty goes back to Plato's conception of the ideas as the sole and perfect prototypes of the sensible world. In Winckelmann's, Schopenhauer's or Adolf Hildebrand's aesthetics one canon of beauty only, and one single standard, that of the Classic period, was acknowledged. While liberal criticism prevents us from judging from one historically fixed point, it may drive us into a relativity that does away with all values. This may turn out to be the new Inferno of our time. If everything one sees merely calls up a subjective judgment, then these subjective judgments must all have an equal justification. Is an evaluation possible at all in that case? Against this apparent fact, life pits a true one in the shape of the personality. It is solely thanks to the personality, to the *fluidum* it sends out and the convincing strength it imparts, that an evaluation is possible. Great art is the art of great artists. They have with their work created values which in all ages kindle new life in new personalities.

The yardstick of the world is man. Was it this that made Buffon write: *Le style est l'homme même*? Man is also the yardstick of the art critic. A blurred medium reflects the objects as dim and blurred, while in a clear mirror they stand out pure and clear. And just as a glass cannot contain the whole contents of a living spring but only an infinitesimal part of it, so a beholder of limited capacity can neither grasp the accomplishment offered by a really great artist, nor understand all that is lacking in a mediocre dauber.

There is little real weight in Picasso's demand: 'Everyone wants to understand art. Why not try to understand the song of a bird? Why does one love the night, the flowers, everything around one, without trying to understand them?' The new, often very personal formal principles of our day rule out the traditional approach and confront the beholder with something which intrigues but at the same time baffles him.

Art criticism has consequently developed with special vigour during the last fifty years. The new Renaissance of art has resulted in the triumph of modern art principles which revolutionized the vision and the artistic feeling of the West. The battle of aesthetic prejudices against new principles was initiated. Emanating from the art centre, Paris, in fulfilment of that city's artistic mission, the change spread to other countries. This new Renaissance in art was accompanied by a slow change in the attitude of art critics. Concepts and methods of visual approach were reassessed, and a new opinion on art matters grew up among the general public.

The necessity of art interpretation is incontestible. To understand and to pass judgment is a primitive need in the man eager for knowledge; and were there no professional criticism there would certainly be that of conversational exchange, the oral criticism of which Sainte-Beuve says: The real criticism in Paris emerges in conversation, and the critic would achieve his most complete and truest results by listening to all sides and making a discriminating compilation of the opinions expressed.

Quality in Art and Criticism

Pas de critique sans une critique de la critique.

Paul Valéry

What are the characteristics of a true critic? The creative power of his intuition and judgment, a deeply-felt relationship with art achieved by personal endeavour, his character and the moral awareness of his task. It is by no means only his method or the lack of it which characterizes a critic—it is personality or absence of personality. Otherwise, a layman would only have to acquire the critical vocabulary to be entitled to criticize. But the true critic, who feels called upon to be a champion of art's sublime mission, and as such to enjoy and use his independence, regards criticism less as a profession than a vocation. Like the artist he must be extremely sensitive, receptive. He, too, is creative. He has daily to contrive afresh a living relation with the work of art. It is not bestowed upon him by any dogma or charter; either he acquires it or he does not. The difference between him and the artist lies in the sphere of their experience—on the one hand art, on the other Nature. The artist interprets Nature, while the critic interprets the work of art. Read Beaudelaire's *Salons* or Ruskin's *Modern Painters*, read what Stendhal had to say on the Italian painting of the Renaissance, read Valéry's essays or Proust's statements on art, follow Jens Thiis in his defence of Edvard Munch, and Julius Meier-Graefe's fight for the recognition of van Gogh, or Roger Fry's for that of the supremacy of French Post-Impressionism; read Herbert Read's and F. X. Šalda's efforts to defend the modern movement in art in England and Bohemia respectively; read the essays August Brunius wrote as champion of the Fauvist generation of Swedish artists in 1909—and you will see what is meant. The true critic fights for honesty, greatness and purity in art; he pricks the dulled conscience, with the high ideal ever before his eyes that *genius* is the spiritual goal of man's life, forming and directing the aspirations of the nation. Generations live from one genius. The true critic knows this. He sees the supremacy of the masters, both past and present, for it is they who provide him with a criterion of greatness and virtue. If the age has no great men, he must cry out for them and criticize the ephemeral tin gods of the day, relegating them to their proper place. It is here that criticism actually begins, for the critic is filled with devotion for the supreme. He solves for the layman the difficult question of who shall and who shall not be honoured. Therefore, true criticism is the natural function only of him who, born for love and admiration of art, has been mocked and betrayed by the meretricious and inferior. Criticism is a form of scepticism, bitter because it is always obliged to pass sentence, yet building up where it tears down (F. X. Šalda). For the demolition of true criticism is a building-up from the idealistic viewpoint. There, too, is a creative element. The critic has a direct function in life in that he influences contemporary judgment. In acknowledging the truly inspired artist he helps to form the spiritual vision of the people. Enough has been said to show that reason alone cannot accomplish a critical work, that no theory can do duty for the living heart and the receptive mind, and that the critic must possess greatness to understand and experience greatness. Criticism is not a purely rational activity; it is a part of the creative process of art itself, and the artist unable to criticize would be pitiable indeed.

If honesty in art is the critic's pursuit, it follows that he must condemn everything that threatens this honesty and adulterates that true enjoyment of art which is one of the purest sources of mankind's rejuvenation and one of its means to liberate itself from the bonds of a world of delusions and violence. Consequently, he must above all consider the formative side, the quality of the presentation, the 'language' used by the artist to express his world. Every work of art conveys a spiritual experience; but in the means it employs it is a product of craftsmanship which can as such evoke joy and love. It is too often forgotten that the most important argument in judging the worth or worthlessness of a work of art is found in its quality, the mastery of the constituent elements and the harmony or disharmony between them; and that this argument must therefore be given pride of place in the critical assessment. Is it not strange that the name of criticism is given to that which is none, where the formal presentation is given no mention among all the secondary characteristics of the work? Let us look at the great works of art throughout the ages in Europe and Asia, whether primitive or highly civilized, romantic or classical—they all bear the hallmarks of quality. This has always been recognized; and countless are the pronouncements such as van Gogh's: 'A painter must work on his technique inasmuch as he wishes to give better, truer, more inward expression to his feelings,' or Max Liebermann's: 'In plastic art, the spiritual perfection is at the same time technical perfection, for here content and form are not only one, but identical.' It is the quality of the work of art alone that makes it a work of art.

It was with regard to this judging of quality that modern art criticism found itself in a changed situation after the new principles of art had become established. For the generations prior to the Impressionists, the aim of art was technical accomplishment. We speak of a perfectionist tendency. Later on the human component was stressed and the expressive quality was given preference. This can be understood from Gauguin's dictum that if his right hand proved to be too skilful, he would draw with his left hand, and if even that seemed to him too easy, he would not hesitate to use his foot. This new principle has, however, also a purely negative aspect. Previously, the critic has seldom been up against a case of a painter's lacking a certain fundamental standard. The artists were always skilful craftsmen who understood their *métier* and, as was customary in every other craft, had been apprenticed to one or more masters. Or they had learnt to control their tools in a school or by intensive self-instruction. The disregard of questions of quality, so important to all true art, was reserved for subsequent generations and their want of patience. The desire for personal expression eclipsed the desire to give this expression a solid artistic form. Such integrity of presentation became increasingly ignored, and works flouting all tradition in this sense were produced on the conscious or unconscious pretext of expressiveness, disregarding the primary rules of art. Even if there is no reason to doubt the sincerity of an inner experience, it must be remembered that the experience does not make the artist. A work's deficiencies can be concealed by endless expedients; the ornamentally-decorative quality, the topographical or the religious content; furthermore, there is the appeal to the sentimentality of the beholder, and last but not least the charm of the sketch. Having been struck with the frequent appearance nowadays of unfinished or half-finished works in exhibitions, and understanding that such substitution of uncompleted for completed work is a phenomenon of the times, we must pity the art that is capable only of these 'feverish attempts'. The attitude of tolerance to unfinished work has gone so far that at present things are put on show that are only fit to serve as a rough sketch in the artist's studio. Everything that is conceived and given form needs time to come to maturity. So much must be discarded on the way—ideas missing the truth by a hair's-breadth, incidentals, mistakes. But nowadays, distinctions are not to the point; and, in the general hustle, the artist seems to have no time to spare for the mature work. This problem, however, has also another side. It is Picasso who once said that an artist has to learn the difficult art of how not to finish a painting.

There is a close resemblance between the way a work of art affects us, and the way in which it was brought into being. If the latter process needs time to mature, the former also needs time to show whether the work is genuine, or merely of occasional or superficial character. How, then, can a criticism be reliable when written down after an often merely fleeting inspection, because the newspaper—the personified demon of the times—requires that 'guide to the evaluation of art' so necessary to the public, immediately after a private view? The purveyance of news, the contact which the criticism of the day must maintain with a wide public not well versed in artistic questions, starts official art assessment on lines other than those indissolubly linked up with serious appreciation.

Journalistic criticism is a spontaneous criticism, often an expression of art-political interests, and its very connection with the daily press gives it a special position. It is for this reason that it often takes its most primitive form here, that of descriptive criticism. Unduly personal perspectives also enter into it, and the review frequently exhausts itself either in undefined attacks or glorification, conveying no positive sense of the viewpoint that prompts them. As a historical example of descriptive criticism, I quote the Greek poet Lucian on a work of the painter Zeuxis:

I am not sufficiently initiated to pronounce on the other beauties of this painting, whether the artist has succeeded in combining the different elements that constitute a perfect picture, such as the accuracy of the drawing, the truthfulness of the colours, the effects of depth and shadow, the exactness of the proportions, and the general harmony; it is for the painter and those who claim to know the rules of art to praise these things. I admire in Zeuxis the ability to display the whole wealth of his genius within a single subject, since he has given the Centaur a fearful and savage aspect.

This is quite intelligent writing—which is not always the case with newspaper reviews—yet it gives no evaluation of the work, but merely the impression it makes. It is noteworthy that Lucian calls himself not sufficiently initiated—an admission that would come hard to a modern critic, who is convinced that when he describes the tone of a landscape and says that it is coarse or sensitive, he has therewith established the artistic value of the work; whereas, in fact, he has merely passed from a description of the subject to a description of the technique. This does not mean there should be no description; description forms part of any art criticism, though less so when there are a fair number of illustrations. Now if, instead of this description, we have an emotional outburst from the critic, are we any nearer an evaluation demanding quite different arguments? Delacroix once wrote of a study by Gautier on the English school:

> He should have had the courage to use *comparison* with other paintings, in which we in France admire the same excellencies, to bring out the merits of the English painters: I find no trace of this. He takes a painting, describes it in his own way, himself produces a picture which is enchanting—but he makes no real criticism. He is satisfied if he can, with a joy that is often conveyed to us, find beautiful words that sparkle and reflect, if he can but quote Spain and Turkey, the Alhambra and Atmeidan in Constantinople. He has attained his goal of being a notable writer, and I fancy he wants nothing further. . . . In such criticism we find neither enlightenment nor philosophy.

Now it is precisely the newspaper critic who has the important task of giving a wide public the first impulse, the first introduction to a deeper penetration into artistic values. Schematic verbalism, a bombastic flow of words, arid enumeration, neglect of artistic evaluation and unreasoning criticism drive the public, the art-dealer, and, above all, the young artist along paths that must in time prove harmful. The great artist imparts a true conception of greatness, and thereby neutralizes those all-levelling, equalizing forces which, nowadays, misunderstanding the democratic tendencies (or perhaps understanding them too well), are always satisfied 'artistically' but never 'economically'; in the same way we require in criticism an authority who, while finding fault, explains why he does so; who educates by passing judgement. But how are we to judge a criticism that is more fully and objectively criticized by the artist than the artist by it? Art criticism should start where the self-criticism of the artist goes astray. Can a non-judging criticism fulfil this demand? Before pronouncing on the work of art, criticism pronounces primarily on the critic himself. It has often been said that a man must himself be a painter to assess painting—as if the epithet painter also implied a qualification to criticize. Were this so, there would be no bad painters.

Criticism plays an enormous part in practical life. The fate of an artist often depends on the criticism he receives. This provides a professional guarantee for the collector, on whom the art-dealer and, on the whole, the ethics of the pursuit of art depend. The critic must feel a responsibility when he knows that, having rather heedlessly helped a young artist to an undeserved success, thereby saving him the trouble of holding his own against criticism and public, and so of maturing, he may be closing his way to genuine art while ushering him into that of easy productivity. Particularly grave demands are put on an art critic in an age when the young artists consider knowledge beneath them and, still immature and ignorant, appear in public with their one-man shows; when they are more imbued with the idea of producing things that are easy to sell than by that of improvement—an age marked by a spreading interest in art among a wider public, in which galleries spring up like mushrooms, each one eager to discover and exploit a new prodigy. Now, is journalistic criticism up to such a task? To be sound, criticism necessarily calls for gradations. Besides the spontaneous brand of the daily press, we must have that of the cultural periodicals and art reviews, concentrating on the quality of the judgments, on formulation and artistic ideals. Formulation is important because it gives the assessment a more definitive form, and because formlessness must not be combated with formlessness. A periodical review that does not answer these requirements is journalistic, in its essence, even when disguised in book form.

It is necessary to keep firm hold of this *idea of quality*, technical and ideological, since it is not important that everything occurring in art shall be dealt with in a periodical; the point is, rather, that everything of value shall be brought out and the faults openly and honestly discussed. Criticism defends the human soul against automatism, and its frequent task, as Brunetière said, is 'to teach man to judge, often contrary to his own taste.'

The critic finds his criterion not in the -ism or the school, but in the distinction between good and bad art. And the qualitative verdict of good or bad implies in itself that it is not the limitation of an artist that evokes a criticism as such. Unquestionably, a painter assumes greater importance if he solves the more important problems of art; and he who paints only landscapes has a narrower range of vision than he who applies himself to both landscapes and figures. A badly painted monumental work has less value than a small still-life displaying pictorial qualities. But if criticism uses the same words for everything, will they not ultimately lose all meaning?

In a time such as ours, when there is a temporary lull in the emergence of new creative ideas, when the young artist should be thoughtfully looking back to see what enduring elements have been thrown up by modern trends, a time which perhaps marks the beginning of a new attitude to art values, the critic, too, must revise his accustomed concepts. Extremes have been abandoned; nobody believes any longer in some one and only dogma of redemption; people are not so artistically keyed up as before, and they often feel at a loss. It is a period for careful assimilation of what has already been gained, of hesitant embarkation perhaps on other courses leading to new heights. An artist who employs already outworn means of expression cannot possibly produce a stirring artistic experience, since such an experience cannot be imparted with these means. An artist of this kind does not create in the true sense of the word; he only reproduces. Moreover, an artist who does not understand that the sole freedom in art is not to do everything he wants but to find his own personal expression, is no artist. Only that measure of strength put into a work can communicate itself to the beholder; and it is also the strength in the conviction of the critic that gives his criticism its value. Qualitative criticism has a qualitative artistic production as a result, and rules out demoralization in the world of art.

The judging of art follows universal rules valid throughout the world. The artist who can nowadays make contact with all artistic products to date through travel, visits to museums and the study of exhibitions and publications, must have at hand a criticism of the same universality. How far would we get if a critique drew a geographical boundary round each country? There is no special English, Swiss or American criticism beside that universally valid.

If an assessment of values disregarded both the great masters of the past and the truly creative artists of the present, the results obtained would inevitably give false perspectives. The national features in art must certainly be observed, but they are on another plane (what is Spanish in Goya and French in Renoir, for example; when we come to El Greco or Chagall, this narrow approach meets with difficulties)—the plane of national tradition, determinative environment, psychological and geographical idiosyncrasy. They do not touch the question of genius and quality.

And Art moves Forward . . .

> But now he discovered unknown beauties in
> works he did not love, and strange faults in
> those he held irreproachable.
> *Gustave Flaubert*, L'ÉDUCATION SENTIMENTALE

I should like to touch on some questions which are closely associated with the revaluation of certain terms and conceptions in the current attitude to art, and whose solution might help us to new and better viewpoints. Above all, there is the question of the artistic *experiment*. It is a sign of the creative will that a work of art is not only labour but also a manifestation of the spirit. The experiment develops, impels the artist to a personal synthesis; it embodies the true valour of the spirit and its challenge to the inclination towards inner ease and outer mass production. In his formulation of the difference between poetry and literature, poetry's eternal value and the temporal one of sheer craftsmanship, Benedetto Croce has made a differentiation which can by analogy also be applied to the plastic arts. If we call the first category artists, what shall we call the second, whose exponents claim that their serial production shall be esteemed art; while, for example, a piece of pottery of outstanding shape and design is to be called handicraft?

Art is the conquest of new values of beauty and form, illogical as life itself, but sustained by an inner necessity. Artistic creation is an act of spiritual discipline, and as such it is in contrast to what is merely spontaneous, expressive, eruptive. It is wrong to think that significant works of art can be produced solely by spontaneity.

The constructive, compositive element, the balancing, ordering, critical spirit is as important to a work as the fire of conviction. If it does not find its pictorial expression, which only attains its personal form by means of experiment, the painting can but aim at creating a mood, and cannot escape the slur of being considered inadequate or limited. It is the lack of these consolidating elements that characterizes the half-finished, merely rudimentary works which were mentioned earlier on. The objection may be raised that the artist is forced to this kind of production on material grounds, as otherwise he would not be able to paint at all: and an artist who has to paint a picture for a low fee cannot give it as much time as a thorough piece of work would require. This objection does not hold water, and merely shows an unduly labile attitude to artistic values. Great artists have been strong enough not to 'sell' themselves; they have followed their vocation under the hardest conditions. The early history of modern art is not that of the easy-going, well-to-do artists mechanically turning out pictures; it is one of saints and martyrs (Courbet, Daumier, Cézanne, van Gogh, Gauguin, Munch, Josephson); this, incidentally, throws a strange light on the idea our modern society has of culture. On the other hand, the Holland of the seventeenth century has shown that a group of artists can live in the best circumstances without detriment to the quality of their production.

The question of the experiment is profoundly connected with the problem of artistic *truthfulness*. When Delacroix broke with the tradition of his time, he did so because he considered its colour muddy, its drawing dead, its ideal rusty. He sought to regenerate painting by the study of Rubens and Tintoretto. When Courbet rose against the literary falsehoods in the art of his time, when the Pleinairists stormed out of the studios and discovered air and light and the lyricism of the atmosphere, when the Neo-Impressionists fought the weak, formal tendencies of Impressionism, they were prompted by no other than purely artistic considerations, with direct bearing on the method of presentation.

The problem of artistic creativeness, the psychology of the artist, dealing with the causes and tensions of the artistic urge, help us to find a new attitude towards that art which is a destiny, a yearning of the soul, in contrast to the mere reproduction of nature—creativeness as opposed to diligence, the inner compulsion as against the mere desire to produce. It was inevitable that depth-psychology should come to dominate when the anthropo-morphic idea of God began to totter. The eye of the artist changed direction and began to plumb humanity. Innumerable modern works of art can be traced back to the influence of 'psychoanalytical' research. This new psychological and humanist approach to artistic creativeness has borne rich fruit. By its help André Malraux has freed himself from his early historico-materialistic viewpoint, to follow Flaubert, Baudelaire and Nietzsche in a new Existentialist formulation of artistic values. Proceeding from psychology and humanism, however, it will be necessary to reach a new attitude to the miracle of life, without which all art and all artistic experience remain a mere substitute.

With every artist, the question of *expression* is posed anew; applicable to each generation is the maxim: *tout reste à faire—tout reste à refaire*. Therefore the age is always waiting for the great artist with the inspired, ordering spirit, who finds expression for his time. And the clinching argument for a *living* art in both painters and critics is that it gives itself passionately to its age, that it produces the only true and palpable present, the most real reality. All else is fluid, an illusion, construction, recollection, without living necessity; tradition without living roots. For this reason the artist's relation to his own time and its reality, to life in general, is of primary importance. Only after this is established does tradition have validity. While the links of tradition can be compared with a long path (horizontally), it is the warm life of the artist that enables him to strike root directly into existence (verti-cally). Therefore, art history and art theory must not lose contact with life either. Is it not precisely because they sprang from the living womb of art that Delacroix's Journal, van Gogh's letters, the aphoristic statements of Cézanne, Gauguin, Braque, Picasso, the programmatic clarity of Matisse mean more for the awareness of art than so many abstract theses written in libraries? By the side of the criticism of the professors and the experts, and the spon-taneous utterances of poets, we have here, as a new factor, the criticism of the great artists.

The question of motif is also one calling for particular attention. Much has been said about non-representational art—that the motif does not determine the true content of the work; while the opposite attitude was called 'literary', meaning that it lay outside the purely artistic approach. Extremes never hold for long. On the one side, time has brought a dissipation of the spiritual content of the work of art, on the other we have—the illustration. Extremes are necessary for a bold thrust forward into hitherto unknown realms of creativeness and inner awareness; the mature art, however, is that of harmony, inner equilibrium, repose, in which the single pictorial elements all work together. The 'human idea', then, has been dispersed, and art was the poorer for it. It seems incontestable that the urge driving the modern artist to expression is the same that brought forth the works of Magic Art, of the art of Byzantium, of Giotto, of El Greco, of Rembrandt. Can the artist leave out man's urge to decipher the hieroglyphics of the eternal mystery of Being when pursuing technical perfection? Certainly not. Nor the serious abstract artist aim at such a goal. Edvard Munch was one of the great painters of our time who had a thorough grasp of the importance of this question. He would never have been able to achieve such strong effects without his technical resources; but without his spiritual profundity his art could not have moved his generation as it did. The same is true of Picasso and Kokoschka.

Though Chardin's Still-life with the Eggs or Manet's Brioches are of sterling quality, the motif in a still-life always expresses another sphere of life than that of ontology. To paraphrase a well-known *aperçu* of Max Liebermann: Even if a badly-painted Madonna has less value as a picture than a well-painted turnip, a well-painted Madonna expresses deeper human contexts than a well-painted turnip. Buth fulfil their function in life—one perhaps in a church, the other in a dining-room or salon. It is the formal imagination which saves the motif from becoming topography or literature. If we think of medieval art and the numerous versions of the Entombment or the Crucifixion of Christ, we see what is meant by the formal imagination of the artist. The motif was there; all depended on the artistry of the presentation and of the spiritual attitude. The generation that ordained motif-less art did not mean it absolutely, for it too had made a choice of motif, and indeed a very precisely defined one. What the Impressionists did—and they stand in the forefront of this development—was to protest against certain historical and literary motifs and conceptions, which in their time had been all-prevailing, the purely artistic viewpoints being pushed into the background. The logical consequence followed: non-representational art. The abstract artist expresses in his style the vacuum created in modern man's consciousness by the absence of an anthropomorphic imagery, forced upon him by an age dominated by abstract scientific thinking. The new artistic viewpoint has triumphed, and from its deficiencies a new art may emerge and reconcile the extremes.

The one-sided acceptance of *intensive colours* must also come in for criticism to-day. Solutions of artistic problems are relative, depending on the exigencies of their time, and they necessarily undergo changes. Colour alone cannot replace the other pictorial elements. A style in which colour predominates will turn its attention to more formal values. From an art-historical viewpoint, the intensification of colour through the Symbolists, van Gogh, Matisse, the Expressionists, Leger, was balanced by the structural ideas of Seurat (Divisionism) and Picasso (Cubism, and Abstract Art). In the realm of expressiveness of colour, no further possibility of development beyond the late van Gogh and the late Matisse is discernible. The periodicity in matters of taste, the natural law of opposites makes itself felt. After dark comes light, after colour form; the two united produce mature, classic art. Thus to-day we are less attracted by that which was revolutionary yesterday, and which perhaps, if it bears the stamp of authenticity, will one day rise again from the darkness of the past as a new truth.

Much has been said about *simplification*, though seldom in connection with the idea of intensification. And yet the simplification which merely uses single pictorial elements with the aim of concentrating their effect is illogical and nugatory without such intensification. As a consequence, shallow simplification has often resulted in a poster-like banalization and attenuation. Is the style of our age to be that of universal simplification and popularization, rendering things easier to grasp, but at the same time spiritually poorer, emptier, more insipid?

The unduly one-sided emphasis on the *elements of rhythmical composition*, such as contrasting and complementary, or warm and cold colours, together with the decorative outline, also contains a certain materialism. For though a picture that satisfies the theoretical demands of Fauvism can be produced by mere routine, without soul, without living warmth, it will remain empty.

We often hear of the English artist's love of *Nature*, of his lyricism and feeling for her. The landscape, often conceived as still-life, and the *nature morte* itself predominate at exhibitions, and the history of modern English art will be primarily the history of landscape and still-life painting. And yet we must be careful about deducing from this fact an absolute national trait. The neglect of figure painting is a serious deficiency, which openly came to light when the movement for a new monumental art set in; artists addicted to the constructive, the ornamental, the expressive, the communication of moods inspired by natural scenery, were confronted with the task of reproducing the human form. The drawing raised difficulties which were not immediately surmountable, and which would not have existed if the young artists had been better equipped for their profession. Their relationship to the human form revealed itself as too superficial, often schematizing, unpsychological, without inner tension, illustrative—this, by the way, and not to our surprise, is also the case with the academic painters who claim the privilege of due instruction in the art of draughtsmanship. One is often astonished to see how the ornamentation on a garment ranks higher than the expression in face and hands or the bodily posture, that flowers are more successfully rendered than the symbolism in an action, that scenery dominates where the human figure should do so. A narrative content glosses over shortcomings in presentation. I have often thought of the words of the old master in Lessing's *Laokoon* to a pupil who painted a very bedizened Helen: 'Since you couldn't make her beautiful, you rendered her rich.'

Many of the deficiencies in present-day art are due to a general lowering of the level of erudition as compared with earlier ages. This is partly connected with the contempt for schooling: either the artist has something to give, we hear, or he has not. And if not, no school will help him. There is no doubt, however, that the artists of former days often had a far richer, more comprehensive and profounder attitude towards spiritual life.

If a man has something to say, it certainly sounds far better if it is not stammered out; a musician's feeling is more clearly expressed if his instrument is in tune and he strikes true notes. Has one ever heard of a genius coming into the world equipped with all the gifts of heaven, and disdainfully passing over everything that others have achieved and known before him? Facts show that this cannot be. Intimately linked herewith is the notion that the artist can draw everything out of himself, rather like a spider. He will owe nothing to any master, any school, any influence. But in reality he is intensely dependent on values of tradition and contemporary creativeness—a fact that never escapes a trained critic. (The critic as detective.) Even if hundreds of thousands of pictures were needed to fill the newlyweds' apartments with colour sensations to enliven the unduly economic and geometric modern architecture, even if the mercantilism of art were to go even farther, the level of artistic quality in the pictures would not be thereby enhanced unless it found its earnest champion in the artist, and a supporter in the critic. The one must paint as if van Gogh, or Picasso or Cézanne, Braque or Klee stood behind him, the other judge as if these masters were to utter their opinion of his ideas.

'Conscious' Primitivism (Naivism) as we meet it to-day embodied, at the start, the aspiration towards a more primordially genuine artistic experience. If the term primitive is made synonymous, however, with genuine, deep, primary, then it applies to all true artists and not only to the primitivists; by this same token primitivism would revoke itself. A link in the officially acknowledged tradition was broken by endorsement of the primitive and popular, and denial of the Renaissance values, by overestimation of the pristine element in pathological art, and in children's drawings. But it was from these very foundations that the resulting primitive mannerism sprang. The concurrent depreciation of technical skill gave rise to the dilemma which brought certain products of art to the brink of dilettantism. Now the same is true of works of art as of human beings: even with the greatest faults they can be lovable. But this must still not hinder the critic from fulfilling his mission. The young artist must find a new synthesis, and the critic must pilot him to a conception of art that gives the qualitative artistic values precedence over the merely subjective ones—this by means of a criticism that is both truly constructive and also didactic. In so doing, he must avail himself of an intensified insight into the history of both art and theory, thereby throwing a bridge from these sciences to the artist and the public. His judgment must be guided both by his sense of quality and his feeling for and understanding of the style of a work as the expression of its inner tension, of the relation of experience and craft—but above all by his *taste*. Like the artist, he must possess *le goût*. Rodin, who had a particular affection for this term, said: 'A man who has knowledge of sculpture or painting without having taste will never make a sculptor or a painter.' He goes on: 'Art is contemplation; it is the pleasure of the thought that penetrates Nature and senses there the spirit with which she herself is animated; it is the joy of the intellect which sees clearly in the universe, and which recreates it through illuminating it by consciousness. Art is man's most sublime mission, since it is the employment of the mind that seeks to understand the world and to render it understandable. . . . Art is, furthermore, taste. It is in all the objects an artist fashions, the reflection of his heart. It is the smile of the human soul over the house and all it contains. It is the charm of the mind and the sentiment incorporated in everything that serves mankind.' Taste is the supreme law, the compass of art.

What is a critic without taste? In one passage in the diary of the Goncourt brothers, we read the following ironic pronouncement:

> The simile is not a lofty one, but allow me, gentlemen, to compare X. to a hunting dog I once had. It foraged, it came to heel, it went through all the business of a hunting dog quite marvellously; the only thing was, *it had no nose*. I was obliged to sell it.

Taste is restricted by the mental limitations of the critic, by his incapacity to adjust his spiritual powers to new artistic phenomena, by the degree of his sensibility. Where is the intellect to encounter the unexpected, if not in art and science? Where is the chameleon-like character of the human mind and heart more forcibly expressed than in its quest of new cross-sections through the riddle of the sensible world? A critic is not worthy of his calling who believes that the constant use of the loud pedal denotes vigour, who does not realize that the strength of a work consists in the artist's having given only a fraction of what he is capable of giving; who does not see the justification in a weak patch or the beauty in an irregular rhythm. A critic who is duped by the mystic or scientific pose of an artist and forgets to judge the genesis of his ideas together with their form, is not worth much. If he does not accept the ineffable that triumphs only in a genuine work, and if he does not set the imagination of the artist above all else, he has no right to criticize.

He is no critic who shies away from making a real critical contribution in the rich, now stormy, now gentle stream of living art, who has a good word for everything he sees. Without evaluation there is no criticism—even if lack of judgement originates in a longing for something extraordinary, because the work in question strikes no chord in the critic (it is the secret of great works of art that they enthrall us and imprint their individuality upon us), and he tries to read into it something that is not there. By his *laissez-faire, laissez-aller* he degrades himself into a mere advertising device for too facile performances, denies through his approval of them the idea of art. Art, which once found its patrons in a circle of persons who were often well versed in such matters, turns to-day to the people as a whole. 'But the ordinary man,' writes F. X. Šalda in righteous indignation, 'does not feel and apprehend the higher values of life; he has only heard their names, he knows of them only by hearsay, indirectly and at twentieth-hand. In this fusty, benighted and base world, there is only one person who enters into and knows reality actively, freshly and constructively, unshakably and positively: the artist.'

Earlier on, the critic addressed himself to the connoisseur and the art-lover rather than to the man in the street. Modern times have put a heavy task upon him. It is the mission of popular education to bring up the people to experience beauty, so that they may share in the creative work of to-day, abolish prejudice and inhibitions more quickly and easily, be a moral support and defender of idealistic interests, guide and influence taste, divide what is essential from what is merely transient, and fight for the genuine and the eternal in art—in all these ways smoothing the path for coming generations.

4

HERBERT READ'S PHILOSOPHY
OF ART

Four Generations of English Art Critics

The great instrument of moral good is the imagination.
Herbert Read: DEFENCE OF POETRY

HERBERT READ deserves his reputation of being the living link in an uninterrupted tradition of thought during four generations of art critics in England. We shall not only find his ideas to be a logical continuation of theirs; together they form an organic unity. We shall also find the reason for it. The present problems of art and education, art and society, art and the harmony of life, have been called forth by the industrial revolution, that working process which has not only changed our way of living but also our mode of thinking, feeling and reacting, the entire status of contemporary human society. We are in the midst of tremendous changes with unpredictable consequences for the whole of mankind. England has been the first country in which this revolution took place and it is therefore natural that England should have produced the thinkers who have seen clearly the danger into which our culture has been thrown. The writings of John Ruskin, of William Morris, of Eric Gill, of Roger Fry and Herbert Read are closely connected with the respective phases of the industrialized society in which they were produced. It would, however, be too narrow to see in Read's works only an organic part of this special English contribution. As has perhaps never been the case before in England, Read is a conscious representative of European thought. He is open to all valuable suggestions from the literature and art of the whole world, of which the main tendency in the sphere of the visual has been the chain of formal revolutions which have occurred during the last five decades in French art. Here he continues the work of Wyndham Lewis, Clive Bell, R. H. Wilenski, but especially of Roger Fry, who was a champion of Post-Impressionism in particular; Walter Pater's interpretation of art and literature, too, resounds in Read's work. Read recognized in the art east of the Rhine a development of the same importance as that of France. He acknowledged at their full value Munch, Kokoschka, Ensor, German Expressionism. The most influential ideas in modern psychology, pedagogy and philosophy come from German-speaking countries: Nietzsche, Marx, Spengler, Freud, Jung, Kretschmer, Prinzhorn, Pestalozzi, Jaensch, Herbart, Cizek—to name only some. Art History and Art Theory have also achieved remarkable results in the German-speaking countries: Burckhardt, Wölfflin, Dvorak, Riegl, Fiedler, Worringer, Schmarsow. They have all contributed to the formation of Herbert Read's opinions, and this English writer might well be compared to a lens concentrating all the relevant ideas of his time on the problem in which he is most interested, namely the problem of art and its function in modern society. It must be mentioned here that a science of art in the sense of the German *Kunstwissenschaft* with its discipline and 'laboratory' work does not exist in England. Through the political development which led to the Second World War, prominent art theoreticians from Central Europe migrated to the U.S.A., where, since then, this branch of science has come to full fruition. In comparison with Germany, Art History has not yet found its full appreciation in the English University either, though conditions during recent years have been more favourable to its acceptance. The first to teach Art History in Oxford was Ruskin in 1869. Roger Fry was Slade Professor of Fine Arts in Cambridge, 1933-34. Herbert Read himself was Professor of Art History in Edinburgh in 1931-33.

What is the most characteristic trend in the leading literature on modern art in England? The English writer on art is an art critic and at the same time a critic of society, using the ideas of contemporary philosophy, psychology and cultural history to support his views. The greatest emphasis will therefore lie on his personality. And *John Ruskin*, with whom we must start, was an outstanding personality. A preacher in the desert one might call him, whose influence in Europe and America has been felt very strongly. His main achievement, but also his greatest weakness, was to emphasize, in Plato's sense, the interrelation of art and morals. Weakness, because his teaching—especially in defending the Pre-Raphaelites—led to the false conclusion that a work of art has to have a direct moralizing tendency or a literary content. Achievement, because there is a connection between art and morals as indeed we see in Plato (*Republic*, 3rd Book and *Laws*, 2nd Book)—a deeper and also more subtle connection than was realized by the Pre-Raphaelites and their standard-bearer Ruskin. Ruskin's crusade against 'Mammonism', his political economy of art, which he developed as a pupil of Carlyle, his social protest, his hatred of industrialism and his love of the fine handicrafts, his educational reform (creative activities were demanded as a part of the curriculum of every student: 'To make carvings, pictures, useful carpentry, not stuffing the memory with gobbets of information, to be disgorged at the next examination') —they all revolve around one ideal, the ideal of beauty. In his introduction to *Modern Painters*, 1888, Ruskin wrote: 'And now, in writing beneath the cloudless peace of the snows of Chamouni what must be the really final words of the book which their beauty inspired and their strength guided? I am able with yet happier and calmer heart than ever heretofore to enforce its simplest assurance of faith that the knowledge of what is beautiful leads on, and is the first step, to the knowledge of the things which are lovely and of good report, and that the laws, the life, and the joy of beauty in the material world of God are eternal and sacred parts of His creation.' This, of course, can be stressed to-day even more than in former times. It happened therefore that, when the Ruskin Society during the last year of the war discussed Ruskin's influence to-day, W. R. Inge pointed out: 'The chief complaint which Ruskin made against our civilization was that it had got its values wrong and, like all Christians, who understood their religion, and all Platonists, he realized most strongly that there are certain eternal, absolute, ultimate values which are generally described as TRUTH and BEAUTY and GOODNESS, which exist in their own right, which cannot be referred to anything else, and which ought to be the aim of every honest man in the world.' This is the real contribution of Ruskin towards the solution of our spiritual crisis, and it was emphasized also by Sir Kenneth Clark in the statement: 'That an age which produces a mass of ugly buildings and ugly objects of daily use must have something fundamentally evil in its composition. An ugly lamp-post is a wicked lamp-post. That, I believe, was Ruskin's supreme discovery.' The aesthetic, and as we see also the moral point of view connected with it, was Ruskin's answer to materialism. He underlined quality against quantity and reached the essence of his philosophy with the words: 'There is no wealth but life; life with all its powers of admiration, hope and love.'

William Morris even more than Ruskin had a direct influence on the development of art as an expression of everyday life, on the appreciation of art's vital importance to human kind. Morris, who had heard Ruskin as an undergraduate in Oxford, not only accepted but also developed his ideas in all directions. We may say that the revival of the *Kunsthandwerk* in all European countries goes back to his ideas and experiments. I remember Oskar Kokoschka telling me that under Morris's influence he not only wrote but also illustrated, printed and bound his first book. On the basis of Morris's ideas the *Wiener Werkstätten* were founded— it was before the First World War—and from it there is a direct line to the *Deutsche Werkbund* and to the *Bauhaus* in Weimar. It is very interesting to note that the *Bauhaus* idea has made a deep impression on Herbert Read, so that we can say that the Englishman has met even English ideas through German mediation. With Morris too we find a close connection between the criticism of contemporary civilization, the notion of art as the only possibility of overcoming the spiritual difficulties, the interrelation of art and morality. Morris spoke of the 'art poverty of the modern world' and he found its roots in the unequal distribution of opportunity for men and women to express themselves artistically, or even to enjoy art. He attacked our civilization in the words: 'Society is based on a state of perpetual war.' And: 'The art of any epoch is necessarily the expression of its social life.' Industrialism was for him a danger, as it contributed to the aesthetic values only with ugliness. He wrote: 'Ugliness of unbeautiful work is dynamic ugliness, for it causes a progressively spiritual deterioration.' Art, for Morris, was 'the divine solace of human labour, the romance of each day's hard practice of the difficult art of living.' It was also 'the beauty of life'. 'What I mean by art,' he wrote in another place, 'is some creation of man which appeals to his emotions and his intellect by means of his senses.' Morris made a distinction between great art and popular art—we would say to-day between art and handicraft. Great art appeals especially to the imagination and is the art of the great masters. Popular art rises out of the wants and desires of men which have to be satisfied by the organized labour of the people. House building, painting, joinery, carpentry, smiths' work, pottery, glassmaking. Morris had a great esteem for this popular art, which is in reality an expression of the health of social conditions. He claimed that 'all things, even the humblest, which are made by man should have this soul-element in them, else they will disgrace the fair face of nature.' It is, in fact, a very unfortunate development which has allowed us to lose the standard of beauty in our activities and, as we shall see, Read claims that only education in a special direction, the education both of youth and of the adult towards an appreciation of beauty, can save us. The education of youth is a slow process, like every growth; a long-term policy, so to speak; the education of the adult must avoid becoming a simple entertainment or leisure, but must lead to opening the minds to the beautiful, providing man with a measuring rod for the comparison of values. Whereas the first method is certain to give good results, if applied systematically, the second is perhaps doomed to remain 'exhibitionist', i.e., cultural values will only decorate an otherwise unbearable way of living, if both do not form a unity. In other words, it will remain a culture which expresses itself only through exhibitions, whereas in a real culture art is the essence of everyday activity. The sculptor *Eric Gill* who, with his friends, formed a little community based on handicraft, once exclaimed bitterly: 'Culture is dope, a worse dope than religion: for even if it were true that religion is the opiate of the people, it is worse to poison yourself than to be poisoned, and suicide is more dishonourable than murder. To hell with culture, culture as a thing added like a sauce to otherwise unpalatable stale fish!' These words: 'To Hell with Culture,' *Herbert Read* has chosen as a title for a booklet in which he deals with new human values. Published during the war, in 1941, it is a paraphrase of the witty statement of Bernard Shaw: 'I am simply calling attention to the fact that fine art is the only teacher except torture,' and a confirmation of the Neo-Platonist's A. N. Whitehead's dictum that 'the most fruitful because the most neglected starting point of philosophic thought is that section of value theory which we term aesthetic.'

The Ethics of Art

In the end art should so dominate our lives that
we might say: There are no longer works of
art, but art only. For art is then the way of life.
Herbert Read: THE PLACE OF ART IN A UNIVERSITY

It was not only the social mentality of the Victorian age during the early stages of industrialism which laid such a blight on all moral and aesthetic values, but also the mechanistic science on which it was based. In his famous lectures on Science and the Modern World, Professor A. N. Whitehead condemned the triumph of materialism and its consequences: 'In the most advanced industrial countries art was treated as a frivolity.' This work made a great impression on Read. He called it 'the most important book published in the conjoint sections of science and philosophy since Descartes' *Discours de la Méthode*. It embodies the material of a revolution in our whole concept of life or being, and seeks to reinterpret not only the categories of science and philosophy, but even those of religion and art.' Revolution, we ask? Was not the revolution against the 'limited moral outlook of the three previous generations' embodied in the Marxian doctrine? We realize now, rather belatedly, that the materialism of one class cannot be fought by the materialism of another class. In his *Critique of Political Economy* Marx wrote: 'All mythology masters and dominates and shapes the forces of nature in and through the imagination; hence it disappears as soon as man gains mastery over the forces of nature. What becomes of the Goddess of Fate side by side with Printing House Square?' To-day we are astonished at the banality of this approach. The fact is that it is people like the philosopher Whitehead, the psychologist Jung, the physicist Schrödinger and others, who are working on that vital mental change which will lead to a new conception of the world—not the champions of class warfare. This new *Weltanschauung* will of necessity be based on the most valuable tradition of European thought. In his aesthetic theories Read, too, goes as far back as to the Greeks. Already in his early work *The Meaning of Art*, 1926, which consists of short studies which he wrote as an art critic for *The Listener*, and which were forged together by his maturing philosophy of art, Read proclaimed: 'The Greeks were wiser than we, and their belief, which always seems so paradoxical to us, that beauty is moral goodness, is really a simple truth. The only sin is ugliness and if we believed this with all our being, all other activities of the human spirit could be left to take care of themselves. That is why I believe that art is so much more significant than either economics or philosophy. It is the direct measure of man's spiritual vision. When that vision is communal it becomes a religion, and the vitality of art throughout the greater part of history is closely bound up with some form of religion. But gradually— for the last two or three centuries that bond has been getting looser, and there does not seem to be any immediate promise of a new contact being established.' He continued: 'No one will deny the profound interrelation of artist and community. The artist depends on the community . . .' It is there that the unity must be achieved, there that education must find a way out. What actually does the artist do to enrich the consciousness of mankind? Read answered this question in his work on *Art and Society*, 1936: 'The artist's primary function, and the only function which gives him his unique faculties, is his capacity to materialize the instinctual life of the deepest levels of the mind. At that level we suppose the mind to be collective in its representations and it is because the artist can give visible shape to these invisible phantasms that he has power to move us deeply.' The problem of the future is for Read 'whether we can preserve art in its essential nature whilst giving it a place in the pattern of our culture. It is dangerous for a society to be too conscious about art; but it is nevertheless necessary for society to support the artist. Art must be regarded as a necessity, like bread and water; but, like bread and water, it must be accepted as a matter of course; it must be an integral part of our daily life, and must not be made a fuss of. It should be treated not as a guest, not even as a paying guest, but as one of the family.' It was in his book, *Education through Art*, 1943, that Herbert Read first developed all his ideas concerned with the definition of art, the natural form of education, the aesthetic basis of discipline and morality, to their full extent and tried to give them a scientific foundation. The book is chiefly concerned with the education of children. The liberation of their natural urge to express themselves is for him the only security for a balanced mind, a mind imbued with the beauty of creation for which modern man in his fierce struggle for life and in his ruthless exploitation of nature has been blinded. In this book we find Read again starting his theory with Plato, whose view of the function of art in education he wanted 'to translate into terms which are directly applicable to our present needs and conditions.' Plato's idea, so neglected through all the centuries, was that art should be the basis of education. In a more recent work which applies the principle of aesthetic education to adults, namely the *Education for Peace*, 1949, Read enlarged upon the Platonic notion that aesthetic training is also at the same time moral training, and applauded Plato for having put forward such an idea with complete seriousness and without any feeling of paradox. And again in his lectures on the Social Aspects of Art in an Industrial Age, given at Yale University during the spring of 1946 and published under the title, *The Grass Roots of Art*, Herbert Read took up this most striking of his problems and came to the conclusion that 'We cannot at this stage of development oppose the machine: we must let it rip and with confidence.' Because the foundations of a civilization do not rest in the mind but in the senses, education through art is the way to provide people with 'those standards which they would carry within their minds, within their bodies (through rhythm, music, dance; see Plato's *Laws*, and the principle of Dalcroze and others in our time), the natural antidote to objective rationality, a spontaneous overflow of creative energies into their hours of leisure.' It is pathetic to read the following words towards the end of his first lecture: 'Our particular trouble, in this air-conditioned nightmare which we call a civilization, is that we have lost the very notion of cultivating the senses, until butter-fingered and tongue-tied, half-blind and deaf to all nervous vibrations, we stumble through life unaware of its most appealing aspects, lost to its intensest joys and communions. Frustrated and brutalized, we drift between the boredom of peace and the self-inflicted wounds of war, and dismiss as lunatic those few quiet voices that speak of love and beauty and of the renunciations we must accept, of power, wealth and pride, if we would have the influence of beauty and love prevail in our lives.'

'I am recommending that everyone should be an artist,' Read claims, 'I am not recommending it in a spirit of dilettantism, but as the only preventative of a vast neurosis which will overcome a wholly mechanized and rationalized civilization. Only a people serving an apprenticeship to nature and art can be trusted with machines. Only such a people will so contrive and control those machines that their products are an enhancement of biological needs, and not a denial of them. Only such a people will be secure from the debilitating effects of mass production and mass unemployment (miscalled leisure). Only such a people, with sensations still vivid and intelligence ever active, can hope to form a stable and integrated society in the industrial world of the future.'

There are more facets to Herbert Read's thoughts, but I must restrain myself and give here only the main line of his aesthetico-social ideas. They will support everyone who works and thinks in the same direction, i.e., on the foundation of a new attitude to the miracle of life and its beauty.

5

ANDRÉ MALRAUX AND GOYA

IT has become almost a commonplace to refer to the trait of
adventurousness in Malraux's character and literary talent;
this same rather superficial catchword has also been taken over
and used in reviews of his work on the psychology of art. How
mistakenly! We need only make a serious effort to get a clear
vision of the problems that preoccupied the author of *La Condition
Humaine* and *Les Voix du Silence* to realize at once that we are in the
presence not of mere adventurousness but of courage, and of
courage in the face of '*Angst*' that overshadows all contemporary
life. And his is not a literary conception like that of a Kierkegaard
or a Sartre. It is the anguish of the twentieth-century man whose
soul is torn between two extremes, between a heaven bereft of its
gods and hell let loose upon life. At first Malraux believed—as for
a time did André Gide—that the solution was to be found on the
social plane, but already in *La condition humaine* the centre of
gravity has shifted from the social Utopian to the enigmatic and
tragic quality of individuation; and from that point onwards, as a
result of Malraux's experiences in the Spanish civil war and in the
French resistance movement, the social-Utopian aspirations fade
from the scene altogether. Malraux is striving for a new orientation towards a spiritual rebirth of humanity, but as yet he has been
unable to give it a shape and a name. He is concerned with man,
Existentialist man, as exclusively as a monk is concerned with
God. For in the field of art history, which for Malraux is the
history of the evolving image of man throughout the ages, he has
changed the whole question, whereas the art historians attacked
him for not having changed the answer.

Spain is to-day for France a rich source of inspiration, a fact
which will, perhaps, not be easily understood in England. And yet
out of the Catholic basis of both French and Spanish culture, and
out of a similar struggle against the predominance of a dogmatic

clerical obscurantism, it may be explained how France sees in certain Spanish problems new possibilities of solution for her own, whereas in the period of enlightenment it was Spain that looked to France for intellectual support. We can here leave out of account the purely temporary admiration for Garcia Lorca, in which, in any case, the whole literary world was associated, and also the permanent impact produced by Picasso who is a universal phenomenon. Let us remember, however, the effect that Paul Claudel's *Le soulier de satin* and Montherlant's *Le Maître de Santiago* made on Paris. And now comes Malraux. It is worthy of note as a happy stroke of destiny that the author of *La condition humaine* should be confronted in his new field of research with a figure like that of Goya, who was the embodiment of all that he himself found equivocal, absurd, and at the same time terrifyingly fascinating in life—fascinating from the point of view of creation, whether that creation is to be regarded as operative in the material of art or of life. That aspect of art history upon which Malraux's interest is constantly fixed is the creative act which bestows upon the artist complete mastery over his formative means. In the fifteen years of his research he has studied indefatigably and with the healthy disrespect of the outside observer the form speech of the art of all peoples and all times, intent upon penetrating the mystery behind its manifold forms; and this journey around the world and through thousands of years of cultural achievement has led him to where the modern artist stands. The freedom of the modern artist symbolizes for Malraux the freedom of the human soul in the act of imprinting its seal on the chaos of the world anew. On the threshold of this new region of spiritual authority he found Goya. In fact, a number of art historians have looked upon Goya as the first of the moderns. It was in connection with Goya that they spoke of creative unrest. Malraux saw more than that. He saw in him the artist who could contemplate the *volubilitas rerum*, the mutability of all relations, the *mysterium tremendum* before which men fear and tremble, with the same courage that he himself displayed on the literary field in his *La condition humaine*, *Le temps du mépris*, *L'espoir* or *Les Noyers de l'Altenbourg* as well as in the reality of war in which he was a volunteer without the support of any precisely formulated human ideal. Here then a poet speaks of a spiritual brother, a painter. No works on Goya have ever yet perceived and expressed so much of the essential man and artist as Malraux's books, although many have contained a greater mass of factual material. Indeed, he is so overcome with the greatness of his discovery in its double aspect of art and life, manifested in the person of a single eminent man, that he brushes aside with a certain disdain all preliminary entry into the material: 'As in the *Psychologie de l'art*, I take for granted a knowledge of the general course of art history, so here I take for granted a knowledge of the life and work of Goya.'[1] In our day when art is at the mercy either of journalistic superficiality, of professorial pedantry or of the scientific scalpel of the art theoretician, Malraux supplies us with a shining example of how to write like an artist about art. He writes without watering down and without disfiguring, constantly out of a personal and therefore living experience; and it is with the intensity of this experience that he guarantees for us his intuitively correct conception of the subject. Not even Baudelaire, for whom Goya was the fantastic caricaturist, wrote with such deep insight and so revealingly on him. This task remained for Malraux a hundred years later and was favoured by the inner relationship between Goya and Malraux and by the similarity of the restless times in which both lived. Malraux approached Goya cautiously. The first words we meet with are several fundamental thoughts on the Spaniard in his *Psychologie de l'art*. Then he plunges into the study of the most intimate of all material that an artist can leave behind him—the sketchbooks. The small Sanlucar sketchbook and the large Sanlucar sketchbook (both 1796-97) confirm his conception of the dark secrets of Goya's character and style. Malraux published this intimate pictorial material for the first time, and with it his first essay on Goya, 'Drawings from the Prado'[2] which forms a unity together with his final work on Goya: *Saturne*. Both are dedicated to Pascal Pia. Not only do the volumes complement each other in their abundance of pictorial material, but also in their texts, inasmuch as the first contains the sketched-in indications of Goya's significance for the understanding of the agony of our time and for the birth of modern art, whilst in the *Saturne* all that was hitherto indicated receives its due expansion and final formulation.

Malraux's attitude differs fundamentally from that of the Romantics, who indeed accepted Goya as the great master of the psychological portrait, of a dynamic colour conception and of

---

[1] André Malraux: *Saturne*. NRf. La Galerie de la Pleiade, Paris, 1950.
[2] English translation by Edward Sackville-West, *Horizon*, London, 1947.

varied graphic techniques, but in respect of his message looked upon him as a symbolist. Malraux declares roundly: Goya does not symbolize; he reveals. But what does he reveal? 'Through him speaks the deep subterranean voice of the unconscious. He assails the order of the world in favour of its mystery.' Neither in the *Disastros de la guerra*, nor in the *Caprichos* nor in the *Disparates* is man for him social man. It has remained for F. Klingender's book, *Goya in the Democratic Tradition*,[1] to maintain this banal thesis. The following passage is its culminating absurdity: 'Goya's *sober materialism* . . . is evident even in the *Disparates*. He repeatedly went out of his way to prove how little he had succumbed to the satanic mysticism which seems to pervade that work.'

Malraux writes in connection with Goya on the absurdity of being human. He writes about the creature, helpless and at the mercy of all the vicissitudes of life; and with reference to the *Disastros*: 'The war is over, but the absurdity continues.' He calls upon us to listen to the deep undertones of what he calls *le chant profond du mal*. Who before Malraux had seen and stated that if Bosch introduced men into his infernal world, Goya on the other hand introduced the infernal into the human world? Goya achieved his anguished style only because his own suffering gave him the power to metamorphose the function of painting—a victory for art, but a tragedy for the man. The knowledge that the Creator is not the true God can only be bought at a heavy price. Separate God from creation and the balance will be restored only by passing the world over to the demonic powers. This is a process easily rationalized, more easily in fact than the representation of society as a demon and of nature as a pure expression of God, as was the practice of many ideologies in Goya's day. The metaphysical absurdity remains intact. The artist can do no other than be reconciled to destiny, which was the Italian solution; or ignore it after the manner of eighteenth-century France; or resist and assail it as did Goya. Why did Goya represent men as he-goats, apes and asses? Why did he draw the lame, the mad, human skeletons, men as chickens, men sawn asunder, flagellants, offices of the Inquisition, nightmares, tortures, monsters, executions, foetuses, gnomes, sorcerers, demons, spectres, prostitution, prisons, famine, shipwreck, conflagrations, the plague? The title

[1] London, 1948.

of Malraux's book gives the answer. This powerful man and artist who whilst he was court painter in 1792 suffered a complete physical and mental breakdown, and afterwards experienced the same failing that darkened Beethoven's later years; this Goya withdrew into his *Quinta del Sordo*, into the deaf man's house, and there in his solitude, and under the urge of his creative genius (fed with *observacion*, *caprico* [phantasy] and *invencion*) beheld the awful and cruel face of the god who devours his own children: 'Saturn'.

There are deeply moving passages in the book, passages that bring home to us the true significance of Goya. Shakespeare, too, called upon the powers of darkness and night. 'In such a night as this, Jessica, when the sweet wind did gently kiss the trees and they did make no noise. . . . O song of love! In such a night, Macbeth, thou heardest, "Thou shalt be kind," and in such a night the forest moved and marched on Dunsinane. It was in such a night that Saul went to the witch of Endor; that Helen saw Troy's first dead brought back, that Alexander crucified the sage who taught him wisdom; that Rome, Persepolis, Alexandria and Babylon burned; that the heiress of Timour threw to her fish in their turquoise basin all the pearls of Samarcand; that the besieged companions of Cortes heard the howls of the Spanish prisoners whose hearts were torn out to the beating of the gongs; it was in such a night that Cervantes learned that he was a slave.'

At the end of the book this dark melody is again intoned: 'In such a night as this, Jessica . . . It was in such a night that the old exile, driven by his deafness from the café table round which his companions foregathered, out to the fairs and the arenas, tried to make that voice heard again which was more eager for the absolute and more separated from it than art had ever known. Perhaps in such a night while sketching, half blind, the sleeping Colossus he remembers having drawn forth from the eternal anguish, above the obscure cries of demons themselves possessed, the other Colossus whose troubled visage dreams among the stars. . . .'

Where Malraux as an art theoretician analyses the style and technique of Goya we follow him less willingly. He says himself in the foreword to *Le temps du mépris*: 'It is not passion but the wish to prove something that destroys a work of art.' All the proof we ask of Malraux is his own heart-beat with which he fills with new life the titanic figure of Goya; and for this all our thanks are his due. We need only think of the art historians with orthodox Catholic views, who have pointed out the destructive influence of Goya on our age, together with certain products of the late Romanesque art, of the hell pictures of the late Middle Ages, of the Mannerists, Bosch, and Breughel, to be fully aware of the value of Malraux's *Leitmotiv*. Malraux shows us a struggling artist, one who, like Rembrandt, is also a prophet, 'only he doesn't know exactly of what.' That is just our own spiritual position and it is also that of Malraux. The attempt to rediscover the world of the irrational or superhuman which had been lost by both man and Christianity, and for which Christian forms were no longer fitted to be the artistic expression, makes of Goya at once our contemporary as well as the courageous forerunner of modern art.

INDEX